Reading
the
Written
Image

CHRISTOPHER COLLINS

READING THE WRITTEN IMAGE

VERBAL PLAY,
INTERPRETATION,
AND THE
ROOTS OF
ICONOPHOBIA

THE PENNSYLVANIA STATE UNIVERSITY PRESS
UNIVERSITY PARK, PENNSYLVANIA

Publication of this book has been aided in part by a grant from the Abraham and Rebecca
Stein Faculty Publication Fund of New York University, Department of English.

Library of Congress Cataloging-in-Publication Data

Collins, Christopher.
    Reading the written image: verbal play, interpretation, and the
roots of iconophobia/Christopher Collins.

        p.   cm.

    Includes bibliographical references and index.
    ISBN 0-271-00763-X
    1. Poetics. 2. Imagery (Psychology) in literature. 3. Figures of
speech. I. Title.
PN1042.G583 1991
801'.951—dc20   90–22295
                                                          CIP

It is the policy of The Pennsylvania State University Press to use acid-free paper for the
first printing of all clothbound books. Publications on uncoated stock satisfy the mini-
mum requirements of American National Standard for Information Sciences—Permanence
of Paper for Printed Library Materials, ANSI Z39.48–1984.

To the memory of
Lily Rasmussen Collins
December 4, 1901–November 1, 1986
My first and best teacher

CONTENTS

PREFACE

The origins of this project lie in my early experience of books. Read to by my mother during the long, tedious childhood illnesses of a prevaccine age, I learned that books—even more effectively than fantasies and almost as effectively as dreams—offered me plausible alternatives to the here and now. But they did so, I found, only when I let myself believe in what I was imagining. Reading was play, I concluded, and, very much like a game or stage play, it was based on the rules of make-believe. When in high school I played baseball, I played as convincingly as I could the role of a pitcher, and when I was obliged to act in the school play I tried to inspire in the minds of those obliged to attend it the belief that I was whoever my Samuel French playbook said I was. Similarly, when I read poems or tried to write them myself, I viewed that activity as play, serious play, but play nonetheless. Could it be anything else but play? Only the conventions of play could allow poets to be truth-tellers despite their making such extravagant statements, presenting to the mind's eye such impossible objects, and connecting all these in a logic that no reasonable person who buys groceries and pays the gas and electric bills would for one moment tolerate in any other context.

I was mildly surprised in later years to find that these miraculous worlds, governed so often by otherwise preposterous laws, were the objects of exceedingly unplayful inquisition. I admired the seriousness of literary interpretation and soon found myself being trained to do it, but I now and then questioned the intent and effect of such activity: whatever clarities it wrested from its texts, it seemed to have scant respect for literary works as imaginative performances. Critics, more often than not, seemed to regard reading, apart from analysis, as a self-indulgence flawed by ignorance and caprice.

A few years ago when, recalling my earliest experiences of being read to and of reading, I resolved to try to ground a study of poetics in the performance of imagery and the principles of play, I quickly found that I needed to place myself in a defensive posture. The received terms of discourse were not simply inappropriate and unhelpful to a study of verbally cued imagery—they were positively inimical. As I began developing my chapters for this book, I found that my situation was very much like that described by W. J. T. Mitchell in his introduction to *Iconology:*

> Every theoretical answer to the questions, What is an image? How are images different from words? seemed inevitably to fall back into prior questions of value and interest that could only be answered in historical terms. The simplest way of stating this is to admit that a book which began with the intention of producing a valid *theory* of images became a book about the *fear* of images.

It is indeed in the context of this fear of images that any theory of imaging must be situated.

Iconophobia, the irrational fear of visual images, has to have been a very ancient response to imitation, especially to the imitation of *living* things, and as such has struck deep roots in the human psyche. I do not speculate here on its etiology beyond assuming that visual and verbal images derive their affective power from their relation to mental imaging, eidetic and dream imagery in particular. Any study of the deeper roots of iconophobia would, I suspect, need to consider such topics as cults of the dead, masked performances, ritual uses of hallucinogens, and delusional states. Often expressing itself as a fear of deception, iconophobia seems connected with the notion that "things are not what they seem" and may without warning slip off their familiar masks or leap out of hiding or transform themselves suddenly into monstrous and malign shapes. Children, who normally pass through a phase of nyctophobia and require the comfort of a nightlight for fear of shadows on the wall or of the unbidden imagery of frightening faces, may be recapitulating a stage of human prehistory when such fears had a universal basis in reality.

By "iconophobia" I do not refer to some sudden panic that overwhelms a person who sees a picture or suffers a vivid recollection. Such extreme reactions are rare. What I refer to is an unease toward and a distrust of images, particularly *mental* images, that seems to be related to a deeper fear, the terror of uncontrolled imagination, the delusional frenzy of "the lunatic, the lover, and the poet," as Shakespeare's Theseus describes it. It is a fear of the power of the "imagination [that] bodies forth / The forms of things unknown."

"Imaging some fear, / How easy is a bush suppos'd a bear"—and reason fears to frighten itself even when, or perhaps especially when, that fear is irrational. We fear no irrationality so much as the irrationality of reason. It is not enough to tell our children or ourselves that when we close our eyes or when we open them in the dark we are as safe as we are with the lights on. The problem we have with the images that are produced in the "dream of reason" is that these apparitions are really not *there* at all, but are *here,* haunting the very mind that observes them.

The particular roots of iconophobia that I attempt to trace in this study are not phylo- and ontogenetic, but cultural. They reveal themselves as inherited biases, age-old attitudes that reemerge in only slightly altered garb in every generation, including our own. Accordingly, I begin chapter 1 *in medias res* with a consideration of the semiotics of images and of some problems that this contemporary approach encounters when it tries to explain—or evade—the phenomenon of the verbally cued image. A cross-reference of Umberto Eco then leads us back to a reconsideration of Plato's and Aristotle's theories of verbal imagery, insofar as one can deduce these from their comments on visual and mental images, and to a distinction, which I feel is crucial, between verbally cued imagery produced in the presence of visible speakers and that generated in their absence—in short, between oral and literate circumstances.

In chapters 2 and 3 my concern is with certain religious uses of imagery, for example, in dream-visions, oracles, and prophecy. Focusing first on Greek divination and then on the visionary practice recorded in the Hebrew and Christian scriptures, I examine the impact of writing on visual and mental imagery and on the orally transmitted accounts of visionary experiences.

Chapter 4, on empirical method and literary interpretation, is the pivot upon which this study turns from a historical to a theoretical direction. Interpretation, as I discuss it in chapter 5, may be divided into two distinct procedures: what I call "enactive interpretation" and "critical interpretation." In enactive interpretation the reader uses the text as an instrument with which to perform *poiesis* and in so doing interprets it very much as a musician interprets a score; in critical interpretation the reader converts the text from an instrument into an object. It is my position that the full cognition of verbal imagery is possible only in the enactive performance of the text and that critical interpretation, when it purposes to examine images, engages the text in a manner so peculiarly inept that its professed aims are frustrated. Without denying the legitimate uses of critical scrutiny, I will suggest that its explication of the written image has not been one of its successes and, further, that the *uncritical* application of its methodologies to the image has often, intentionally or not, conformed to a hidden iconophobic agenda.

Chapters 6 and 7 elaborate a theory of the written image and of the literate imagination grounded in the conventions of poietic play. They take as their inspiration Coleridge's definition of "poetic faith" as the "willing suspension of disbelief" and apply to it the play theories of D. W. Winnicott and Gregory Bateson. I conclude with a model of the written image as a construct formed by the symbolic code of words but invested by the conventions of verbal play with the power to assume in the mind of the reader a quasi-spatiotemporal existence.

In addition to the authors I have already mentioned, I need to acknowledge my general indebtedness to the work of Murray Wright Bundy, Eric Havelock, Stanley Fish, Roman Ingarden, Wolfgang Iser, Walter Ong, Allan Paivio, Michael Riffaterre, and Michael Polanyi.

I am personally grateful for the advice and encouragement of Michael Heller, Una Chaudhuri, and John Maynard of the Department of English, New York University; I also gratefully acknowledge the helpful comments of Paul Vitz of the Department of Psychology. I wish to thank Bettina Knapp of the Department of Romance Languages, Hunter College, City University of New York, and Michael Bishop of the Department of French, Dalhousie University, who suggested to me a number of useful lines of enquiry, and Susan Drucker-Brown of the Department of Anthropology, Cambridge University, who shared with me some of her research into the function of sacred architecture. I am especially grateful to Michael Brown of the Department of Anthropology and Sociology, Northeastern University, for his friendship, encouragement, and intellectual energy. My thanks to Zachary Munzenrider of the Penn State Press, who, in the process of proofreading my manuscript, offered a number of judicious and felicitous suggestions. Finally, I wish to thank Philip Winsor of Penn State Press for his long-term diligence in realizing this project.

LITERACY AND THE OPENING OF THE INNER EYE

As readers of what is sometimes termed "imaginative literature," we prize the verbal skill of poets and novelists to "portray" persons and settings so vividly that we seem to view them with what some have called an "inner eye." The issues posed in a literary text may be identifiable with those presented in a philosophical tractate, but our apprehension of them is qualitatively different principally due to the polysemous resonances produced by its more particular, that is, imaginal, level of reference. Nevertheless, when we are called upon to analyze the content of literary text, we are obliged by the nature of this task to subordinate (if not completely suppress) the concrete-imaginal function of this language to its abstract-propositional function. The literary text, this message from an absent sender, is thus regarded as a superfluity of secondary qualities awaiting the discerning eye of the hermeneut to reduce it to its essential primary properties.

Before we perform this critical interpretation of a work of poetry, however, we must persuade ourselves that no concrete-imaginal element, untranslated into abstract-propositional terms, is significant. The hermeneutical profession has never quite come to terms with or satisfactorily accounted for writers' and readers' commitment to imagery and the thematic obliquity that this entails. Why should literature depend on images? The Horatian maxim that the skillful poet mixes the sweet with the useful, the ornamental image to catch the attention while the valuable lesson is inculcated, has been one perennial explanation. The other, somewhat more satisfactory view maintains that imagery should not be superadded to abstract propositions but should be made to function *as* abstract propositions through such figurative devices as metaphor, metonymy, and allegory. According to this view, verbal images are tropes subject to a rhetorical analysis capable of opening them up and preparing them to be unfolded in the language of critical discourse.

Literary interpretation has therefore come to be considered a means by which images, the particular perceptlike representations evoked by language and scanned by the inner eye, are either sequestered from or assimilated into abstract-propositional discourse; once these obstacles to thematic clarity are dealt with, the entire text can be translated into nonimaginal, categorical prose. But in so doing, hermeneutics, even the negative hermeneutics of deconstruction, neglects not only the image but the process by which the image forms in the minds of readers: it fails to examine the implications of the fact that texts, whatever else they can be made to be, are notated scripts composed to be played by readers and that, though scripted in a public code, these works are performed on a private, inner stage. In a literate culture the presence and authority of the oral performer is deeded over to the solitary reader, and it is here within this theater of the mind that the *poiesis* of reading is performed. It is here, out of the bare suggestions of abstract verbal signs, that persons and settings are concretized in ways that inevitably differ from reader to reader of the same text and from reading to reading by the same reader.

Hermeneutics, both biblical and secular, has made this difference a problem—as indeed it always is for a project premised on the univocal meaning of discourse, whether it be a divine or a human semiotic code. This difference in interpretive performances is no less a problem for those who have recently discovered the "undecidability" of literary discourse. This problem of hermeneutics has led it down through the centuries to devise different tactics, but one aim has been constant—to regulate the reading of writing and, as a literate discourse, to reestablish the *magisterium* of oral authority. Though the problems of hermeneutics need not be the problems of poetics, those who have demanded of a poem that it dutifully unpack its contents for inspection have imposed this problem on poetics. The nature of this imposition and several moments in its history are the topics of this chapter. For reasons that will become apparent, I will begin in recent times and then from this vantage point look to the past.

Umberto Eco and the Imaginal Interpretant

Semiosis is social play. Though every semiotic game has its own set of rules, the tacit premise for each of these innumerable games is: *A* shall in circumstance X not be regarded as A but as B. Participants know that A is not B, but choose for the immediate purposes of play to simulate the belief that A really is equivalent to B. Its A-ness, which we know it *has,* remains but is effaced by its conventionally assigned B-ness, which we choose to believe it *is.* This unstable equilibrium of knowledge and simulated belief, from which is derived the double identity that marks every sign, is the essential awareness that every social player must maintain.

The rules of social play in every game situation establish the function of certain classes of signs. According to the system of semiotics associated with the writings of Charles Sanders Peirce, signs are either *icons, indices,* or *symbols.* An iconic sign—a picture or a diagram—resembles in some manner the object it stands for. On the other end of the scale, a symbolic sign—a word or number—does not look like, sound like, or in any other sense resemble what it represents: it is an arbitrarily designated cue that in a given conventional code evokes a particular concept.[1] Since its immediate sensory presence is not *naturally* associable with its meaning, the symbolic sign must be strongly coded. Between the two, the indexical sign draws attention to itself but only to convey that attention elsewhere to an object or concept beyond itself with which it is associated.

Icon, index, symbol—each constitutes a particular kind of maneuver. In iconic play, participants agree to regard one sensory (most often visual) object as analogous in its perceptible properties to another object: the perceived object A is accepted as a surrogate that represents the absent object B (a particular or a generic B). An index, on the other hand, suggests, but does not represent, the absent entity: like a pointing index finger or the index of a book, it refers us elsewhere. Indexical play characterizes games of detection, such as hide-and-seek; unlike iconic play, which associates its objects by resemblance, indexical play associates through contiguity and causality: A, the present object, stands for B, the absent object, because A bears upon it the traces of B.

Of the three classes of signs, however, symbol is the preeminent mode of human social play and offers, in the form of speech and writing, the readiest and most adaptable of all play-equipment. In primate evolution the emergence of this class of signs must have immediately separated the human from those related species that still had to rely on a repertory of iconic gestures and

1. We will need to keep in mind that the word "symbol" will in this study regularly denote the verbal sign and not the "literary symbol" of eighteenth- and nineteenth-century poetics. Whenever "symbol" is used to designate the latter, I will carefully mark that usage.

recognitions and indexical problem-solving methods. Wherever it evolved, speech became a species-specific, therefore secret, code by means of which the human animal could communicate with its kind about animals of other species without betraying its true intentions. The human could now name and classify them, but, most important, it could *deceive* them. The display of iconic and indexical signs could mean one thing, while the words shared with fellow hunters or herders could mean something quite different. Even within the species, among those capable of symbolic signifying, linguistic symbols could be used to segregate and deceive. The distinction between semiotic participants (grammatically: first and second persons) who share information and nonparticipants (third persons) about whom information is shared applies to all three classes of signs, but, being a system of arbitrary ciphers, a natural language could be a secret code from which non-speakers could be excluded.

The preeminence of symbolic signification derives from its capacity to convey abstract relationships and qualities. Generally icons and, to a lesser extent, indices need to be interpreted, that is, their signification needs to be sifted from their incidental aspects. A photograph, for example, might at first seem to be an arrangement of colors, then a landscape, then a view of a particular place one visited ten years ago—and all the while it remains a three-inch paper square in one's hand. It never totally evanesces into that set of verbalizable memories that it signifies. A picture is worth a thousand words because it is semiotically overdetermined: every place on the pictorial plane that we fix our gaze upon is potentially an iconic sign and may also serve the function of an indexical sign. By contrast, a *verbal* description of a sloping field, a line of trees, and a chain of hills beyond seems to vanish at once into the scene it evokes and then, like Prospero's masque, quickly dissolves, leaving not a rack behind.

However, while the words instantly vanish into thin air, the representations they may evoke in the minds of listeners or readers dissolve more slowly. It is in its power to assimilate icons and indices into its baseless fabric that symbol abjures part of its magical power, for it induces us to evoke imagery that is not wholly abstract, not wholly conventional, not wholly disentangled from what to the imager seems incidental sensory experience. With its protean ability to represent whatever it can name, symbol can simulate, that is, "play," the two other types of sign and absorb, but not wholly assimilate, their essentially *non-symbolic* functions. These residual functions of icon and index within the play of symbolic signification allow language to simulate the same universe of objects that, without verbal mediation, the body knows and the senses engage.

Peirce seems to have accounted for this play-within-a-play by his concept of the "interpretant." This subsequently much-disputed term Peirce variously defined as a representation of a representation (1:171), a mental effect or thought (1:303), and a sign created by a prior sign.[2] As a representation of an absent referent, the concept of an interpretant implies an imaginative act, albeit a momentary apprehension of an "idea"; when this idea assumes the form of a visual schema or image, I propose to refer to it as an "imaginal interpretant."

Those who have concluded that Peirce created distinctions without differences in respect to his concept of the "interpretant" have preferred to read into his system the simpler model proposed by Ferdinand de Saussure (*Course in General Linguistics*) with its relation of signifier (*signifiant*) to signified (*signifié*). According to the Saussurean tradition of European semiology, human signification is in every instance language-like, what Peirce would have called "symbolic": icons and indices arrive, thanks to this all-pervasive medium of language, already inscribed with conventional meaning.

Umberto Eco in his essay "Peirce and the Semiotic Foundation of Openness" (in *The Role of the Reader*) expresses the uneasiness many semioticians have felt in regard to the Peircean "interpretant." To make it a "fruitful notion," he says,

> one must first of all free it from any *psychological* misunderstanding. I do not say that Peirce did it. On the contrary, insofar as, according to him, even ideas are signs, in various passages the interpretants appear also as *mental events*. I am only suggesting that from the point of view of the theory of signification, we should perform a sort of surgical operation and retain only a precise aspect of this category. (198, emphasis added)

His next sentence describes the postoperative state of the patient, one in which interpretants have become "the *testable and describable* correspondents associated by public agreement to another sign" (198, emphasis added). From

2. Charles Sanders Peirce. *Collected Papers,* ed. Charles Hartshorne and Paul Weiss, (vols. 1–8) (Cambridge, Mass.: Harvard University Press, 1931). Elsewhere he categorized interpretants as "immediate," "dynamical," "final," "emotional," "energetic," and "logical." Commentators have all agreed that the interpretant is the meaning or concept evoked by the sign and that in turn it evokes another meaning that is *its* interpretant, but they have disagreed as to how such an interpretant could also be final or be called an "interpretant" instead of simply a "concept." (See, for example, Eco, *The Role of the Reader,* 184.)

the point of view of his, and most semioticians', theory of signification, it is important to interrogate a sign. The interpretant, or conceptual sign, that a sign evokes in an interpreter begins a process of elucidation of that original sign but only by attaching other significances to it, which themselves ought not to pass uninterrogated. If they were purely "mental events," and not "associated by public agreement" to their precedent sign, they could not be "testable," but, as Eco suggests, if only they were public enough to be testable they could be described, and, once verbalized, they would be ipso facto removed from the shadow realm of the private mentalistic "self." Is Eco addressing a problem of imprecision in Peirce's semiotics or a problem in semiosis itself? This is not completely clear, but what is clear is Eco's goal: to situate the signification of signs wholly within publicly coded discourse. Peirce's concept of the interpretant obstructs this goal by suggesting that there occurs at the very midmost relay point of this semiotic process a perilous instant when the interpreter performs an immediate cognition of a sign and forms an image that may not appear sufficiently public to be interrogated and successively glossed. If only an imaginal interpretant did not emerge unpredictably at this inconveniently central point of the process, if only the semiotic loop did not pass for an instant through the privacy of human brains, we would all publicly know what we meant. Eco's next sentence describes this happy state:

> In this way the analysis of content becomes a cultural operation which works only on physically testable cultural products, that is, other signs and their reciprocal correlations. . . . Thus one is never obliged to replace a cultural unit by means of something that is not a semiotic entity, and no cultural unit has to be explained by some *platonic, psychic, or objectal* entity. Semiosis explains itself by itself: this continual circularity is the normal condition of signification and even allows communicational processes to use signs in order to mention things and states of the world. (198, emphasis added)

Eco's modest proposal that for theory's sake we neuter the interpretant with one swipe of Occam's razor obliges us at the very least to seek a second opinion, for it simply fails to account for the phenomenon, specifically the disposition of iconic and indexical signs within the discourse of symbol. If imaginal interpretants could retain their cultural inscriptions intact, these imaginal signs would be relatively unproblematic and there would be no rupture in the circuit of semiosis. If, however, weakly coded information—imagery that does not neatly match up with cultural iconography—should be found to constitute an interpretant, then semiotics should confront this and try to account for it, rather than wish it away. To use an electrical analogy, signification at this crucial interpretant juncture passes through a material of low conductivity and thus at that point emits informational energy. If one's theoretical ideal is smooth, superconductive, undiminished transmission, then such interpretants "lose" energy. But if one is willing to take semiosis as a somewhat more problematic process, one may view this entropic moment as an event of great consequence—as nothing less than the epiphany of the image.

To use another analogy: semiosis is the relay of a message via a messenger, that is, a signified via a signifier. The messenger carries burdens, verbal and perhaps also objectal, that within the social context are interpretable by the addressees as meaningful. These burdens pertain to circumstances temporally and spatially absent from the addressees, whose effort must now be to reconstitute the meaning of these burdens, adapt themselves appropriately to this news, and determine a proper response. The act of reconstituting these absent circumstances corresponds to the function of the interpretant, and that must precede any chain of responses consequent to receiving this piece of information. The human messenger's function is indexical, and the iconic content embedded in the indexical signs he delivers to his addressees is the imagery he has stored, the imagery he now verbalizes and induces them to form mentally.

Since Peirce in his writings has associated the interpretant with "mental events," he has, according to Eco, occasioned "psychological misunderstanding." Peirce and his readers have apparently misconstrued the interpretant as having the aspects of, or indeed as being, a "platonic, psychic, or objectal entity." In specifying these three, Eco has projected the problems of the interpretant into the history of Western thought and implied that this "psychological misunderstanding" is some two-and-a-half millennia old. Since the foundations of our poetics and our theory of the written image were first established in the elementary schoolroom of Western philosophy, it is fitting that we take Eco's cue and ask ourselves what a platonic, a psychic, and an objectal interpretant might be.

The Oral-Mimetic Message

If, as Eco asserts, "continual circularity is the normal condition of signification," fifth-century Greece was a model of public coding. Hellenic culture, as Eric Havelock has described it in *Preface to Plato,* was founded on a thoroughgoing practice of mimesis. Human beings were the living repositories of communal knowledge: only what could be transmitted orally, rehearsed mimetically, and stored mnemonically could become "cultural units." Verbal learning was a kind of *catechism,* a process in which the student repeated (literally, "made to echo") the words of the teacher.[3] It was not until the third century B.C. that writing began to supplant mimesis as a technique of information storage and transmission, though, of course, it never wholly succeeded in doing so. The transitional fourth century, according to Havelock, experienced the full implications of this shift from an oral world dominated by Homer and Hesiod to a new, literate world of philosophers and historians, from one of traditional belief to one of free and skeptical inquiry, from one of poetry to one of prose, from the cult of *mnemosynē* to the school of *logos.*

Plato's grand plan was to teach a new generation how to examine this "unexamined life" that had been relived generation after generation and to question the mimetic institutions that sustained it. Since poetry, which had always played a crucial role in the mimetic *paideia* of Greece by providing it with representations of reality, was a mnemonic art that also perpetuated *mis*representations, poetry was perhaps not worth reinstituting in the ideal state. Though Plato seemed ambivalent on the matter of literacy, the truly philosophical *politeia* would seem to depend on the production of written prose, even if this were merely a device to jog the memory, as Socrates seems to permit in *Phaedrus* (274–78). Whether or not he viewed writing as the technology of the future, the oral poetics of the past had not succeeded in enlightening Greek society. In the tenth book of his *Republic* he argues that, while culture in all its artifactual manifestations had always used poetry as its model, poetry had slavishly used culture as *its* model and too few interrupted this mimetic transmission to consult actual experts in particular crafts and disciplines. For that reason, even Homer's representations were weak and

3. The Greek and Latin words for memory, *mnēmē* and *memoria,* also duplicate the *m*-sound and thus seem to reenact the opening, closing, and reopening of lips. Might one not speculate that these words are somewhat linked with such words as the Greek *mermerizein* (to ponder, reflect, imagine), the Latin *murmur,* and the English *mumble?* (Cf. also the almost universal *mamma* and the duplicative *B*s, also bilabials, of the onomatopoeic *barbaros* and *babble.*) In the age of printed school books we tend to forget how important unison mumbling has always been in preliterate education.

distant imitations of an imitation. Imagery in all its manifestations had thus come to be associated in Plato's mind with an infinite and vicious regress of mimetically generated types. His concept of the archetypal forms became his answer to this dilemma.

Every modern study of "mimesis" acknowledges how resistant to translation this word is. Plato, having introduced it as a philosophic issue, used it as though it normally denoted a process that included "the artist's 'act' of creation, the performer's 'act' of imitation, the pupil's 'act' of learning, and the adult's 'act' of recreation" (Havelock, 36). If one were to identify a contemporary term that partially corresponds to "mimesis," one might choose perhaps "cultural coding"; similarly, the body of cultural artifacts that the Greeks called *technē mousikē* has some striking definitional overlap with our "textuality." If we may try out these translated terms: Plato's ultimate design was not to pursue the paradoxes and aporias of textuality, though other contemporaries did so with relish, or to interrogate the cultural code that produced them, though his Socrates constantly did this and died for doing so, but rather to preclude this coding process entirely by eliminating sensory experience once and for all from the dialectic of reason.

What would a "platonic interpretant" be? If we were listening to a speech or reading a text, a platonic interpretant would presumably be the idea, the real form, that lay behind the phonic or graphic sign of the word. This timeless, absolute, verbally denoted essence would for an instant reveal itself to the highest mental faculty, the *nous* (in Latin the *intellectus*), and then vanish as its meaning entered the contingent structure of the sentence. In a semiotic system that might conceivably be derived from Plato's anti-mimetic statements, a "platonic interpretant" would therefore be an image that is transcendent to any publicly examinable cultural code, a form allied to verbal abstraction, geometry, and intuition rather than to perceptual experience, resembling Peirce's "iconic diagram," but one that is mentally scanned and of purely ideal provenance.

Eco's second "non-semiotic" entity he calls "psychic." By this term he may be referring simply to a "mental event," but, associated as it is with "platonic," a specifically psychic interpretant would be an impression made upon the invisible inner world of the thinking subject. The platonic psyche, though it preserves the knowledge of the transcendent forms, is nevertheless forced to participate also in the work of mimetic representation, undergoing daily the impressions of actual objects and receiving nightly the shadowy images sent to it in dreams. The embodied psyche, though preoccupied with the imagery of mimesis and therefore "fallen," was nevertheless the rightful domain of the sovereign intellect. A "psychic interpretant," as distinct from a "platonic interpretant," would from Plato's point of view be an impure form, an image that still bears upon it the incidental traces of sensory experience, that is, of personal memory. It would be a mental icon derived from the sensory knowledge of mere objects, that is, objectal entities. What Plato would spurn as mired in mimesis and insufficiently ideal, Eco would ban from his semiotic republic for the opposite reason—because it is insufficiently mimetic and therefore mentalistic, unreplicatable, and not firmly inscribed within a public system of signs. While they would obviously disagree as to the value, and indeed the reality, of "platonic" entities in semiosis, they would both deny the validity of "psychic" entities.

Plato's pupil Aristotle in his *Poetics,* having found a way to reinstate mimesis and declare poetry to be "more philosophical and serious than history," installed poetry as the superior handmaiden in the service of philosophy. His reasoning was that, while the historian describes particular human aspects, only the poet describes universal aspects, for, though both imitate, only the poet abstracts behavioral traits and reassembles them in new composites. Since the *poiētēs* does not merely reproduce, but *makes,* this imitation, Aristotle chose to call his theoretical treatise the *Poetics,* rather than the *Mimetics,* a title that his master might well have assigned to such a work.

Yet for all his pointed, anti-platonic praise of poetic mimesis, Aristotle the poetician has very little to say about mental imagery, the psychic aspect of this process that Plato found so objectionable. That he was not obliged to discriminate between pure and impure forms, between transcendent and natural images, explains only part of his reticence. Having relegitimated verbal mimesis, we might suppose he would have celebrated the skill by which poets induce mimetic—in this case, imaginative—states in the minds of their audience or readers, but the words for "mental image" (*phantasma*) and "imagination" (*phantasia*) do not even appear in his *Poetics.* As far as he is concerned, apparently, they belong to the private, shadowy realm of *psyche,* for him the impressionable lower mind, and these phenomena he reserved for his separate treatises on the soul and the functions of memory (the *De Anima* and *De Memoria*).

This was no oversight on his part: modern concepts of "imagination" and "imaginative literature" are completely alien to Aristotelian poetics. In his *Rhetoric* he casually summarizes his psychological position when he defines imagination as weakened sensation (*phantasia estin aisthēsis tis asthenes*). In the very first sentence of his *Poetics* he announces his intention to "consider poetry in itself, its various genres, and the constitutive powers of each [*dunamin hekaston*]." It follows that for a critic who praised poetry for its *dunamis,* any inherently weak element would be hardly worth mentioning. Our conclusion is unavoidable: in an oral-mimetic cultural context, verbally evoked imagery, central though it is to the literate experience, is a minor byproduct of poetic performance.

As we have noted, Plato would have agreed with Eco in denying the relevance of "psychic" entities in the relay of information, but, for Aristotle, who seems to have accepted wholeheartedly the mimetic process as the most efficient means of *paideia,* psychic factors were simply less salient than other factors. *Katharsis* was partly an effect of imagining oneself as the tragic hero, but if Aristotle believed this empathetic role-playing was mediated by spectators' mental imagery, he did not choose to say so. Like most Greeks, he acknowledged that people experienced these mental images, for example, wraithlike representations in dreams, but, though the gods could send very vivid *phantasmata* to poets and diviners, the imagery publicly conveyed by language was quite another matter. The reason for this is quite simple. In what was still a predominantly oral culture, verbal imagery was normally accompanied by a far more attention-demanding fact, the visual presence of the speaker. Written texts were indeed read, that is, decoded directly from their graphic characters, but when these works were poems, they were so received only *faute de mieux.* Aristotle alludes to such reading in privative terms, referring to effects that tragic or epic works can have *even without* enactment or recitation (*Poetics* 1450b19, 1462a11–13), and when *graph*-words do appear in the *Poetics* they invariably refer to painting, not writing, as though the fact that poets chirographically composed tragedies was an incidental matter. The prospect of curling up in bed at night with a good scroll or codex seems to have been as unappealing to the ancient Greeks as settling down to access a novel on a computer monitor would be to us. Certain kinds of writing, it is true, were being composed to be read in private, yet in that phonocentric world, still dominated as it was by the aesthetics of oratory even when oratory had little or no political effect, the verbal arts were skills associated with the agora, the theater, and the recitation hall and embodied in the rhetor, the actor, and the rhapsode. Aristotle's royal pupil could sleep with the *Iliad* under his pillow, but only wartime conditions could force such expedients.[4]

---

4. Aristotle acknowledges literacy as a cultural factor: even tragedy, he says, can, if necessary, be read as closet drama and still preserve some of its *energeia* (*Poetics* 62a12, 17), and in the *Rhetoric*

The distinction between poetic *mimesis* (acting out a text) and *diegesis* (telling a text), when applied to the culture that first defined them, is often misunderstood. True, mimesis was the imitation of human actions staged in drama and diegesis was narration and description as components of epic and lyric poetry (see Plato's *Republic* 92d2, 92d5, 93c1–9, 93d7, 94b1), but Aristotle took pains to characterize all *poiēsis* as mimetic. Even the diegesis of epic was mimetic, as he indicates by the twice-used phrase "diegetic mimesis" (*diēgēmatikē mimēsis, Poetics* 59b33, 37), which clearly implies that narration, being publicly performed, must convey mimetic effects, that is, iconic and indexical information.

The Messenger as Objectal Entity

In the *theatron,* or "viewing place," the verbally generated mental image, be it a "platonic" schema or a "psychic" picture, is necessarily forced into the background by the sensory object—the speaker. Eco's "objectal" entity, corresponding to Peirce's "existent" or "dynamic object" plus its mental counterpart the "immediate object," was provided by the living, breathing, gesticulating human relay in the public semiosis of Greek culture, who persisted as dramatis persona to interpose himself as a visible object between his audience and his words, thus superimposing upon and partially occluding the mental images that his words might otherwise evoke in the psyches of his addressees.

This objectal factor, patently true in the case of the dramatic actor, was also true of the professional reciter. As Plato tells us in the *Ion,* the rhapsode's performance fully participated in the skills of mimetic portrayal. The yearly festival of the Panathenaea was devoted to the performance of Homer's epics. Judging from Plato's account and those of others, rhapsodes trained them-selves to impersonate witnesses to these exploits and would seem to relive these scenes with hallucinatory excitement, to mime with gesture and voice the strokes and epic taunts of the protagonists. Through the agency of the rhapsode's skill, an audience could imagine itself present on the plains of

---

(III.xii.2) he speaks of poets whose works are meant for reading (*hoi anagnostikoi*). This trend would increase as papyrus production increased in the Hellenized eastern Mediterranean, but writing intended for the silent, isolated reader would not appear before the invention of moveable type.

Troy or in the royal hall of Ithaka, but if mental imagery in the form of what might be termed second-order mimesis could be diegetically evoked, it still had to compete for attention with mimesis of the first order—the physical presence of the speaker. Though the rhapsode was not strikingly costumed, masked, ringed with a dancing, chanting chorus, or backed with a visually arresting scenic design, he had his own attention-fixating means, for, being unmasked, his facial expression could change with each emotion and with each character he diegetically mimed.[5] His performance thus required iconic skill—he signified others—but in the display of this skill the iconic signifier became himself an objectal signified: the obvious fact that the rhapsode was a portrayer distinct from a portrayed allowed a spectator to focus somewhat less on what he said than on how *he* said it. In every fundamentally oral culture—and Greece in the fourth century was no exception—every audience tends to be an assembly of connoisseurs. Alert for evidence of technical prowess, they will consider the mental imagery evoked by a literary declamation as of secondary or tertiary importance.

Not only did professional narrators imitate actors and thus draw visual attention to themselves, but actors, whenever their script directed them to tell a story or describe a scene absent to their interlocutors, regularly impersonated narrators. Only one stock character, however, the so-called Tragic Messenger, had this as his primary function. In so doing, he, too, became a peculiarly objectal entity. For, though his diegesis (in this case the indexical function of his symbolic signs, that is, his words) strove to efface his mimesis (the iconic function of, for example, one who had witnessed a marvel or a horror), when he appeared, he immediately became an object of the intense visual focus of the other actors and the chorus, whose reaction to his diegetic action was usually powerfully emotive. Needless to say, their concentrated

5. In their treatises on oral performance rhetoricians regularly shifted in their references from oratorical to dramatic and recitational techniques. See Quintilian *Intitutio Oratoria* XI.3 for a very detailed inventory of vocal and gestural signs. Here he alludes to Cicero's *De Oratore* III.59: "Est enim actio quasi sermo corporis," and asserts that actors add so much grace to poets' works that the same passages are infinitely more effective when recited aloud than when merely read (XI.iii.4). See particularly sections 72–81 on facial gestures. For a curious study of manual gestures, see John Bulwer's *Chirologia: or the Naturall Language of the Hand Composed of the Speaking Motions, the Discoursing Gestures thereof. Whereto added Chironomia: or the Art of Manuall Rhetoricke. Consisting the Naturall Expressions, Digested by Art in the Hand, as the Chiefest Instrument of Eloquence.* See also Aristotle's *Poetics* 62a where he censures reciters for exaggerated gestures. It should be noted in passing that Aristotle's word for gestures is *sēmeia*, "signs," and that for him a *sēmeion* was a piece of evidence, an object from which some other fact could be inferred. (See Wartelle, 142; and Eco, *Semiotics and the Philosophy of Language,* 26–29.)

attention would draw the attention of the audience to him as well. Signifying a crucial juncture in the plot whenever he appeared on stage, the Tragic
Messenger was himself a visible message, a focal point that reassembled the
personae of both stage and orchestra about himself.[6]

As we have seen, Eco's three banned entities are each deeply implicated in
the cultural context of classical poetic theory and each corresponds to a
separate kind of visuospatial cognition. The "platonic," with which I began,
corresponds to a schematic image (cf. Peirce's iconic *diagram*), a generalized
form that we regularly produce in response to common, unspecified nouns,
the concept, or "idea," of such entities as "dog," "house," or "chair." The
"psychic" corresponds to a more detailed image or one based on well-
remembered experience (cf. Peirce's iconic *image*), an internal visual simulation that may be prompted by descriptive language. The "objectal" corresponds
to the perceptual image (cf. Peirce's *immediate object,* one's mental response to
a *dynamic object* — something "out there"), a visual image with which we are
presented in a performing art and that may function as an icon or an index or
both.

Those who would wish to valorize the mental icon would certainly find
no encouragement in Plato or Aristotle. Plato, of course, privileges the
"platonic entities" and contemns the "objectal." Aristotle respects the "objectal"
and denies the ultimate reality of the "platonic." Both, however, argue that
the "psychic entities," those wraithlike images of *phantasia,* are negligible
factors in human intercourse, for while ideas are endorsed by the Divine
Intellect and objects validated by the human senses, mental images are
unsharable, subjective experiences.

If we take a broader view of Greek culture as dominated by another dyad,
philosophy and the arts, we also find the discourse of the imagination
pointedly excluded. Despite their epistemological differences, Plato and
Aristotle, like all philosophers, deal in logical, categorical entities. Therefore
when they mention a sensible object by way of illustration, this reference is
meant to evoke a schematic, not a particularized, image — an *idea,* be it real or
nominal. Broadly defined as abstract schemata, "platonic entities" were no
less Aristotelian than Platonic. Now, if Greek philosophers invested their

6. The Messenger speech allowed the chorus to respond emotively to a revelation, a response that
was "not an extension of the story but rather a reaction to it. If this was so, the Messenger speech might
well have been much more of a visual highlight in the production than is generally assumed. This in
turn would seem to explain why the device is used more frequently and more evocatively in the later
plays." J. Michael Walton, *Greek Theatre Practice,* Contributions in Drama and Theatre Studies, no. 3
(Westport, Conn.: Greenwood Press, 1980).

thoughts in abstract schemata, Greek poets embodied theirs in the perceptual objects of actors and rhapsodes. As our survey of Greek mimetic practice has shown, the percept, because of its dominant presence in the attentional field of an audience, forced the issue of mental imagery into the periphery of poetic theory. Even when this issue later appeared in rhetorical treatises, the mental image was regarded as a minor element compared with debating technique (logic and paralogical figures) and delivery (voice and gesture). (*Figurae* were momentary comparisons and verbal substitutions used to further an *argumentum;* when a speaker pretended to see an image before him, using the device of *enargeia,* or *illuminatio,* his audience focused less on this image than on him and his quasi-hallucinatory frenzy.)

The Opening of the Inner Eye and the Hermeneutical Reaction

Marginalized though it once was, the visual image was eventually to become the focus of literate culture and regarded as a dangerous energy that needed to be carefully managed. As oral compositions became written texts and as hand-copied texts became printed texts, the cues to imaging became progressively more fixed and bound, yet conversely the images that they evoked became more indeterminate and open. As written copies became more numerous and the private, solitary reader emerged into history, this psychic entity became liberated from the constraints of traditional oral culture. As *written* image, it was summoned into being by the public code of language; but as written *image,* it enjoyed a freedom heretofore untasted by the human psyche. The destabilizing effects of this new literate freedom therefore triggered the hermeneutical reaction. Images, especially those contained in canonical texts, both sacred and secular, could not be left open to individual interpretation. A hermeneutocracy is the inevitable institutional response to an expanded literacy and to the liberated subjectivity that its imagery naturally engenders. The interests of institutions and dominant classes in regulating the reception of texts is too large a subject for this space, but, as Foucault and others have amply demonstrated, the self-defensive motives of such groups are not difficult to uncover. Their need to disambiguate, to their advantage always, the polysemous image—to identify and repress interpretations that threaten their authority—is also obvious.

I chose for two reasons to take exception to Eco's reading of Peirce. My first reason is general: semiotics, of which Eco is a leading exponent, is at present the *novum organum* of the human sciences, and therefore how it is defined is crucial to how we define our work within our separate disciplines. The second is the specific focus of this chapter: in restricting the "interpretant" function to a recognition of exclusively culturally coded units, Eco ignores the phenomena of mental imagery—without which literature would become a less problematic, but also a far less powerful, art form—and would thus increase the domination over this function by one or another interpretive establishment.

Of his three "non-semiotic entities" most of us would be willing to rule out platonic ideas: medieval realists are for the most part in their crypts and modern essentialists are currently in hiding. The phrase "platonic entities" is therefore something of a red herring. This leaves "psychic" and "objectal" as viable survivors of Eco's scalpel. For some of us the phrase "psychic entities," which I have interpreted in a Greek philosophical context, is also charged with pejorative connotations, "psychic" being commonly associated with "spiritualistic" and "mentalistic." As we have seen, neither Plato, Aristotle, nor Eco has much tolerance for "psychic entities," or what we might call "imaginal interpretants," but, as I hope to prove, these entities are the essential figments of fiction, the "fictive things" that literate communication generates. "Objectal entities," on the other hand, are the very demonstrable data that accompany face-to-face oral communication, including all of early Classical poetry and all of visually performed dramatic literature down to the present. Though Eco regards them as mere objects, deficiently coded in their loose and fuzzy thingness, their presence, as I have suggested, looms large in oral-mimetic cultures.

Though our principal concern will be with "reading the written image," let us one last time consider the objectal aspects of "attending the oral performance."

It would be absurd to deny that costumic, gestural, and intonational signs abound in drama, but are such signs all that happens, all that is communicated? Can all perceived theatrical phenomena be accounted for as techniques of signification and parsed out into culture-specific signifiers? To rephrase this question, do we value a performance only for what we can find to say about it afterwards? Those who ascribe to the absolutist view that Eco seems to support would declare that every recognizable detail of such a performance was inscribed with determinable meaning. Given a moment to review their compendium of coded signifiers, they would produce another similar instance and announce that this intertextual linkage proves once again how seamless is the web of semiosis. The possibility that you or I might not make this same ingenious association does not seem to matter. But if this is a *public* code, it should matter. Who is this public that has such ready access to this cultural code? All of us may be public, but some of us are apparently more public than others. Interpretive communities, given a bit of authority, quickly pick up the rhetoric of Humpty Dumpty and the etiquette of the Mad Tea Partisans.

What I have proposed in regard to oral performance, that visual data always accompanies it and is intrinsic to it, is also true of the reading performance of written texts. The principal difference is that, whereas the visual data of orality is perceptual and processed by the outer eye, that of literacy is imaginal and processed by the inner eye. In both cases visual construal is a learned skill: the audient spectator of an oral performance must know how to look and what to see; but the reader of a written text must do all this through the mediation of graphic symbols and, moreover, contextualize these verbal cues with supplementary, extratextual details.

To explain what I mean by this constructive process of the inner eye in reading, let me resort to that faithful old example, "dog." When we encounter this word in a text and no specific breed is mentioned, what kind of image do we form? If this noun is only mentioned in passing as I have just done, there is no time and no justification to form a specific image of it: it has the imaginal status of a mere schema, like Peirce's "iconic diagram." But if the text tells us that it wags its tail, barks, or lays back its ears, we are obliged to construct a somewhat more particular animal. Is the breed undecidable? Of course it is, if by that we mean that no evidence exists to determine which breed of dog is intended. But intended by whom? The author? The genre? The text? If we can all agree on the undecidability of such a text in respect to this particular noun and also agree that its tail and ears have to be of a certain length, its bark of a certain volume and timbre, and its body of some certain magnitude between that of a Chihuahua and a Saint Bernard, then we have also implicitly agreed that verbal signs can be weakly coded and require some degree of imaginal supplementation. This would be no small agreement. Where would readers go to supplement this weakly coded sign? This reader-constituted "dog" may be drawn from a public store of types—a field guide of schemata—or from a private childhood recollection, but in any case this imaginal construct is constrained by the dictates of the text: since most texts seem to assert dominion over their contextual reference, the game rules dictate that image-supplementation should observe the rule of parsimony.

Without presuming to rewrite a text in the act of reading it, readers are nonetheless on their own when they confront a page of writing. As Plato's Socrates reminds us in the *Phaedrus,* writing makes us disciples without masters. These texts do not respond to inquiry. No speaker interposes a physical presence as interpretive mediator between the meanings and the audience. Reader and text enjoy a perilous freedom and a solitude that it is now two-and-a-half millennia too late either to lament or to ignore. But, as though this freedom within this image-thronged solitude were too dreadful and dangerous to entrust to us, we still have masters who accompany texts, not the authors but the executors of the authors' estates, that kind of oral governor who, in the quaint but timely language of Thomas Elyot,

> can expound good authors, expressing the invention and disposition of the matter, their style or form of eloquence, explicating the figures as well as sentences and words, leaving no thing, person, or place named by the author undeclared or hidden from his scholars. (*The Book of the Governor,* 1.15)

It is ironic that these Polonian schoolmasters of "validity in interpretation" have come to be regarded as the champions of literacy, when the truth may be that literacy, to the extent that it empowers individuals to construct fictive entities, is what they most fear. The fictive things individuals make when they read writing wink when they will. Like the inner eye that opens in the dark and enlightens that dark with "psychic entities," these fictive things wink most when hermeneuts wince.

The Image of the Messenger

This "image" may mean the visual presence of a messenger, for example, of an actor who portrays this character, or it may mean the imagery that the messenger has come to deliver, that is, the imagery that the words portray. As banal as this distinction may seem, it has continually blocked, or at least diverted, advances in the poetics of imagery. This primary distinction between the perceptual and the mental image, a distinction that must be established before any useful discussion of this topic can proceed, has too often been weakly made or, by some sort of amnesia, has been dissolved in premature considerations of semiotics and rhetoric.[7]

As I have suggested, our understanding of visuality, both perceptual and mental, has been confounded by a misreading of Plato and Aristotle. Whenever theorists have, explicitly or not, built theories of the literate imagination upon these foundations, they have built upon sand. At the heart of this problem has been the shift from oral to written transmission of information, a shift of which these philosophers were themselves only partly aware, a shift that to this day is uncompleted, for neither of these two cultural technologies has proven absolutely victorious. The two have persisted in a stand-off, for no matter how literate we may be, as long as we speak with one another, as long as we attend lectures, recitals, and dramatic performances, we will also live in an oral culture in which the presence of the speaker, the perceptual image of the messenger, will always be overlaid upon his or her verbally conveyed mental imagery. Conversely, as long as we read, we will always visually address ourselves to sequenced pages of left-to-right symbols, the presence of which as printed page will in its own way also condition our mental imagery. In oral and in literate settings the mental image is mediated, and at the same time partially obscured, by perceptual orders—and quite differently in each setting.

Diagram 1 illustrates the differences between the way in which oral and literate messages are mediated and their mental imagery—that is, imaginal interpretants—simultaneously evoked and inhibited. The two major categories of information, *epē* and *drōmena,* useful terms derived from the study of Greek religion, constitute strongly coded elements (*epē*) and somewhat more weakly coded performance elements (*drōmena*). As I pointed out earlier, the actors and the staging (here combined as *opsis,* or "spectacle") constitute the "objectal entities" that interpose themselves as "messengers" between the audient spectator and the meaning of the spoken discourse. Thus the imaginal signifieds of the *epē* are occluded by the perceptual data of the *drōmena.* The fact that the latter include embedded iconic and indexical signs ("action," or as Aristotle carefully calls it, the *praxeos mimēsis,* the "imitation of action") does not make them the more transparent: on the contrary, when, as Hamlet counsels, the action is suited to the word, the word to the action, the

---

7. "Just as the shrillest sort of Platonic idealism serves to reveal the excessiveness of Platonism, an exaggerated Aristotelianism shows through most in its empiricist heritage: its recognition of a Signifier but poorly masks its confusion between *thing* and *image of the thing....* " René Lindekens, *Dans l'espace de l'image* (Paris: Aux Amateurs de Livres, 1986).

EPĒ (things said)		DRŌMENA (things done)	
writing	speech	movement	forms
4.	3.	2.	1.
document	narration	action	actors as objects ORAL CULTURE
(grammata)	*(diēgēmatikē mimēsis)*	*(praxeos mimēsis)*	*(opsis)* "objectal ⟸ entities"
A.	B.	C.	D.
LITERATE CULTURE text as object	narration	dramatic scene	mental imagery
⟹ "objectal entities"			"platonic" (i.e., schematic) and "psychic entities"

Diagram 1

perceptual array is all the more riveting.[8] Narration in the oral performance was essentially a turning away from the visually presented *drōmena*.
Though this is the specialization of the messenger-as-character, any persona
could initiate this apostrophic, purely verbal procedure of *epē*. That is, any
actor could turn from the realm of iconic and indexical objects (*opsis*) to an
absent realm defined solely by the symbolic code, a purely mental realm in
which purely mental icons and indices are evoked. The one somewhat
anomalous category is "document," by which I mean a written text used by
the performers as a source of stored and retrievable information. Needless to
say, this element when it is used in the dramaturgy of an essentially oral
culture, or one dedicated to celebrating its age of heroes, serves more as a
prop than as an informational source.[9]

8. *Actio,* in this context, was the Latin term for "delivery," whether it was the technique of the *actor,*
the public reciter, or the orator. *Hupokrisis* was the equivalent term in Greek.
9. The one direct reference to a written document in Aristotle's *Poetics* is to a letter written by
Iphigeneia (in Euripides' *Iphigeneia at Tauris*) and meant to be sent to her brother via one of two
strangers who have mysteriously appeared at Tauris. Pylades, the prospective messenger, asks her to
unseal it and read it to him lest by chance his ship be wrecked on the way to Argos and he escape only
with his life—a typical oral reliance on the human memory over the fragile missive. The oralizing of

The status of the document is of course reversed, as is all else, in the literate situation. Here the text (the scroll, book, page, etc.) is the primary object of attention; its *grammata* are the visually coded *epē,* the symbolization of phonemic speech, which itself symbolizes through diegesis a realm of sensibilia — of dramatic action and imaged objects — that must be constructed in the mind of the reader. These symbolized doings, these mentally represented *drōmena,* are the "platonic" (here understood as "schematic") and "psychic" entities of which Eco spoke. The printed page is the "objectal" entity, the missive that in a literate culture has become the surrogate of the messenger. It too can inhibit mental imaging, but only when the reader decides to convert the text from an instrument of performance to an object of hermeneutical analysis.

---

the document effects the *anagnōrisis,* because the other stranger is her brother Orestes himself. The oralizing of documents is of course a theatrical necessity in any culture unless writing is made large enough for a literate audience to read it.

VISIONARY PLACES

In the first chapter we examined the semiotic act in which the visual imagery present in the mind of the Messenger is orally made present to the addressee. In this chapter we consider the genealogy of mental imagery. Philosophical and literary concern with the imagination as a constructive, intellectual activity does not much precede the eighteenth century, but religious concern with it is as old as religion itself. Since religious thought has exerted such a passionate and perennial influence on culture and has universally recognized the powerful implications of imagery, our concept of the imagination comes through history to us as a palimpsest inscribed and reinscribed with conflicting beliefs and practices. We cannot hope to understand its modern literary usage without tracing, however briefly, its religious origins.

The Chamber of Horrors

A mentally stored image is a burden. It may be a pleasant burden—a wish-fulfillment fantasy, a gratifying souvenir of the past, or a hopeful plan for the future—but to the extent that this image urgently needs to be communicated to others, it is a matter of serious general concern. It is news, and if, as folk wisdom has it, no news is good news, then all news is bad news. This proverbial expression and its corollary imply that natural cycles and human routines, boring as they may be, are preferable to any event that destabilizes them and thereby induces anxiety. The more emotionally troubling an event is, the more likely the imagery accompanying it will be remembered and transmitted to others as news; hence I think we are justified in generalizing that the imagery humankind chooses to store tends to reflect human experience at its most intense. If no news is good news, if on the societal plane news is experienced as history, and if the happy people is the people without history, then this happy people, should they ever be discovered, would have few images that even they would deem memorable.

To a stable community, the bringer of news is the herald of history, a necessary but dread announcer of change. Even if he has been sent out by that community to gather news and return, his arrival, though awaited, will yet be a surprise. If he has been sent to it from somewhere else, his arrival may find it totally unprepared. Whatever its momentary state of readiness, the community he enters will be *com-munis,* that is, enclosed literally or figuratively by a wall, a rampart that protects its presence from the absence "out there," from the spatiotemporal elsewhere out of which history emerges.

Drama has always drawn its themes from this tension between the here-and-now with its perceptual arrays (iconic, indexical, and incidental) and the elsewhere with its verbally (symbolically) conveyed images. Greek tragedy, for example, is veritably transfixed by the anxiety of absence: somewhere else, some time already or some time soon, something has happened or will happen the news of which has not yet reached the persons sequestered on the narrow, walled stage. The gods know what this is. Even the birds may know. But the persons most passionately concerned are left waiting, waiting and speculating in a present that is as narrow as the *proskēnion* they stand upon. All that they need to know or fear to learn is elsewhere. The wall to their back divides the here-and-now from this unknown elsewhere, and only three doors—variously specified as leading to the country, the city, the harbor, an interior, and so on, depending on the play—permit communication between these two realms. The persons of the drama look down from their platform, which is also called the *logeion,* the speaking place, and address the chorus ranged below on the semicircular *orchestra,* or dancing place, in the midst of which stands a low altar. But they cannot see the spectators, who, knowing the mythic scenario, bear a certain resemblance to the gods who, invisible themselves, view all the absent realm that environs these baffled agonists. Seeing into, or rather, mentally imaging, the absence of past and future and elsewhere, these persons of the *theatron,* or seeing place, are true seers.

The spatiotemporal universe represented by the Greek theater is divided into two sectors: that which is now presented to the senses is the Manifested, whereas the equally real world absent from them, be it past, future, or elsewhere in the temporal present, is the Unmanifested.[1] The *proskēnion* and the *orchestra* represent the manifested world, which the agonists try their best to manage, while behind them lies the wall of the *skēnē*, or "tent" (an archaism that was kept even after theaters became permanent structures of masonry). This backstage area was a storage- and tiring-room for the actors, but to the audience it was a forbidden chamber, like the sanctuary (the *naos* or *adyton*) of a temple. Events simultaneous with the events on the *proskēnion*, but deemed improper for viewing, took place in this chamber.

The *skēnē* was often therefore the place of uncanny and terrible goings-on, often a veritable chamber of horrors, to be imagined but never uncovered to the bright, rational light of day. It is, for example, from the darkness of the *skēnē* that the Messenger toward the close of *Oedipus Tyrannos* emerges to say:

> The sorriest part of what had happened
> Is not for you, no viewing [*opsis*] is permitted.
> Still, what I can remember you shall learn now:
> The fatal ending of that sorry woman.
> (lines 1237–40)

But if one sense was forbidden to cross that threshold, another was allowed. The cries of Medea's sons, the groan of Agamemnon, the shriek of Clytemnestra, the thunder at Colonus: such sonic effects must have prompted vivid imaging on the part of the audience. Sometimes one of the doors was left open and, whether or not the audience could glimpse anything within the *skēnē*, dramatis personae could gaze in, view, and comment on the shocking sight.

The only beings that were unconstrained by this epistemological division were the gods, who, normally unmanifest to mortals, surveyed a cosmos of time and space in which all was, or could be, manifest to them, even the secret thoughts of men. They were privileged beings who, when necessary, could be represented above the *proskēnion*, even above the *skēnē*-wall, flying or hovering, thanks to workmen who hoisted them up there by means of a crane, or *mechanē*. Butcher in his translation of the *Poetics* has his Aristotle use the time-honored Latin expression:

---

1. Cf. Benjamin Lee Whorf: "The Hopi metaphysics . . . imposes upon the universe two grand cosmic forms, which as a first approximation in terminology we may call the MANIFESTED and the MANIFESTING (or UNMANIFEST) or, again, OBJECTIVE and SUBJECTIVE." "An American Indian Model of the Universe," in his *Language, Thought, and Reality*, 59. The reader familiar with Whorf's essay will note that I have taken some liberties in appropriating his terms.

> The *Deus ex Machina* should be employed only for events external to the drama,—for antecedent or subsequent events, which lie beyond the range of human knowledge [what I have been referring to as the absent, the elsewhere, in short, the Unmanifested], and which require to be reported or foretold; for to the gods we ascribe the power of seeing all things. Within the action there must be nothing irrational. If the irrational cannot be excluded, it should be outside the scope of tragedy. Such is the irrational element in the Oedipus of Sophocles. (54b2–8)

"Within the action" means "within the action presented on the *proskēnion*"; the irrational "outside the tragedy" in reference to the Oedipus must therefore refer to the self-blinding of Oedipus in the *skēnē,* which, he declares, he did at the prompting of Apollo. Thus the divine and the human irrational collaborate in this extreme expiatory act.

The irrational, the *alogon,* was whatever could not be discussed and comprehended by *logos,* by verbal reasoning. The gods were superior to human logos; the impulses of the sensory "lower soul" were inferior to logos; and together they constituted an alogical alliance in which the gods made their wills manifest through dreams and divinatory procedures that depended on the susceptibility of the alogical lower soul to divinely sent visionary messages.

At this point we are ready to form a more comprehensive image of this model of the universe. Imagine a circle within which the known resides, the Manifested. Imagine it surrounded with the unbounded Unmanifested. Now imagine a small chamber attached to the inner circle, a chamber with doors that will permit communication between the two epistemological realms. When the divine *alogon* manifests, only a threshold separates the two realms. In the structure of the Greek theater, we thus have a schematic model of the Greek universe in the oral stage of its cultural development. We also have a model of the Greek psyche: the concealed space of the *skēnē* represents the faculties of memory and imagination, the public space of the *proskēnion* represents the faculties of speech and reason; the one associated with the *pathē* of the lower soul, the other with the conventionally adjudicated business of the agora, the arena of *logos* and *themis;* the one a subjective realm of affectively toned mental images, the other an objective realm of public icons and public language.[2]

---

2. The notion of the mind as compartmentalized by "faculties" is, of course, an ancient one. Long before Freud's so-called hydraulic metaphor of mind, even before the mechanistic models, philosophers

The *skēnē,* then, is the elsewhere, the absent, the Unmanifested made contiguous with the here-and-now, the present, the Manifested. It is the uncanny Absurd that adjoins the canny Rational.

Oracles and Dreams

Humankind, restricted to the Manifested, must wait for things to happen. Even when we act, we have to wait to learn the full consequences of our actions. This imprisonment in the sensory present has always provoked a yearning for the knowledge of the future, a power that we ascribe to beings of the Unmanifested, who can "see the future" with as much ease as we see the present.

Just as certain locations could afford greater perceptual vistas than others, certain locations seemed to induce greater visionary feats. (It is remarkable, by the way, how often the same places have seemed to foster both kinds of visual experience.) Legends spring up about such places. Some hero of the past had fallen asleep there and had a dream-vision that later proved to be true, or someone met a person there who seemed to have preternatural powers. However it acquired its reputation as a visionary place, it had become a place where those troubled with uncertainty could go to receive prognosticative dreams or hear sounds that a firm believer could interpret as speech. In its basic form, divination was a message from the Unmanifested to the Manifested transmitted either in an analog code (iconic and indexical signs through the medium of mental imagery visually hallucinated) or a digital code (symbolic signs in the medium of oral language auditorily hallucinated).

As Oedipus encountered Apollo in that terrible moment when he saw his mother-wife hanging in their bedchamber, so did the Delphic priestess, the

---

visualized the mind in architectural terms—lower and higher stories, front rooms facing the outer world, back rooms where things were stored, and a shrine-room where the mind drew down upon it the illumination of the gods. For a remarkably introspective study of memory as a storeroom see Augustine's *Confessions,* X. The psychologist Bertram Lewin traced the storage-room metaphor all the way back to the paleolithic caves of Europe; in *The Image and the Past* he proposed the theory that the cave paintings were ceremonial experiments with inside-the-skull visualization; the cave, being a model of the mind that one could actually enter, became, in effect, humanity's earliest temple.

Pythoness, meet this same god in her oracular chamber, one of the most sacred visionary places in the Hellenic world. Even Socrates consulted her. But she, after all, was a specialist, unlike the common horde of soothsayers with their credulous clients.

Most ancient Greeks, like most other contemporary cultures, believed that the gods communicate with humankind through dreams and waking visions. Their fourth-century philosophers, however, were not so sure. As for mental imagery generally, they regarded it as having certain practical applications. An artisan formed a mental image of a bed, for example, then measured and cut his lumber accordingly. This was termed *eikasia,* or likeness-making. Another practical use was in a system of mnemonics devised by the poet and orator Simonides of Ceos (556–468 B.C.): a speaker would commit to visual memory the details of a place—a temple or street—and then associate key words of his speech with the series of images that he would perceive if he were walking in an orderly fashion through that environment. Just as *eikasia* helped one plan one's actions, this mnemonic system helped one organize one's thoughts.[3]

Spontaneous imaging, however, if we judge from the remarks of Plato and Aristotle, was regarded with great circumspection at times with suspicion and open hostility. In their writings they display a curious ambivalence: though imagery is a function of the lower, sense-mired soul, it is nevertheless the medium of divine communications, and, though it serves a traditional social function, it is nevertheless potentially disruptive. *Phantasia,* the term most often used for spontaneous imaging, was associated more often than not with dysfunctional and lessened, rather than enh nced, states of consciousness. The lessened state of dream-consciousness, an occasion for *phantasia* that all persons could experience, was experimented upon by some temple cults that promoted techniques for enhanced lucid dreaming. After suitable preparation, a vision-seeker would spend a night lying upon the temple floor (*incubatio*), hoping to be visited by the divinity of that cult and given a prognosticative message. This dream would be a representation of perceptual experience, a *phantasma,* that is, a *seeming.* In respect to sensory modalities it was usually a combination of visual and auditory signs, that is, icons and indices, that were shown or enacted (*drōmena*), plus symbolic signs—words—that were spoken (*epē*).[4] From the point of view of established Greek philosophy, *phantasia,*

---

3. See Frances Yates, *The Art of Memory.*

4. For an interesting late-Classical account of dream-divination theory, see Macrobius's commentary on Cicero's *Somnium Scipionis.*

or as we would call it "imagination," was clearly an alogical phenomenon: perhaps for that reason it was so little recognized for its creative and problem-solving potential.

True, poets continued to speak as though they were often overcome by the powers of *phantasia* and, like the initiates of the mystery religions, had been eye-witnesses (*epoptai*) of theophanies. But it is debatable whether these accounts, expressed as they were in culturally determined formulae, recorded actual altered states of consciousness or were simply examples of conventional hyperbole. It is also true that earlier poets, such as Homer and Hesiod, invoked the Muses, but their testimony seems more an elegant allusion to an even earlier vatic technique than an accurate transcript of their own experiences.

The vatic practice that we actually find documented in Greece took the form of what was called *mantikē*, or divination, and appears to have been practiced under careful institutional restraints. Except for the occasional shaman from Scythia, sorceror from Thessaly and the Carpathian hinterlands, magician from Egypt, and gymnosophist from beyond the Indus, "barbarians" all, the Greeks consulted only their own diviners, principally those who were tenured, as it were, at such shrines as Delphi, Eleusis, Dodona, and Cumae. Plato's comment on diviners in the *Timaeus* makes an interesting distinction between the message the diviner receives and the message that is to be relayed to the inquirer:

> And herein is a proof that God has given the art of divination not to the wisdom, but to the foolishness of man. No man, when in his wits, attains divinatory truth and inspiration; but when he receives the inspired word, either his intelligence is enthralled in sleep, or he is demented by some distemper or possession. And he who would understand what he remembers to have been said, whether in a dream or when he was awake, through divination or possession, or would determine by reason the meaning of the apparitions which he has seen, and what indications they afford to this man or that, of past, present or future good and evil, must first recover his wits. But, while he continues demented, he cannot judge of the visions which he sees or the words which he utters; the ancient saying is very true, that "only a man who has his wits can act or judge about himself and his own affairs." And for this reason it is customary to appoint spokesmen [*prophētas*] to be judges of inspired divination. These are themselves called "diviners" [*manteis*] by some who are quite unaware that they are only the interpreters of dark sayings and visions, and

are not to be called diviners at all, but only spokesmen for those who practice divination. (71e–72b, adapted from the Jowett translation)

The two realms, the Unmanifested and the Manifested, apparently communicated in different codes. The principal officiant at a Hellenic visionary place was called a *mantis* and was often a priestess (sometimes called a *sibylla*). Sequestered from the public, her visionary statements would be mediated by institutional hermeneuts. The interpreter or college of interpreters would translate her ravings, as they were called, into elegant metered language. After her struggle with the unseen being who gave her her knowledge, we may picture her in the *adyton*, drenched with sweat and sleeping off the physiological effects of what, by all accounts, could be a strenuous encounter, while the official interpreter was relaying to the questioner the divine will and receiving the fee.[5]

Plato's and Aristotle's views of *phantasia* have more than their share of ambiguities. For Plato it was a higher power in that it could be divinely inspired, yet its place of operations in man was the lower soul, its organic location the liver.[6] As for Aristotle, in the *De Anima* he contrasts the lower with the higher cognitive processes and assigns to each its own type of *phantasia,* the sensory (*aisthētikē*) and the deliberative (*bouleutikē*). The first we share with most higher animals, the second is purely human and is used to plan future actions and foresee the consequences of such behavior. It is this higher *phantasia,* a sort of rational *eikasia,* that we rely upon when we construct theoretical models and ideal forms, be they statues or dramatic personages. The higher, or *noetic,* soul produces ideal forms by generalizing the products of sensory *phantasia.* Aristotle's main criticism of Plato was that the older philosopher had virtually deified these ideal composites, while willfully demoting the data that actually constitutes them to the status of copies.

---

5. See also Plato's *Philebus* 71C–72; also Plutarch in his antiquarian dialog "Wherefore the Pythian Priestess Now Ceases to Deliver Her Oracles in Verse," *Moralia* 75, 94. The picture Plutarch gives us of the Pythoness at work is that of a less violent, less managed visionary technician, but then again it comes to us five centuries after Plato.

6. In the *Phaedrus* (50D) he speaks of divinely inspired visions that he calls *phasmata* (singular *phasma*) in apparent distinction to ordinary mental images, or *phantasmata* (singular *phantasma*). These veridical visions, he says, are memories of the soul's preexistence and correspond to the Pure Forms, or Ideas. It is perhaps worth noting that the initiates of the Eleusinian Mysteries were said to witness the *phasma* of Persephone. See Wasson, *Road to Eleusis,* 80. Plato's use of this technical term suggests that he regarded the preexistence of the soul as a prenatal initiation into a theophanic mystery that the philosopher must spend his earthly days attempting to recollect and comprehend.

According to Aristotle, it was the lower sensory soul that was responsible for the formation of spontaneous imagery, the non-deliberative *phantasia* of dreams and divination. On this point Aristotle agreed with Plato and was, if anything, more distrustful than his master of the art of *mantikē*. For one thing, it was absurd, he said in *De Anima* (462B–464B), for any reasonable person to believe that God sends visionary messages, for, if he did, he would certainly pick out the "best and the wisest" and not behave as he seems to and send them to just anyone (*tois tuchousi*)—and to animals, as well, for some of them also seem to have dream imagery.[7]

Nevertheless, in the heroic age (the remote past from Aristotle's vantage point, apparently) only the most exceptional men were granted divinatory experiences. The legends surrounding the founders of ancient cities always told of encounters with local divinities in dreams, in waking visions, or face-to-face. A covenant of some sort was usually struck in which the supernatural being promised to support a newly founded enterprise in exchange for adequate worship—the famous *do ut des* formula. If the city proved successful, its founder and his god would be honored ever after and the place where the vision was received would become sacred ground.

Such a place becomes reputable when someone reputable sets up a memorial or is said to have done so. Jacob, who was later to become the eponymous hero of the Israelites, received a vision on a particular visionary location according to the legend recounted in chapter 28 of the book of Genesis. Having defrauded his elder-brother Esau of his patrimony, he hastily left home to seek temporary refuge with a kinsman several hundred miles to the north. During his desperate flight, he lay down one night on a hillside. He took a stone for his pillow and in his sleep beheld a ziggurat-like ladder stretching to heaven with its procession of divine messengers, or angels. Suddenly he saw his ancestral god, Yahweh, standing beside him and promising him and his descendents land and prosperity. When Jacob woke from his sleep, he said:

---

7. Skeptical as he is, Aristotle nevertheless acknowledges the powers of dream phantasia to generate veridical imagery that may be of help, for example, in diagnosing disease, and in a concession to the conventional opinion of the day he even grants that such relatively unbidden imagery can provide insights into future events, but again it is only to the simplest-minded of us and at that person's simplest-minded moment that such visions arrive. The distinction Aristotle draws is between the ordinary man (*ho tuchōn*), who is a sensitive medium for impulses and stray impressions because his mind is vacant and unemployed, and the intellectual (*ho phronimōtatos*), who is a poor receiver because his mind is too alert and active.

"Truly the LORD is in this place, and I did not know it." Then he was afraid and said, "How fearsome is this place! This is no other than the house of God, this is the gate of heaven." Jacob rose early in the morning, took the stone on which he had laid his head, set it up as a sacred pillar and poured oil on the top of it. He named that place Beth-El [House of God]. (16–19)

This sacred pillar is in Hebrew a *matstsebah,* an object of veneration popular among the Baal cults of Canaan and later resolutely destroyed by the Israelites (who in the reign of Josiah even destroyed the pillar and shrine at Beth-El). Then he made a vow: if this vision was a true vision, then this god would protect him in his exile and would bring him safely home again, and he would accept this god as his own, declaring, "And this stone which I have set up as a sacred pillar shall be a house of God." But since a shrine and a cult need funds, Jacob added, "And of all that thou givest me, I will without fail allot a tenth part to thee" (Genesis 28.22).[8]

Eventually a place (like Beth-El or Delphi) becomes the center of an amphictyonic league. Often a hill or mountain, this raised site becomes regarded as the *omphalos* of the world, the place where the human ecumene is joined to the lifegiving divine realm. (Jacob proclaimed this visionary place the "gate of heaven," and many other ancient cities were so regarded: Babylon, for example, literally meant "the gate of the gods.") To honor the divinity's revelations of the future, the neighboring communities would join to honor and preserve that other temporal absence, the past, by instituting regular public remembrances of the god's providential acts. What had been, when they first occurred, divinations of the future, would now be placed among the oral chronicles of the past. In addition to these digital-coded memorials, the devotees would produce analog-coded memorials—icons (paintings, statues, and carved articles such as the *matstsebah*), sacred buildings, and outbuildings to house the more well-to-do pilgrims who would visit this place. In time, additional permanent buildings would have to be constructed to house the workers who would serve the physical needs of the visitors.[9]

8. Unless indicated, as for example KJV for the King James Version, all biblical passages come from *The New English Bible* (New York: Oxford University Press, 1976). In this version LORD (capitalized) signifies the Hebrew "Tetragrammaton" YHWH, usually rendered by modern scholars as "Yahweh."

9. As for the sacred character of ancient cities: even if they were not founded as a response to a particular local apparition, they were always developed according to the advice of oracles, auguries, and the like. See Fustel de Coulanges, *The Ancient City,* 138–42. "Every city was a sanctuary; every city might be called holy" (141).

At length a "holy city" would form about this visionary place, dedicated to preserving analog representations of that orally preserved past, a city whose iconically designed architecture would rise above a landscape itself engraved with features that function as indexical signs: a spring created by a magician, a pool where the waters of chaos rise from the underworld, a cave where a demon lies imprisoned, a cleft in a hillside that the enraged sky god once opened with a blast of lightning. Thus the amphictyonic shrine would become a city of visible testimony.

The House of the Wind

As part of the campaign of consolidation waged by David and his supporters, it was decided that Israelite religion and Israelite political power should be centralized in the "City of David," Jerusalem. This meant that the numerous hill-shrines, like Gilgal, Shiloh, Gibeon, and Beth-El, would have to diminish in importance. In order to accomplish this, he had to transport the Ark of the Covenant, the most sacred of the Mosaic relics, to the royal capital.[10]

The Ark, a chest containing the Decalogue and other tokens, had been kept in a small tent, the Tabernacle, which itself was enclosed in the Tent of the Presence. The hill-shrines had their altars, but the Tent of the Presence was as nearly a formal temple as the Israelites had until David's son Solomon completed the Temple on Mount Zion in Jerusalem (c. 950 B.C.). The Ark was believed to be a place where Yahweh would be present, standing invisibly upon its gold cover. The Ark and its enclosures had an advantage over temples of stone and wood: it could be carried into battle and serve as a sort of command post for the Lord of Hosts, who, like other divine rulers of Bronze and early Iron Age theocracies, was thought to battle for his people against the gods of other nations. This portable Holy of Holies also harked back to the Bedouin past, a legendary patriarchal age of innocence and independence, when the Hebrew clans and tribes moved continually with their sheep, goats, and cattle over the grasslands west of the Arabian Desert.

When Solomon completed his Temple, the Kingdom had its supreme

10. Between the Conquest of Canaan and the reign of David, Shiloh had been the principal amphictyonic center. See Joshua 18.1 and 21.2, Judges 21.12, 1 Samuel 1.4, and Jeremiah 7.12.

amphictyonic shrine, a building that faithfully reproduced the Tent of the Presence and the Tabernacle, but on a monumental scale.

> And Solomon said: O LORD who hast set the sun in heaven,
> but hast chosen to dwell in thick darkness, here have I
> built thee a lofty house, a habitation for thee to occupy
> forever.   (1 Kings 8.12–13)

This installation of the Ark into the Inner Shrine, the Holy of Holies, took place appropriately enough at the Feast of Tabernacles (Sukkoth).

The "thick darkness" of the Holy of Holies is not unlike the dark recesses of other sanctuaries throughout the ancient world: the direct visual presence of gods was intolerable to mortal eyes. The myth of Zeus and Danae was a Greek exemplum. All gods were in essence invisible beings, dwellers of the Unmanifested realm, but nearly all were able to assume some visible appearance—anthropomorphic, theriomorphic, or dendromorphic—and be depicted as such in iconic representation. But Yahweh had chosen not to do so. He who was who he was, as he named himself in that much-disputed phrase (Exodus 3.14), later told Moses that no man could look at him and live (Exodus 33.23). Though in many passages of the Bible this divinity is characterized in anthropomorphic terms, he is never fully described as such. The god for whom Solomon built this new residence, while never seen, is observed in his effects, his theophanies associated with sudden environmental changes—earthquakes, storms, lightning, and, most consistently, wind.

The Hebrew word *ruach* means both "wind" and "spirit." In itself, this double meaning is not exceptional: the Greek *psychē* had a comparable semantic extension, as did the Latin *anima* and *animus*. What was exceptional was the way the Hebrew word encompassed the concepts of "life-breath," "psychological attitude," "incorporeal creature," "divine power," and "wind" (in the ordinary sense of air in motion). In the second verse of Genesis, for example, is it a mighty wind sweeping over the waters, is it the Spirit of God hovering over them, or is it *a* spirit sent by God? The "Creation Psalm," Psalm 104, could be used to support all three of these interpretations; it also includes several instances of *ruach* as vital principal, or "life-breath" (see especially verses 3, 4, 29, and 30). Ancient Hebrew evidently conceptualized *ruach* as a cosmic causative force that only appeared to be different in its different manifestations (cf. the speculations of the Milesian Presocratics), whereas modern languages make sharp distinctions between these phenomena. *Ruach* seems, therefore, to be a term that denotes *invisible power, the intensity of*

which can only be gauged by its visible effects. The invisible god who could come
down from heaven and graciously sojourn in the darkness of the Holy of
Holies was, when abroad, the rider on the wings of the wind.

Yahweh ruled inanimate nature as the furious storm-*ruach.* He ruled
animate nature by his life-giving breath-*ruach,* the withdrawal ˙ f which
caused death. But he ruled culture and history by allotting to individual men
and women a particular kind and amount of *ruach.* These adjustable allot-
ments could be spirits of wisdom, of jealousy, of judgment; they could be
lying, faithful, good, perverse, new, unclean, proud, patient, humble: the
psychodynamics of *ruach* could thus be appealed to when faced with the
question, What was it that possessed him that he behaved that way? Where a
polytheist might attribute unusual behavior to the momentary influence of a
particular god, the monotheist Hebrew would explain it as a kind of spirit
sent by Yahweh. (We can easily see here the perennial tendency in monothe-
isms to detach subaltern "spirits," some obedient and some rebellious, from
the Divine Spirit.)

This invisible energy, when it is specifically designated as the *"ruach* of
Yahweh," could produce states that the Greeks called *enthousiasmos.*[11] As such
it spurred to action such popular leaders as Samson and Gideon in the period
of the Judges. More typically it produced ecstatic trances and prophetic
utterance. The Hebrew word for prophet, *nabi,* appears to be related to a
verb meaning "to pour forth" and meant a person capable of episodes of
uncontrollable mediumistic speech. It therefore seems to denote a psychological state related, if not identical, to the *mania* of the Greek *mantis.* When, in
Numbers 11, the starving Israelites murmur against Moses, he assembles
seventy of their elders around the Tent of the Presence and enters the
Tabernacle. There Yahweh withdraws part of Moses' *ruach* and distributes it
to the seventy, who immediately fall into a prophetic ecstasy. The next day, a
ruach from Yahweh springs up, in English translations a "wind," and drives a
great number of quails into the Israelite encampment. As the wind comes
literally from God-knows-where, so also comes the prophetic spirit. Like the
future, both are elsewhere until they arrive. (Cf. Jesus' comment: "The wind
[*pneuma*] blows where it wills; you hear the sound of it, but you do not

11. Albright (355) speculated that toward the end of the second millennium a charismatic practice
was introduced into Greece and into Palestine from Anatolia and that Dionysianism and Hebrew
Prophetism were two branches of the same movement. According to Jewish tradition, at least,
Prophetism ceased with the beginning of the building of the Second Temple. The dates that bracket
this period correspond to the beginning of the Iron Age (c. 1200) on the one hand and, on the other,
the introduction of Semitic ("Cadmean") script and the first compilation of biblical texts (c. 600).

know where it comes from, or where it is going. So with everyone who is born from spirit [*pneuma*]" [John 3.8].) As though the Deuteronomic law of primogeniture could apply to spiritual as well as fleshly sonship, *ruach* could also be inherited, as we learn from 2 Kings 2.9, where Elisha begs and eventually receives a "double portion" of Elijah's *ruach*.

From the time of Elijah on through the time of the Babylonian Captivity the effect of this invisible force on history becomes increasingly a verbally mediated effect. The famous episode in which Elijah reenacts the archetypal Mosaic confrontation with Yahweh on Mount Horeb points this up:

> Suddenly the word of the LORD came to him: "Why are you here, Elijah?" "Because of my great zeal for the LORD the God of Hosts", he said. "The people of Israel have forsaken thy covenant, torn down thy altars and put thy prophets to death with the sword. I alone am left, and they seek to take my life." The answer came: "Go and stand on the mount before the LORD." For the LORD was passing by: a great and strong wind [*ruach*] came rending mountains and shattering rocks before him, but the LORD was not in the wind [*ruach*]; and after the wind there was an earthquake, but the LORD was not in the earthquake; and after the earthquake fire, but the LORD was not in the fire; and after the fire a low murmuring sound [*gol*]. When Elijah heard it, he muffled his face in his cloak and went out and stood at the entrance of the cave. Then there came a voice [*gol*]. (1 Kings 19.9–13)

The voice, or sound, repeats the previous question and Elijah repeats his previous answer, after which Yahweh gives him some very specific political advice.

The significance of this passage for our study of verbal imagery lies in its pointed shift of emphasis from natural theophany to the prophet-mediated word. From 1 Kings on, the frequency of "word" [*dabhar*] increases, as does the expression "the word of the LORD," that is, of Yahweh, attaining its greatest degree of frequency in the Book of Jeremiah. The later twelve, or minor, prophets employ that phrase less often simply because all, or nearly all, these texts are explicitly presented *as the word of Yahweh;* the books of Hosea, Joel, Micah, Zephaniah, Haggai, Zechariah, and Malachi, for example, simply begin with this attributive phrase. This is not surprising. No longer wonder-workers or king-makers, the prophets had become relayers of the divine word—in short, messengers; the name of the last prophet in the canon, Malachi, in fact means "Messenger of Yahweh."

The significant relationship between *ruach* and *dabhar* is that both are invisible aerial entities that can proceed from a mouth and can thus become the invisible manifestations of an invisible Creator. As the symbolic code of language does not resemble its signifieds, it is a fitting vehicle for an aniconic deity. The burden of the messengers' messages was also aniconic in the semiotic sense — either a call for spiritual renewal (symbolic signs performing their abstract work) or the presentation of what we might call the "imagery of consequence": in the past, when the patriarchs, Moses, and the good kings did *A,* the successful consequences were *B;* when the unfaithful people and their wicked leaders did *C* (as they are doing now), the catastrophic consequences were *D* (as they are now or shortly will be); and if a repentent Israel does *E,* Yahweh has promised to revise the future and produce the glorious consequences *F.* The prophetic message thus points to the visible evidence — that is, the indexical signs — of invisible acts. When misfortune occurs, the prophetic mind searches for an intelligible cause and traces that cause back to the divine unmanifested source of all this manifested world, the spirit-wind that brooded over the waters and quickened them. For the sake of this visible world, it brings its petitions to the god who invisibly stands upon the Ark, his throne within the darkened Holy of Holies, within the Temple, within the Holy City.

Celestial Messengers

The concept of the messenger is crucial to this study of mental imagery. Before we continue to examine it in a biblical context, I think it would be useful to take several steps back from our cultural scrutiny to place the messenger in a broader rhetorical context. Hence the following excursus.

In the *Rhetoric* Aristotle distinguishes between the written style (*lexis graphikē*) and the agonistic style (*lexis agonistikē*), the confrontational style of public debate, characterizing the former as more precise and the latter as more histrionic (*hupocritikōtaton*) (III.xii.1–2). Obviously the written style was the more recent development and the agonistic style was the mode of the older, traditional, oral harangue. This distinction can be further elaborated if we assume, as I did in the first chapter, that "style" can mean information supplementary to the sign-function of words. Aristotle's "written style" would add to the words of a message a tone of detached observation and inquiry, whereas the confrontational style would convey an emotionally charged relationship between a given speaker and a given addressee. Before returning to our study of Hebraic visionary practice and its impact on theories of mental imaging, it would be useful in marking our progress through this territory of language and mental imagery to draw up a short list of situational contexts that generate different verbal activities.

Aristotle's agonistic style of oratory is based on the situational context I will term Direct Presence, the perceptual presence of a speaker to one person or to a group. It may be a direct oral statement ("I–Thou") to a single addressee, a dialog ("I–Thou-I") between two or among several persons, or a general address to a public ("I–You"). What distinguishes this verbal activity from every other one is that it includes only those persons acoustically present at the time of utterance. It excludes all others, who, if they are ever to learn what was said, must depend on the Indirect Presence of an informant.

These persons absent from the original speech must have faith in the representations of a messenger (in Greek an *angelos*), a person-sent-from-a-presence (an *apostolos*). In Indirect Presence a believer participates in the originary presence through the messenger, or a relay series of messengers, who thus connects him with the speaker. But this re-presentation process can never actually reinstate the original speaker; moreover, the messenger necessarily occludes that speaker by interposing his own presence and by unavoidably interpreting the message in the act of re-presenting it. The message itself is revised by the fact that this is an orally transmitted text that depends on its memorability and on the mnemonic skills of the messenger. These deficits notwithstanding, the importance of Indirect Presence as a substitute for Direct Presence is evident in most religions (cf. the *Torah she-be'alpeh* of Judaism and Apostolic Succession in Christianity).

The third degree of removal from actual presence may be termed Epistolary Presence. Here the message is committed to writing and the messenger becomes a letter-carrier. At this point we are at a stage that is technically literate but still stylistically agonistic: assuming this is not an "open letter" or a general manifesto, the speaker is addressing a particular person or persons and writes as though he or she were present to them. The epistle is a written intermediary as the apostle is a human intermediary; both require of the receivers an act of faith. (Other kinds of coding and storage, for example, photography and audio recording, are in this sense also "epistolary" [see Ong, *The Presence of the Word*, 176–91].)

The last of these four informational emanations is Scriptural Presence, that is, the link-up with the authoritative source through the collection, transcription, and compilation of the oral texts of Indirect Presence and the written texts of Epistolary Presence. Here again writing is only a storage mechanism, not a stylistic factor. Especially when an alphabet is used, this writing is a phonetic notation that is activated only when it is re-oralized by being read aloud, the motoric and auditory process of articulation physically re-presenting the original speech-act. To those who trust its authenticity this writing is the written message concerning the messages of messengers who have received the speech of originary speakers, and its purpose is to reinstate the presence, however attenuated, of these now-absent speakers, to make forever manifest the mind of the now Unmanifested, to perpetuate the long lost face-to-face, I–Thou relationship of Direct Presence.

This essentially theurgic project contrasts sharply with a verbal practice that abandons the agonistic style and applies the written style to what is *now* present or potentially present to the senses. We might call this the quest for Empirical Presence. Converting indexical imagery through analysis into evidence, this project seeks another path toward the causes that underlie phenomena. History, philosophy, and science, despite the levels of logical abstraction to which they are known to attain, may all be regarded as discourses of Empirical Presence.

Contrasting with religious and scientific quests for presence is the impulse of poiesis, which, though not necessarily opposed, is nevertheless quite distinct and produces quite different verbal products. Instead of the question, "Can I now and forever accept this on faith as a true revelation of what lies beyond our ken?" or "Does the evidence support this conclusion?" the question is, "Will I temporarily *pretend* to believe this?" The fictive presence of poiesis and its implications for imagery we will consider in subsequent chapters, but before we can deal directly with this topic we must complete the process of defining and excluding the verbal modes that do not produce the written image. We began with a consideration of oral poiesis in Greek culture; we must now resume examining the implications of verbal presence in Hebraic culture.

At this point in our study of the written image it is essential that we look at the effect of a writing—that is, a *scripture*—that does not imitate the act of writing but rather the act of speaking. The agonistic style, solidly based on an oral system of information, will, even when read in solitude, generate something of an order *similar* to what I have earlier called the objectal image of the speaker, an image that tends to occlude the mental images that the words evoke. Drama places the visible presence of actors before the eyes of the spectators, but what sort of objectal image is presented in writing?

Moreover, what sort of image is obtruded when the writing declares the speaker to be an unimageable divinity or, if he be angel or man, simply neglects to describe him?

To try to answer these questions, let us first imagine the sort of "real-world" situations that writing composed in a traditionally oral society strove to record.

The perceptual presence of a speaker can affect our mental imaging of the words in various ways. A speaker's appearance may be intimate and familiar and therefore less distracting—a story told by a friend might readily lend itself to our visualization. On the other hand, a speaker's presence can be quite imposing and deliberately enhanced for effect. In an oral culture in which messages must be conveyed in person, a man of superior authority would be surrounded with emblems of power. Anyone being ushered into his presence would be likely to see guards and servants and a display of opulence. The lord might also place himself in a position spatially superior to his auditors, who, when they hear his words, are obliged to "listen up," a kind of hearing that the ancient oral world knew all too well. To "listen from below," an idiom that has entered numerous languages, reflects the social conventions of orality. It meant to hear carefully and to act accordingly, in short, to obey.[12]

"Listening from below" could also be a natural consequence of the lowering of the hearer, as in the ceremonial practice of prostration. Abraham and Lot bow low to their angelic visitors, Joseph's brothers bow low to him, the Israelites are warned not to bow down to false gods, the fugitive David bows low to Saul, who later bows to the ground before the risen ghost of Samuel, the prophets of Jericho bow low to Elisha—with how much greater humbleness was one expected to approach the feet of the Most High! Perhaps the aniconic character of Yahweh was a mark of extreme visual deference. Accordingly, to believe that Abraham and Moses were allowed to speak with Yahweh "face to face" (however that expression was understood) is to accord them the highest possible honor.

Hearing the words of an unseen or, if seen, undescribed speaker is the typical biblical mode of reporting speech. Whether or not it derives from a posture of deference toward the speaker, this narrative style, nonetheless, does not diminish the sense of *presence* of the speaker. In an oral context all

---

12. Cf. the Greek *hupakouein,* the Latin *obaudire* —whence our "obey"—and the German *Gehorsamkeit;* the Hebrew *shema* meant both "hear" and "obey." Even our word *understand* can imply subservience as in: "I want you to do that, do you understand?" "I understand."

discourse is in the agonistic style. For words to be heard, there must be a speaker somewhere nearby; the less visible the speaker, the more awesome and worthy of obedience that speaker is.

According to one traditional doctrine every word of the canon was dictated or inspired by Yahweh's own *ruach,* making him in effect the omniscient narrator of the Bible. Questions of authorship aside, we may regard the Bible as a written record of the uneven compliance of a people with the terms of a covenanted lease on their land and, indeed, on their very lives. In this light, Yahweh becomes the principal speaking character in the narration. Even when he is not speaking to or through his heavenly or earthly messengers and even when other speakers are not directly addressing concerns of the covenant, his presence and his power orientate all discourse. His role is that of universal landlord, that is, universal king, and the king, when he is not speaking through his agents to the people, is being spoken of by his people.

Compared with this invisible king with his court of powerful spirits, all earthly kings and kingdoms were pale imitations. The Tent of the Presence and the Tabernacle it enclosed were said to be modeled on a heavenly prototype revealed to Moses on Mount Sinai (Exodus 25.40). This double enclosure suggested the dwelling of a divine patriarch or sheikh who was to all the creatures of the earth what Abraham or Moses were to their nomadic followers. The Temple, which reproduced the basic design of the earlier movable shrine, befitted a firmly settled monarch who was to the Heavenly Host what Solomon was to the militarily secure Israelite nation. Kingship in either case was an authority orally wielded. Kings conferred face to face with their advisors and personally dispatched their own messengers. Three passages afford interesting insights concerning the heavenly council over which Yahweh presided.

Before Ahab, king of the Northern Kingdom—then known as "Israel," as distinct from the Southern Kingdom, "Judah"—decided to engage the Aramaeans in battle, he called in his prophets to advise him. As he sat upon a throne set up by the gates of his royal city, Samaria, all urged him to launch an attack to recover the town of Ramoth-Gilead. But one, Micaiah, under pressure recanted and divulged this vision:

> I saw the LORD seated on his throne, with all the host of heaven in attendance on his right and on his left. The LORD said, "Who will entice Ahab to attack and fall on Ramoth-Gilead?" One said one thing and one said another; then a spirit [*ruach*] came forward and

stood before the LORD and said, "I will entice him." "How?" said the LORD. "I will go out and be a lying spirit in the mouth of all his prophets." "You shall entice him," said the LORD, "and you shall succeed; go and do it." You see, then, how the LORD has put a lying spirit in the mouth of all these prophets of yours, because he has decreed disaster for you. (1 Kings 22.19–23)

We see here a two-tiered universe reminiscent of the Homeric world-picture, and note how closely the procedures of celestial diplomacy parallel those of earthly kingdoms. Needless to say, the lying *ruach* does succeed: Ahab locks up Micaiah and rides east to meet his unkingly end. (Cf. the false dream sent by Zeus to Agamemnon, *Iliad,* 2.6.)

A more famous instance of a envoy sent from the divine court appears in the Book of Job. It begins during a festival time, perhaps New Year's Day. The children of Job have assembled and received their father's blessing. Simultaneously in heaven the "sons of Yahweh" (usually glossed as his "angels") assemble about their father who asks them for news of the earth. Satan, apparently an investigatory angel (modeled, some speculate, on the Persian secret police), when asked concerning Job, volunteers to test the faith of this up-till-now fortunate man. Besides the parallel settings, what is important to note here is that spirits not only transmitted verbal messages (symbolic signs) and induced visions (on the surface level, at least, iconic signs), both veridical and false: they also effected perceptible changes on the earthly plane that were to be interpreted as *indexical* signs. After Satan communicates these disastrous signs, Job, his wife, and his "comforters" undertake to interpret them, only to learn in the end that these two planes, though parallel, are incommensurate. From the human point of view, the deliberations that take place in the celestial *skēnē* are, to use Aristotle's adjective, *alogoi* — irrational and unspeakable.

The final enthronement setting that I will cite is the vision of Isaiah (chapter 6). This takes place in the Holy of Holies, the *skēnē* of the Temple. Isaiah reports seeing Yahweh above the Ark, attended by seraphim, who shade their eyes from his glory. Isaiah is abashed that he, a "man of unclean lips," should behold this vision, but a seraph (a spirit of fire) touches his mouth with a burning coal from the altar and he becomes purified. "Then I heard the Lord saying, Whom shall I send? Who will go for me? And I answered, Here am I; send me" (6.8). Isaiah, a human, has volunteered to be a messenger of God, a *malak.* When he leaves the *skēnē,* this visionary place where heaven intersects with earth, he will reenter the manifested world and appear upon the stage of human history with a message from the Unmanifested One.

From Cosmos to Microcosmos

I began this chapter with a consideration of the Greek theater as an epistemological model of the Greek universe, the *proskēnion* and *orchestra* as the Manifested, the *skēnē* that lay behind the doors of the back wall as the Unmanifested. Perhaps it is mere coincidence that the seventy Jewish elders who produced the first Greek translation of the Bible (the Septuagint version) translated the three words *ohel* (the outer tent), *mishkan* (the Tabernacle, the Holy of Holies), and *sukkah* (tent or booth) as *skēnē*, which of course the writers of the Christian New Testament also adopted. The word *skēnē* was, after all, a common term not necessarily laden with liturgical connotations. But the architectural isomorphy of palace, theater, and temple appears to have been more than coincidental and, I would submit, represents the communications model of every orally administered government.

As far as the public was concerned, the ruler of a non- or semiliterate kingdom was at any given time either (1) hidden, (2) conferring with his council, or (3) executing his will via his messengers. In the first state he was totally unmanifest and his thoughts inscrutable; in the second, he became present to a select few and in a special place, for example, his throne room; in the third, his representatives proclaimed, interpreted, and enforced his decrees. The ancients reasoned that a Divine King of the cosmos would similarly comport himself, but on a divine scale. He would normally reside in bliss, removed from the cares of cosmic sovereignty, enjoying the delights of a heavenly garden (cf. the *pardes,* or paradisiacal pleasure garden, that the writer of Ecclesiastes said that Solomon planted). But when need be, he would confer with his advisors—lesser divinities such as those whom Zeus assembles on the Homeric Olympus or the "sons of God" whom Yahweh meets with in Job 1.6–12. At these conferences the god would reveal what he had kept hidden in his heart to these lesser beings, who, of course, were not omniscient. Then he would charge one or several from among them to intervene in affairs elsewhere in his universe. As below, so above—when anthropomorphic religion reversed this formula, it made the divine oral-communications network the prototype of the earthly one.

	UNMANIFESTED	VISIONARY PLACE	MANIFESTED
1. General models: celestial prototype	Hidden Divinity	Divine Assembly	Angelic Mission
earthly type	Hidden King	Royal Council	Sending of Agents
2. Sacred places: Greek Oracle	Hidden Divinity	*adyton, naos*	*mantis,* or *prophētēs,* representing *mantis*
Greek Theater	Hidden Divinity	*skēnē*	Messenger
Jewish Temple	Hidden Divinity	Holy of Holies (Tabernacle, or *skēnē*	Priest
Jewish Prophecy (its setting)	Hidden Divinity	anywhere, often in presence of angelic visitor	Prophet, as Messenger
3. Intra-psychic "places:" Microcosm	Inner Self (*psychē*)	Imagination (*phantasia*)	Utterance (*logos,* spoken or written)

Diagram 2

Diagram 2 illustrates each visionary place as a chamber between the Unmanifested and the Manifested. At the top is the divine prototype with its earthly counterpart. Below these are the institutional structures that derive from them. In the case of the Greek oracle the *mantis* becomes the instrument by which the god becomes present; her incoherent words are heard, interpreted, and proclaimed by her spokesman, the *prophētēs.* In the Greek theater, as we have seen, the adyton is the *skēnē,* the dark inner sanctum dominated by the divine and the subhuman *alogon;* through its doors enter the messengers to announce what the manifested world cannot immediately know. Like most oracles and temples, including the Tabernacle of Moses and the Temple of

Solomon, the theater had its altar outside and opposite the entrance leading to the inner chamber.

The Jewish Temple, said to have been built on the celestial model, was by some believed to *be* that celestial palace. "The LORD is in his holy temple, / The LORD's throne is in heaven" (Psalm 11.4). Here is an iconism of place that surely makes up for an aniconism of the divine person. If the Creator Spiritus, who knew all the secrets of his creation and had made prophets by simply "pouring out his spirit upon them," resided in this earthly temple, it ought to have been the visionary place par excellence. Despite its cultic centrality, however, it never precluded the having of visionary experiences elsewhere—the whole world, as Jonah found, was Yahweh's—and prophets could be accosted by envoys from the court of heaven anywhere (consider 1 Kings 8, Solomon's sermon at the dedication of the Temple).

The final isomorph is that of the microcosm. If heaven is the spiritual cosmos and earth the material cosmos, then man is the little cosmos, and—if there is an Unmanifested, a visionary place, and a Manifested in the first two cosmoi—these three epistemological sectors also coexist in man. Conceived of as a power of, or a place in, the psyche, the imagination could produce either visual or verbal representations or, as was often the case, a combination of both. Finally, if temple architecture is the universal paradigm, its structure is also human, and the human body, as Jesus and Paul declared, is the Temple of the Holy Spirit.

SCRIPTURE AND POIESIS

Having noted the importance of visionary places and procedures in the ancient world, we have to account somehow for the relative paucity of descriptive writing these cultures produced as they made the transition from orality to full literacy. I have suggested that oral transmission of narratives and oral performance of written texts tend to inhibit the presentation of verbal imagery, but, as we examine the writings of the Bible, other reasons seem to emerge. It is certainly not my intention here to present a biblical poetics or anti-poetics, even if I were able to do so, but rather to sift through this large and various set of texts for clues that might help us answer the initial question I posed in my preface: what are the cultural roots of literary iconophobia?

When one addresses this question to the Hebraic tradition, the first response is likely to be that the ban on iconic representation of the Deity has somehow marked Judaism and to some extent Christianity with an underlying unease in respect to mental imagery and hence to any writing that deliberately evokes it. Such a hypothesis would suggest that hermeneutics, when it turned from scripture to écriture, carried with it an iconophobic bad conscience that disabled it from constructing an adequate theory of the written image. Without denying the persuasiveness of this position, I would argue that the problem is more complex than this. It is too simple an explanation to say that because the god of Moses and Elijah inveighed against the visual depictions of his rivals and of himself, he conditioned all those subsequent generations that feared his wrath to turn the mind's eye from the products of their own fantasy.

In this chapter we need to ask, What in the scriptures is fully described and why? And what is not described and why? As we shall observe, cultic artifacts are described in extensive detail, whereas persons are described only when a feature, like hair or stature, is significant to the narrative. We know, for example, exactly what the trolleys looked like that carted the sacrifices to and from the altar in Solomon's Temple but have not the least idea what Solomon looked like. Except for cultic objects and architecture, nouns are notable for their lack of adjectival modification, being customarily elaborated only by synonyms and antonyms in parallel constructions. Flora and fauna are designated by their specific nouns and customary verbs and usually left at that, as are other natural phenomena.

Grass grows, fire burns, stocks and stones stand, but what of human beings? Conscious human life is characterized by its vast choice of dynamic options. For that reason, perhaps, biblical narrative typically shows persons in action. When we speak of Hebrew writing as deficient in imagery, we mean deficient in the static portrayal of living beings. As we proceed in this study of the written image, we must resist narrowing our notion of imagery to static pictorial representation. We must remember that verbs are precise grammatical means to depict nouns in significant movement. If, in a given culture, men and women are judged by their actions, then human imagery will be kinetic and indexical. If, in that same culture, cultic artifacts signify by their formal and representational aspects, then artifactual imagery will be static and iconic.

The Written City

According to the biblical tradition God had an original design for Creation that Adam and his descendents spoiled. This design might in human terms be called a mental image, the sort that Plato says a carpenter forms by the process of *eikasia* before beginning to build a piece of furniture, or the Demiurge before making a cosmos. When God determined that postdiluvian mankind was ready, he began to reveal to Abraham and his descendents the outline of his original purpose. To do so, he chose semiotic means comprehensible to his fallen creature: (1) indexical signs in the form of portents, "Acts of God," augural signs (cf. the Urim and Thummim), (2) iconic signs in the form of dreams and visions (sent to and/or interpreted by the seer, or *roeh*), and (3) symbolic signs in the form of speech (especially the ecstatic speech of the *nabi*). The latter could be interpreted as the direct transmission of the word of God or of his angelic intermediaries and could accompany the visionary revelation of iconic and indexical signs. Since symbolic signs can encode icons and indices, these linguistically mediated, orally transmitted messages produced a sizable body of gnomic and narrative compositions. Some of these oral texts—the Decalogue surely—were written down in alphabetic script as early as the twelfth century B.C., but most scholars agree that the transcription of most of the then-extant oral accounts did not predate the seventh or sixth centuries.

Born into a fully literate culture, we might at first find it strange that a people who had always the means to do so did not commit their national epics, songs, proverbs, prophecies, cultic regulations, and etiological myths to writing as soon as this means was available. That the Israelites did not do so during the almost four centuries that they securely dominated the land suggests that they did not *need* to do so, that the memorially stored and orally transmitted information that constituted their cultural code could be preserved through the institutions locally in place. The apparent fact that much of this information was collected and transcribed beginning during the latter half of the seventh century and systematically edited and copied and recopied during and shortly after the Babylonian Captivity suggests a crucial relationship between place and memory: as long as a people can store its traditions orally in association with a familiar environment and a culturally coded amphictyonic city, it will not need to encode its oral traditions in writing or promote general literacy. By analogy, private collectors of artworks are not normally inclined to have them professionally photographed unless they fear their damage or loss.

For an oral people, indexical signs (geological formations, tumuli, ruins, and so forth) and iconic signs (visual representations) are sufficient aids by which to store and retrieve symbolic signs, that is, verbal discourse. In such a society there is a story that goes with every monument and every unusual topographical feature. The visible world is everywhere coded by divine and human hands. As we observed in the story of Jacob on his visionary hillside, throughout the world the most common means of commemorating an unusual event is the erection of a monument. If the event has been a theophany, the monument has a double purpose: it reminds the people of the miraculous occurrence and it also reminds the divine being, who is thereby invited to reveal her- or himself at that place again. Temples and shrines, when they are built on such sites, become places of visitation for the divinity because they are both human and divine mnemonic devices. To destroy such a marker is to strike at and scatter the contents of a people's national memory, perhaps even to cancel a god's memory of them. Like many a conquering nation, the Israelites in their early history therefore undertook a campaign of cultural genocide that included the tearing down of the monuments of subject nations in order to "blot out the name of them from that place" (Deuteronomy 12.3), a policy that others in 722 and in 587 were to turn just as brutally against them.[1]

Place is indeed a powerful preserver of names. Once inscribed with meanings, visual objects continue indefinitely to prompt particular memory data. We have only to return to our childhood hometowns to recall more names, events, and feelings than we may wish to remember. Throughout the world prior to encoding of concepts and speech in graphic symbols, place was deliberately encoded to assist memory storage. Avenues, walls, temples, statuary—all these could be made to embody associative meanings. If cathedrals were encyclopedias for the semiliterate Middle Ages, megalithic structures from Stonehenge to Teotihuacan served the same purpose for their preliterate communities. Architecture, thus constructed to memorialize the past and symbolize the meanings of the cosmos, provided a visual array that an onlooker could take away in the form of visual imagery and meditate on after returning to the profane, everyday world. If place is intrinsically memorable, and monumental places are inscribable with particular meanings, it follows that the mnemonics of Simonides could not have been an original invention but rather a shrewd adaptation of a much more ancient art of memory.

The importance of urban architecture as image in the ancient world cannot be overestimated. The ancient city was a fortified place, a repository of food and weapons during times of famine and war, but, as Fustel de Coulanges pointed out, it also stored the nation-making cultural artifacts of the people. The inner city with its central temple was thus in symbol and fact the final refuge of the people and was itself a visible profession of faith. To center oneself within such precincts was to situate oneself within the significances of a complex diagram, dense with meaning. Yearly pilgrimages to that architectural complex refreshed one's mental image of it and of the significances it embodied. Male Israelites, for example, were expected to visit Jerusalem three times a year, at the Pilgrim Festivals of Passover, Shevuoth, and Sukkoth. Should an enemy succeed in blocking these pilgrimages or indeed in destroying the city and its holy places altogether, it might hope to wipe out forever those significances and with them the nation that those significances integrated—unless, that is, the dispersed communities had a way to remember the holy places and, like Simonides with his mnemonic of the

1. See also Leviticus 26.1, Deuteronomy 16.22, and Exodus 34.13.

"mental walk," could set forth upon a mental pilgrimage to that once and future city.[2]

For a preliterate culture this mental reconstruction is difficult: dependent on orally transmitted narrative, such a people, once uprooted, cannot retain in transgenerational collective memory the complex structure of meanings that had been built into such architecture, not to mention the rich anecdotal content associated with actual visits to such sites. For such a people, the Aztecs for example, doctrinal tradition after a few generations becomes folklore and the subjugated nation has its options narrowed either to marginalization or to assimilation. For a people with a literate option, however, the destruction of these architectural symbols does not "blot out the name of them from that place," but transfers instead that name to another code and transforms that place into a mental "place."

The question of remembering seems to have been crucial in the years immediately following the destruction of Jerusalem in 587. Psalm 137 focuses on the pain of remembrance, then the necessity of remembrance ("If I forget you, O Jerusalem, let my right hand wither away," 5), then on a theme that often accompanies such protestations, the prayer that *God* will remember, as though God might "turn his face" from them and forget them as he had done with the Israelite Northern Kingdom that had been devastated by Sargon in 722 and totally dispersed.[3]

Psalm 74 is entirely structured around a plea to God to "remember the assembly of thy people" for

> The shouts of thy enemies filled the holy place,
> they planted their standards there as tokens of victory.
> They brought it crashing down, like woodmen plying their
>   axes in the forest;
> they ripped the carvings clean out,
> they smashed them with hatchet and pick.

2. See Psalms 46, 48, 76, and 84; also 120–34 ("Songs of Ascents"), especially 125, where topography becomes iconic, the hills enfolding Jerusalem as the Lord enfolds his people. Note too how the bitter Psalm 137 is placed after a series of exultant evocations of this amphictyonic center.

3. See also Lamentations, chap. 5. On the question of literacy in the Northern Kingdom: there was no doubt as great a proportion of literate persons in Samaria as in Judah, but whether or not in the short years prior to the Assyrian conquest they strove to preserve the common oral heritage is doubtful. Samaritan scriptures, somewhat different in details from the Jewish canon, exist, but when and how they were compiled is unknown. Most scholars agree in crediting King Josiah of Judah with the first systematic efforts to write down and edit the oral texts of Ephraim and Judah; this was a full century after the destruction of the Northern Kingdom.

> they set fire to thy sanctuary,
> tore down and polluted the shrine sacred to thy name.
> They said to themselves, "We will sweep them away,"
> and all over the land they burnt God's holy places.
>
> (Psalm 74.2, 4–8)

This apparently depicts the state of the largely nonliterate population left behind in the hills and caves about the ruins of Zion. Transported east to a small town in Mesopotamia, Ezekiel and the other literate Jews in exile felt this same need to remember. Perhaps one mnemonic strategy for him was to sketch an aerial plan (a diagrammatic icon) of the city on a tile to be a "sign to the Israelites" (4.1–3). But a far better way was to reproduce the image of the city by encoding it in language that his literate compatriots could use to prompt its mental reconstruction.

> In a vision God brought me to the land of Israel and set me on a very high mountain, where I saw what seemed the buildings of a city facing me. (40.2)

What follows for two chapters is the description of an angelic architect who measures and seems by that very act to bring into being a new Temple within a new Jerusalem. The measurements, in cubits and handspans, are elaborately precise—tedious details for most modern readers, but for an exile familiar with the architecture of that time, this essentially ekphrastic text could be used to form a three-dimensional image of that lost holy city, a written image that in turn could be used to retrieve the meanings that had been built into its symbolic architecture.

The power of written language to preserve abstract discourse was by the sixth century a well established fact, but its power to evoke the imaginal meanings of *place* was discovered only when this literate elite, uprooted from its sacred city, was forced to encode that city and the rich record of its liturgy in writing, to establish a Scriptural Presence, a connectedness with the "fathers" and with the god that had once cherished them. The power to transmute indices and icons into words that in turn could evoke *mental* indices and icons was a literary invention of epoch-making proportions. The Pentateuch had contained precise ekphrastic descriptions of the Ark, the Tabernacle, the Altar, and so forth, but with the visions of Ezekiel we have the first of a series of ekphrases of the Temple and the city that were to preserve vividly in the minds of the exiles the imagery of that lost kingdom.

Another moving example of the power of prophetic imaging and of the writing that it produced is the Book of Tobit, classified by Jews as belonging to the Apocrypha. It is the story of a pious Israelite of the Northern Kingdom who in the past had made all the prescribed pilgrimages to Jerusalem but now could not: first, he had been transported to a far-northern settlement by the conquering Assyrians, then he became blind. Now in Job-like despair, feeling the judgment of God on him and on the whole Diaspora, he prepares for death. But through the help of the angel Raphael and the resourcefulness of his son Tobias, Tobit regains his sight, beholds his family with joy, then in his mind's eye visualizes the restoration of Jerusalem. His blindness had been an outward sign of an inner blindness of the imagination.

The Book of Tobit is often regarded as a romance, that is, a composition in the style of the Hellenistic novella, a narrative enlivened by the adventures of a young hero (Tobias) who with supernatural help (Raphael) battles with an evil demon (Asmodeus) who has cast a spell over a beautiful maiden (Sarah). This internationally popular genre undoubtedly represented a stage of literacy and chirographic book publishing that could not have existed before the second century B.C., when urbanized populations could indulge a taste for verbal imagery as a form of vicarious observation. Any local tale, any traveller's story, any legendary miracle could be woven into this fabric. Writers of romance could with the stroke of a pen create any wonder their minds could conceive. Anything imaginable was possible and absolutely nothing in the world of Hellenistic romance was unimaginable.

Perhaps because of its frankly imaginative elements, Tobit was not accorded canonical status. Its image of the restored Jerusalem, however, involved imagination of quite a different nature. Jerusalem and the Temple of Solomon, though they had been destroyed and were only partially reconstructed, had truly existed and had been repositories of meaning. Distant memories they may have been, but they were not mythic constructs. They existed in God's memory, and, thanks to writing, they were also forever present in human memory. This was a writing-down (a *scriptura*), not a making-up (a *poiesis*)—a distinction crucial to our understanding of classical Hebraic descriptive writing.

We might assume that classical—that is, pre-Hellenistic—Greek authors, by contrast, would be unconstrained in their descriptive imagery. But when we compare the two, we do not find in Homer, Hesiod, and the tragedians appreciably more description of specific persons and places than we find in the Hebrew canon. These two classical literatures are more like one another in this respect than either is like post-Renaissance Western literature. One reason why Homeric similes stand out so prominently is because these self-contained little pictures are so very different from the linear sequence of narrative events.

We might also assume that the Hellenes, whose national identity was always geographically diffused when compared with the Israelites, would have little concern for storing in words their cultural artifacts. This assumption is correct, but there is one Homeric description that is comparable to the extended "written cities" of the Bible: the description of Achilles' shield in book 18 of the *Iliad.* Upon this shield is depicted, among other details, that ultimate human structure, the city, in this case two cities—the city at peace and the city at war. When we compare these with the written city of Ezekiel and Jeremiah, these cities of Homer are generic, not specific. But, like the scriptural Jerusalem, their prototypes are coded human artifacts; that is to say, since every ekphrasis is by definition the verbal encoding of an artifact, its coding in symbolic signs has been necessarily preceded by its coding in non-symbolic, that is, indexical and iconic, signs. Not only are the signifieds on the shield examples of cultural activities, but the signifier (the shield), itself the signified of the poet's words, is a complex graven image, an icon. In both Hellenic and Hebraic writings, prior to the second century B.C. we seldom find extended descriptions that evoke mental imagery that are not based on already coded artifacts. The normal prototypes of written images in classical Hellenic and Hebraic writing were visible art works, either geometric or representational. Of all formal, geometric artifacts, the temple and the city that environed it were the most encyclopedic repositories of meaning, and for the Jews the preservation of the Temple—even as mental image—was a national necessity. But as for representational artifacts, Mosaic law had placed upon them considerable prior constraints.

Human Imaging and Divine Speech

While the prohibition against representational art (Exodus 20.4) has usually been interpreted as applying only to representations of the Deity and to temple-worship, some literalists extended it to include all representations, especially of the human form.[4] Since publicly displayed images of the

4. The "Birds' Head Haggadah" produced in South Germany in the late thirteenth century went so far as to depict men with birds' heads in order to comply with a strict interpretation of

human form have always been recognized as having a power to stimulate private images, most religions have utilized them in exercises of controlled visualization. After meditating upon an icon of some sort, usually a highly conventionalized figure, the devotee in sleep or in a state of lessened perceptual acuity might "see" this depiction appear and even "hear" it speak. The Greeks made a distinction between *eikōn,* the artifactual cue, and the *eidōon,* the divine visitant. The idol is therefore the icon "come to life" in the visionary state, the spiritual being in the form of a *phasma* (apparition) that displays the power to move, gesture, and speak and seems to conduct the devotee over a mystical landscape of symbols in which appear the images of things to come. *Idolatry,* therefore, properly signifies the worship of mental images that appear to one after contemplating icons and should not be confounded with iconolatry. The biblical ridicule of idolators as worshipers of stocks and stones could have been correctly aimed only at the most unsophisticated adherents of iconic cults and justified in response only to the grossest forms of religious showmanship.[5]

Perhaps the underlying reason why the One God could not be represented was that unlike other gods he was claimed to be the source of *all* powers, constructive as well as destructive, loving as well as wrathful, maternal as well as paternal. Pantheons, though they seldom begin so, inevitably become cosmic divisions of labor, systems of allotted and delegated authority in which separate divinities specialize in particular powers. But how could a single, omnipotent, omnipresent divinity ever be depicted, without depicting him or her as having some particular characteristic, that is, without delimiting its attributes. If it were depicted as a storm-god like the Baal of the Canaanites, would it not need the partnership of a god of the stars or of the seasons or of the waters under the earth? If it were shown and subsequently imagined as a loving protector, would this not strip it of its divine cruelty?[6] Would not other gods be called in to fill such vacuums in the cosmic economy?

---

the commandment. By contrast, the third-century-A.D. mosaics of Dura-Europos on the upper Euphrates depict human figures, albeit standardized; God is represented synecdochically by intervening hands.

5. The apostle Paul (1 Corinthians 10.20) recognized this distinction when, alluding to Deuteronomy 32.17, he identified *eidōla* with *daimones,* spiritual beings other than, and presumably opposed to, the god of Jews and Christians. *Eidōla* were to be negatively shunned because their worship was ineffectual (Hebrew *hebel,* Greek *mataios*) but positively condemned because it was disloyalty to God or, in the metaphor of Hosea, spiritual adultery.

6. Those who wince at this attribute should reread Job or at least consult Deuteronomy 32.39–42.

The only representation of this god would have to be a living likeness, not a lifeless artifact, a person who would bear a "family resemblance" to God, as the creation account says Adam bore. In chapter 5 of Genesis, which appears to be a self-contained account of human creation and genealogy, God creates man in his likeness (Hebrew *demuth,* Greek *homoiōma*). Then, ignoring the story of Adam's first sons, Cain and Abel, this account goes directly to his begetting of Seth in his "likeness and image." This son of man (*ben adam*), when he engenders a child, begets Enosh (like "Adam" another Hebrew word for "man"), a living likeness of God thrice removed.[7] The language used to describe the visionary imagery of Ezekiel is quite exact. When he sees the throne-chariot, Ezekiel sees *living* creatures that bear the *likenesses* of humans and animals. Is this the phantasmagoria of a mind intoxicated by the cultic glyphs of Babylon? The text does not interpret them as *phasmata* or *eidōla,* but as genuine beings. Which is to say, this is not a vision of mere likenesses of living creatures but a vision of actual living creatures who in turn bear the likenesses of particular species that artists happen to have observed and made into culturally coded icons. This distinction is important. The creatures that Ezekiel sees and describes are originals, not copies, and their apparition is therefore offered as a true glimpse of the Unmanifested realm of God, which in this visionary place has erupted into the human Manifested.

God, as the Lord of Life, permitted the sons of Adam not only to bear his "image and likeness" but to replicate it through sexual generation. But man could not *create* living likenesses of himself. If, as the Hebraic tradition resolutely emphasized, the common property of the divine and the human was oral utterance, the speechless omnipresence of God was an everyday, unexceptional condition. If, on the other hand, God had a message to impart, he, or his angel, would unmistakably announce himself. According to the ethnocentric comparative theology of the Jews, Yahweh spoke but could not be seen or visualized—unlike the gods of the gentiles, who could become visible and be visually represented but could not really speak. This verbal presence was propitiated by all believers through proper conduct, by the

---

7. There seems to be a significant relationship between sonship and imagery in Hebraic thought. At least in its later usage, this phrase, "son of man" (or "son of Adam"), takes on a more than merely generic connotation. Cf. the use of this phrase in Ezekiel and Daniel. I will not speculate further on the meaning of the title "Son of Man" assumed by Jesus in the Gospels. Orientalists have traced the phrase to many different sources, Assyrian, Babylonian, Iranian, even Indian. Whatever its provenience, however, it is generally assumed to have gone through a process of esoteric doctrinal definition in the first and second centuries B.C. and is associated with the Essene cenobites of the area about Khirbet Qumran.

priests through cultic service in the Temple, and by the prophets to whom was revealed the year-to-year compliance of the people to their covenant with their divine landlord. As Creator of the process of natural generation, he could be recognized in his living icons; as Preserver and Destroyer, God of history and of nature, he could be perceived everywhere in his indexical signs; but as Lord of Language his most sublime, and most human, theophanies were symbolic signs, the words he confided to his human messengers.

There were no creative-writing workshops in ancient Jewry. Humanly generated words constituted, from the religious vantage point, a lesser language. The writing down of this lesser, merely human language, a skill that could preserve anything that flitted into the consciousness of any one possessed of a reed pen and a sheet of papyrus, was a wearisome technology, as the last three verses of Ecclesiastes tells us. The notion of literary inventiveness and originality of any sort was discouraged because the true value of words, spoken or written, lay solely in their linear descent from the past and ultimately from their association with the only speaker that really mattered, Yahweh. Hence, if a new composition was to be introduced to the literate and necessarily religiously trained elite, it would have to be attributed to some worthy of the past—to Enoch, for example, or Moses or Solomon or Isaiah. This self-abnegating gesture would not, of course, guarantee its acceptance, but, for an author lacking conspicuous prophetic credentials, to claim it as his own would certainly have been an unwise promotional strategy.

Though we may now view the Hebrew scriptures as a rich treasure of poetic invention, it is doubtful that its writers ever thought of themselves as inventors. The only one who legitimated thoughts, words, and consciousness itself was Yahweh, the bestower of that invisible energy, *ruach*. The thoughts that humans were capable of generating were, as the Bible usually characterizes them, sly, evil thoughts. The various Hebrew words used in reference to the self-initiated activities of the mind tell us that, to the religious writers of these texts at any rate, thought was man's principal means of separating himself from God and his fellow men and of living a secret selfhood. The utterances that issued from such private thought were "lying," "wicked," and "vain" words. "Why do the heathen rage, and the people imagine a vain thing?" asks the Psalmist.[8] Why indeed, since Yahweh reads the hearts of all

8. Psalm 2.1 (KJV). In the King James Version the noun "imagination" is used nineteen times to translate three different Hebrew words and three different New Testament Greek words. The verb "to imagine" is used fourteen times to translate five different Hebrew words and one Greek word. The

men. He had done so in the Garden of Eden when he called Adam to account. He did so when he condemned humanity to the Flood, for he saw that man's "thoughts and inclinations were always evil" (Genesis 6.5). He brought the Israelites to the Promised Land despite knowing how each of the impious among them had planned to "follow the promptings of [his] stubborn heart" (Deuteronomy 29.19). Looking back, he tells Jeremiah how the forefathers of the present generation had rebelled: "Obey me, I said. But they did not obey; they paid no attention to me, but each followed the promptings of his own stubborn and wicked heart" (Jeremiah 11.7–8), and because the present generation had not changed, he would now deliver them to the Babylonians (Jeremiah 16.12).

If one were to derive a theory of the imagination from the Hebrew scriptures, it would have to start from the basic distinction between productive and reproductive imagination. The remembrance of the history of the people—the escape from Egypt and the entrance into Canaan, especially—and the remembrance of Jerusalem and the Temple were acts of reproductive imagination, or memory-imagery. This sort of imaging was positively enjoined on the faithful. Productive, or combinatory, imagination, however, was viewed as the worthless work of merely human thought. Now we call this "creative imagination," and so it seemed to the writers of the Bible, but since only one god created the universe, the creations of human minds could only be blasphemous parodies of Yahweh's work. And of course there were those stupid enough to do exactly this—and then fall to their knees and worship these images.

To understand the reasoning behind the extreme enmity of the Hebraic tradition toward the "creative" imagination, we need to appreciate the sharp distinction it made between the divine and the human thought processes. Although thoughts and their attendant images are attributed to God and to humanity, God's hidden thoughts, as soon as he utters them in words, begin to become actions. Either his *ruach* effectuates them instantaneously, his angelic spirits undertake to do so, or, if his plans require human cooperation, his prophets relay his words to the people and their leaders.

This latter, unfortunately, was his least efficient way of executing his designs, for humans, unlike angels, have a peculiar difficulty with words. When humans decode the revealed signifiers, the signifieds that they generate

---

New English Bible rarely uses "imagination" and "imagine" in these instances. For example, the above quote reads: "Why are the nations in turmoil? / Why do the peoples hatch their futile plots?" King James's translators evidently regarded the imagination as the prime mental faculty of subversion.

in their minds become contaminated with their own private thoughts and images, and even when the pious repeat God's words, these words get contaminated with the sly, crafty discourse of mortals and become misrepresentations (*shav*). Instead of hearing-and-obeying (that single-word concept in classical Hebrew and in other orally based communication systems), humans go their own way with the result that all they think and achieve becomes empty and ineffectual (*hebel*).

When humankind tries to form a mental image of the divinity, the result is, like Nimrod's tower into heaven, an ineffectual folly, an emptiness—*hebel*. The only god that the human mind can construe by its own unaided efforts is a god it creates and, as Deuteronomy 32.21 declares and Jeremiah reiterates, this parody of a god is *hebel*. Similarly, when one visualizes a desirable object or situation, this too is *hebel*, or so the Solomonic preacher of Ecclesiastes declares: "Emptiness, emptiness ... all is empty. ... emptiness and chasing the wind" (1.1, 11). It is *hebel* to try to pursue the wind; it is also *hebel* to try to pursue that invisible energy, the spirit ("wind" and "spirit" are designated by that one word, *ruach*), for only God controls the *ruach*. Likewise it is *hebel* to fantasize an imaginative ideal: every human ideal is an idol, an idol of the mind, as Francis Bacon two millennia later and arguing from quite different premises was to call it. If you could do and possess whatever you imagined, as King Solomon could, you would be even worse off because you would be burdened with the materialization of *hebel*, a monument to your own emptiness.[9]

The foibles of human kings notwithstanding, the model of kingship was divine; the truly godly monarch was supposed to be the earthly vicar of Yahweh and the faithful shepherd of his Lord's straying people. No king, despite his strengths, had proven perfect, but every king was enthroned with the hope that with the oil that anointed him, God's spirit would transform him into the monarch that could protect his small flock surrounded as it increasingly seemed by armies of wolves. From the Psalms to Isaiah and thence to later apocalyptic writers, the figure of the Anointed One, the Messiah, loomed larger in the minds of the believers as the political prestige of their nation dwindled. Here was a human image, as human as their beloved King David, but, as the supreme human messenger from God to humanity, this ideal leader seemed to embody the very image of God, in

9. 1 Kings 11 remarks on the power of Solomon to indulge his royal desires. He had seven hundred wives and three hundred concubines. His political marriages with neighboring royal houses led him to indulge the religious traditions of these princesses to the extent of sanctioning the worship of Ashtoreth of Sidon, Milcom and Molech of Ammon, and Kemosh of Moab.

which the unfallen Adam had been formed. Whenever he appeared or was sent from heaven, humankind could put away its mental images of the godhead, for in this warrior-king they could contemplate the authentic manifestation of the unmanifested Lord of Hosts.[10]

Parousia: The Once and Future Presence of the Word

According to Jewish tradition the earthly vicar of Yahweh would be a king in the lineage of David and rule the world from Jerusalem. In the language of Psalm 2, the anointed king (Messiah) of Israel is said to be "begotten" by Yahweh and, as his son, to rule over all the nations of the earth. As the Israelite nation shrank in dominion and prestige, this notion of divine filia-tion seemed more and more important, for as time wore on it seemed that only a member of Yahweh's own household could intervene to save the Jewish nation from total submergence and assimilation and its scripture and laws from becoming of interest only to Hellenistic antiquarians. Only such a Messiah could mobilize and lead the faithful remnant on the terrible "Day of Yahweh," the day when their hidden god would burst forth and reassert his suzerainty over the cosmos.

The Messiah, as son of God, would represent his father's will and wield such spiritual energy that his very word would annihilate his enemies (Isaiah 11.4). Since the Messiah would be the messenger par excellence, possessed of the authority of God *by birth,* not by human faith, the word he would utter would be the undiminished word of him who sent him. That privilege that Abraham and Moses enjoyed in some degree and for brief moments, the privilege of face-to-face communion with the Most High, would be his by right and be perpetually enjoyed. He would not need to learn from writing, because he would be able somehow to participate in the Divine Assembly with those spiritual beings, sometimes referred to as the "sons of God," who were commanded directly by God.

According to those who identify Jesus of Nazareth as this Messiah (Greek *Christos*), a brief synopsis of the completion of worldly history is as follows: the Christ was born in the birthplace of King David, of whose lineage he was

10. In the Christian New Testament see the Gospel according to John, which is emphatic throughout on the proposition that in seeing Jesus one saw the Father. See also 1 Corinthians 15.49; 2 Corinthians 4.4; and especially Colossians 1.15.

(c. 3 B.C.). In A.D. 27 he began to preach the coming of the new age, gathered a following of disciples, but was executed in 30. His disciples reported that he rose from the dead and after a few weeks with them disappeared into the sky. Shortly thereafter, God sent his *ruach* to strengthen and inspire them to proclaim to the world the imminent return of Jesus, who would destroy the enemies of God's people, rule a reunited kingdom for a thousand years, raise the dead, judge the living and those who had died since the creation of Adam, and create a new, harmonious, heavenly universe. While they awaited this second and final coming, they strove to persuade both Jews and Gentiles to enter their fellowship, or "church." In order to preach this "good news," or *euangelion,* to as many persons as possible, they needed to communicate with distant communities of Christians through writing. The earliest extant Christian writings, the letters of Paul, date from the period 48–63. He was executed in 64. In 70, after an unsuccessful revolt in Judea, the Romans under Titus destroyed the Temple and Christians and Jews alike were persecuted throughout the Roman Empire. In the period 70–100 the oral and written accounts of Jesus' sayings were collected and published in what came to be four versions, the three Synoptic Gospels and the more esoteric Gospel according to John. By the latter half of the fourth century a new scripture was established that constituted a written testimony of a new contractual relationship—a new testament, or covenant—between God and humanity. This scripture began with an account of the first coming of the Christ, detailed the growth of his Church, and ended with a precise revelation of the second coming. In Greek, the language in which this New Testament was written, each of these two comings was called a *parousia,* that is, an arrival, a return, a becoming present, or simply a presence. The interval of the Church was thus understood as a period of absence between two presences.

This theory of history influenced the writings of the early Church Fathers, and their so-called Patristic writings in turn reinforced this scenario. The concept of messiahship, or christology, central of course to these writings, left a particularly strong impress on traditional Western concepts of mental imagery. Like the earlier defined doctrine concerning idolatry, it entailed an authorized relation between a signifier in the Manifested and a signified in the Unmanifested, a relation between presence and absence. Mental imagery, however, even when it is prompted by conventional written signs, enacts itself on an inner stage and resists external authority. It is a presence that is at the same time an absence. Our task now is to try to understand from this new scripture what function, if any, it assigned to verbally cued imagination.

The validity of the New Testament as a covenant between God and humanity is based on the authority of the words of Jesus. Though he was literate (Luke 4.16–20), his teaching seems to have been exclusively oral; at least none of his writings has survived and none is explicitly mentioned. He claimed to have received from God, his real father, the authority (*exousia*) to say what he said. As the word implies, *exousia* is the quality of "being from (someone or somewhere else)" and is a delegated power. The first impression he always made upon religious Jews was his way of assuming an *exousia* that the *grammateis,* the scribes or doctors of the written law, could not or dared not exhibit. They were obliged to consult scripture and its commentaries, whereas he spoke as though he directly executed the legislative voice of the living God. In a community now dependent on the written word of God, Jesus represented the spoken word of God, the vitalizing *logos,* not the deadening *gramma.* The episode of Jesus' healing the centurion's son (or servant) is to the point. When Jesus is about to enter the man's house to see the boy, the centurion stops him and says that, as a military man, he understands *exousia:* when he tells a lower-ranking soldier to do something, that thing is done, for legionary authority is a line of command orally transmitted and unquestioningly obeyed. If Jesus has the authority from God to dispel the malady, he can do so simply by the oral word. Jesus does exactly this and commends the centurion's faith to others. In the ultimate development of the christology of the word (John 1.1), Jesus was said not simply to possess but to *be* the living word of God, the word that issues from the very mouth of God—the oral word that at the creation brought the world into existence and ever afterward transmitted the numinous presence of God to all who heard it.

The contrast between the living *logos* and the dead *gramma* continued to be a doctrinal issue after the death of the young Messiah. The Christian scriptures reveal the development of a profound conflict between the message of the directly perceived messenger and the later written transcripts of that message. On the one hand the credibility of this messianic messenger was based on a correspondence between his life and the predictions set forth in prophetic writings. (Old Testament history also came to be viewed as prophetic, that is, as a chronicle of "types" that prefigured the redemptive drama of the New Testament.) On the other hand, if he was the authentic Messiah, his presence should have been sufficient proof. If the Unmanifested that apocalyptic writings described had become present to the senses within the Manifested, then the purpose of those written images was at an end ("consummated," "fulfilled") and prophecy, as a revelation of the Unmanifested, was itself obsolete.

This latter point is important to stress. If the Unmanifested was here and now in the Manifested, then a visionary place between the two realms should no longer exist. No special *skēnē* or Tabernacle would be needed. As proposed earlier, the *skēnē,* or visionary place, was the central point linking the Manifested with the Unmanifested. If a group rejects this dualism either by declaring these two to be interpenetrating realms or by denying the reality of one of them, that group denies the necessity of the *skēnē.* This appears to have been exactly what the primitive Church did. Its immediate focus was the Second Temple rebuilt and adorned by the hated Herod I and controlled by the Sadducean party—less the central holy place of Jews than a royal chapel (Albright, 293–94). Jesus himself had inveighed against abuses in the Temple cultus and had predicted its destruction and his own ability to rebuild it in three days. The report of this statement weighed heavily against him at his trial before the Sanhedrin.

When the Gospels recount such predictions, however, they add that by the "Temple" he meant his body and that he was really predicting his own death and resurrection. Nevertheless, by transferring the concept of the Temple (that is, the *skēnē*) to his body he struck a blow at the edifice of stone and its monopoly of access to God's spirit. If, as Paul later said, every Christian's body had become a temple of the Holy Spirit, then the microcosmic *skēnē* had come into being. The kingdom of God that is within each Christian (Luke 17.20) could at the moment of spiritual illumination appear to one even in the trammels of this world of darkness.[11]

In addition to the small human temples that now walked the earth, each filled with the Spirit of God—each pledged, if called, to give testimony (*martyrion*) to that indwelling by suffering sacrifice as Jesus did—there was the largest and the most ancient temple of all, the sky and the earth. The macrocosm would stand established until the end of time. Isaiah 40.21–22 ("Deutero-Isaiah") calls the sky the tent where God abides in his majesty, hidden to earthly eyes, and the earth is his footstool. This persistent concept had always been a humbling afterthought to temple builders (I Kings 8.27). In the Revelation of John, at the end of the universe this macrocosmic temple

11. This was frequently the experience of the Christian martyrs, if we are to believe the accounts circulated among the early churches. Stephen's vision at the end of his trial in Acts 7.54–56 is representative. For references to the body as a tent, see 2 Corinthians 5.1–5 and keep in mind that the *skēnai* (tents) Paul refers to were made of skins (an etymological linkage?): as skins covered the wayfarer in his tent, the human integument enclosed the soul on its pilgrimage to heaven. See also 2 Peter 1.13–14.

is at last thrown open, its sanctuary revealed, and a wholly new reality created.[12]

All this would come to pass in a "little while" (John 16.16–23). Since everyone would shortly see God's Messiah and his glorious army of angels face to face, there would be no need to imagine a world beyond this transfigured world—what would be left to imagine? This ultimate non-dualistic heaven on earth would be the parousia of complete presence: nothing would be absent and, for the elect at least, nothing could possibly be imagined. When John envisioned the New Jerusalem, he "saw no temple in the city; for its temple was the sovereign Lord God and the Lamb" (Revelation 21.22). "The throne of God and the Lamb will be there, and his servants shall worship him; they shall see him face to face" (22.3–4). The Kingdom of God would neither be within nor without but everywhere at once. Divinity would no longer be invisible: the Unmanifested would be the Manifested.

Though no one, not even Jesus, could know precisely when this day would dawn, it would occur during the *present generation.* In the three Gospels where this statement appears it is followed by the solemn oath: "Heaven and earth will pass away, but my words will not pass away."[13] When this apocalyptic change occurred, the saved would see differently, said Paul. Now, when we wish to "see" God, we are dependent on the indirect reports of messengers, the testimony of those who, unlike Paul, had directly perceived the Messiah. Peter, for example, could write: "It was not on tales [*mythois*] artfully spun that we relied when we told you of the power of our Lord Jesus Christ and his coming [*parousian*]; we saw him with our own eyes" (2 Peter 1.16). For those who heard and saw Peter (who had heard and seen Jesus) the messianic presence was indirect; for those to whom his letter was sent it was epistolary; and for those who later read this epistle in their New Testaments it was

12. A scant three decades before the destruction of the Second, and final, Temple, Stephen was brought up before the Sanhedrin, charged with having blasphemed against the Temple. When he repeated his preaching against it as a building that tried to enclose the *skēnē,* he was led out of the city and stoned to death by a mob organized by Saul, the tent-maker (*skēnopoios*) from Tarsus who, as Paul, was later to preach the Protomartyr's sermon to the Athenians on the Areopagus (Acts 17.19–23). See also Hebrews 9.2ff.

13. Matthew 24.34–35; Mark 13.30–31; Luke 21.32–33. However we translate *genea* (generation or century), early Christians were urged to expect the parousia during their own lifetimes; see 1 Thessalonians 4.15–18. The destruction of the Temple in 70 must have intensified this vigilance, for Jesus had prefaced each of the above eschatological discourses with a prophecy of its stone-by-stone destruction.

scriptural. The attenuation of presence necessitated the strengthening of faith.[14]

This attenuation that grew in the months and years after the passing of Jesus was counterbalanced by charismatic phenomena that encouraged the faith of Christians in the promise of imminent cosmic revolution. The Holy Spirit, they believed, had come to the disciples shortly after the ascension of Jesus into heaven to comfort them in their loss and to impart to them the power of prophetic speech and vision. When inspired by this charismatic power, Christians could derive strength from the prophetic images they spontaneously envisioned or formed in their minds when they read or heard the accounts of others who, like Paul, had had ecstatic experiences. But this nonetheless was only an indirect and blurry vision, "puzzling reflections in a mirror" (in the more familiar KJV "through a glass, darkly").[15] At the parousia "we shall see face to face" (1 Corinthians 13.12). As for the damned, they would be punished by removal from the face of God, a Hebraism denoting total and irrevocable rejection (2 Thessalonians 1.9).

The period between the two parousias was accepted as an indefinite interruption in the unfolding of the Day of God. Yet Paul does not seem to have envisioned an interval of more than a few decades. The destruction of the Temple in 70, followed in three years by the horrors of Masada, must have seemed a certain prelude to the Second Coming. But whatever explanations theologians over almost two millennia have proposed for this delay, one thing is certain: it meant a continuance of Paul's mirror-vision or, as I have termed the rhetorical presences of the agonistic style, the Indirect Presence of the oral relay, the Epistolary Presence of the writer to one or more specific addressees, and the Scriptural Presence as a compilation of indirect and epistolary accounts. It meant a reliance on mental imagery, much of which, like the Book of Revelation, harkened back to the apocalyptic imagery of the postexilic Diaspora. The written imagery of scripture was a poor substitute for the Direct Presence, but until God arrived that longed-for presence would remain an absence re-presented only by continual acts of faith and creedal affirmations. In that state of temporary separation the written image became a support for the Church Suffering and a powerful tool in the apostolic work of the Church Militant.

14. But even for Peter the recognition of Jesus as son of God required an extraordinary act of faith (Matthew 16.13–17), for the Messiah was himself a messenger who brought what was for his disciples the Indirect Presence of God.

15. Paul's allusion *di' esoptron en ainigmati* is to Numbers 12.8 (Septuagint) *en eidei kai di' ainigmatòn,* a passage that Augustine also found highly significant and to which I will refer shortly.

Nevertheless, the practice of visualization and the use of the written image have been marked by troubling contradictions and ongoing controversies. Christians have been roused to violence over the use of visual icons. But beneath the question of icons lay the ancient issue of the *eidōlon,* the mental image aroused by the perceived image.

Related but semiotically distinct was the subtler issue of the written image. God's Spirit, which was said to have controlled the pens of the evangelists and writers of the rest of the canonical scripture, was also said to dwell within the Church and to inspire prophecy. But did he inspire Christian poets? If so, how can we tell in a given textual instance that the Spirit has really done this? How do we discern the true Spirit from the false spirits? What is the purpose of a writing that does not inspire a vivid visualization of eschatology—of Death, Judgment, Heaven, and Hell? Poiesis, the merely human making of mental images, can only fashion false images of fear and desire—the idols of false gods, that is, demons. Christians must discern such spirits "for our fight is not against human foes, but against cosmic powers, against the authorities and potentates of this dark world, against the superhuman forces of evil in the heavens" (Ephesians 6.12). Poiesis, should it aspire to the inspired status of scripture, would become diabolical.

When the parousia happened, mental imaging, even that inspired by the Holy Spirit and enshrined in the Holy Scripture, would be cast aside. When the actual voiced word of God was *heard,* not merely read, writing would become obsolete and the written image prove itself to be the mere shadow it has always been. But how did one know that this cosmic event would come? The written image, the lowly shadow, had given that assurance. But the day that the scripture with its written images asserted would soon come had not come. Could it be that the prophetic images were *distorted* shadows and the mirror of the prophetic mind a blurred and confusing surface that had all along only reflected the images of our fallen humanity? If scriptural signifiers were lowly when compared with their divine signified, they would be even lowlier if they proved to have *created* their signified, in this case the atonement of humanity with God. Scripture, should it turn out after all to be mere poiesis, becomes mere vanity.

The Augustinian Approach

For Augustine (354–430), there had always existed two organized realms, the City of God and the City of Man.[16] The City of Man is the visible society, the Manifested, which because of its intellectual blindness had always fallen prey to the invisible powers of Hell. The City of God had now evolved into the Church, the community of all true believers in union through grace with Heaven, that is, with the Unmanifested of God. Jerusalem, the Holy City of the past, had only been a shadow of the true City of God (15.2). When at the end of time Christ comes again to judge the living and the dead and Heaven appears to the transformed senses of humanity, there would be but one city, the fully manifested City of God. As for the delay in the second parousia, he speculated that the millennium of peace had arrived already, begun at the first Pentecost when the Holy Spirit entered into the Church (20.3–29). There had been no delay: the City of God was now the millennial city. For, though exiled in a doomed society that evil men constantly struggle to dominate, "The City of God has a peace of its own, namely, peace with God in this world by faith and in the world to come by vision" (19.27). For Augustine "faith" meant a trust in the written testimony of the Church and "vision" meant face-to-face communion with God after the parousia. "Face to face—this is how the holy angels . . . already see" (22.29), he reminded his readers, alluding to Matthew 18.10: "In the way, then, that they see, we also shall one day see. But we do not see in that way yet."

How do *we* see? Augustine's answer is that in our corporeal state we now see only *sensibilia,* but at the parousia our nature will be so exalted that we will see with the inward vision, the "eyes of the heart" of which Paul spoke in Ephesians 1.18, and behold *intelligibilia,* that is, realities that now we can comprehend at best only intellectually. This appeal to a Platonic concept effectively bypasses the dilemma of the image, prophetic or otherwise, by classifying all forms of imagery as carnal modes of representation. At the close of the fourth book of his *Confessions,* he seems to allude to Plato's allegory of the cave when he asserts that when we contemplate the representations of the world that we find in books we do so with our back to the light that enlightens them: only when we turn to face that light will we ourselves become enlightened.

In his commentary on Genesis (*De Genesi ad Litteram*) he makes a histori-

16. *The City of God,* trans., Gerald G. Walsh, et al. (Garden City, N.Y.: Image Books, 1958). abridged version, ed. Vernon J. Bourke.

cally important set of distinctions between "corporeal," "spiritual," and "intellectual" visions (Bundy, 167–72). Corporeal *visiones* are purely sensory events, what we would call indexical signs, that is, the "signs" that skeptical Jews required of Jesus, portents that seem to point to some sort of meaning but are often misinterpreted. The example Augustine chooses is Exodus 19.18:

> Mount Sinai was all smoking because the LORD had come down upon it in fire; the smoke went up like the smoke of a kiln; all the people were terrified.

Whether or not another observer would have agreed with Moses that this was a theophany, no one, we might suppose, would deny that something loud, fiery, and smoky was happening atop the mountain. To understand exactly *what* such phenomena meant would require a person skilled in reading these signs, an expert who would be able to situate them within an interpretive code.

A spiritual *visio,* on the other hand, appears not as a percept but as a mental image communicated to a single person, who is usually in a dream or trance state. From the examples that Augustine chooses, the Revelation of John and the vision of the enthroned Yahweh in Isaiah 1.6, spiritual visions are transmitted directly as iconic signs. Like corporeal visions (indices), spiritual visions (mentally displayed icons, i.e., *eidōla*) require interpretation, and the person who is capable of interpreting such *visiones,* the Joseph or the Daniel, is superior to the person who receives them. We have already encountered this distinction in Plato, who contrasted the oracular ravings of the *mantis* with the wise interpretation of the *prophētēs.* Had not Aristotle already disparaged the veridicality of divination by noting that almost anyone could have what seemed a prognosticative dream and that the most reasonable of men were the very ones least susceptible to such messages?

If the true prophet was one wise enough to unravel the meaning of one's own or another's vision and then impart it for the benefit of others, then the principle that Augustine proposed here was the primacy of the interpreter of indexical and iconic signs over the mere experiencer of them. If we understand written images as the recodings of indices and icons in linguistic signs, then, according to Augustine, the interpretation of written images is a necessary activity inherently superior to the reading and imaging of these written cues. Imagining thus becomes in every way an inferior preliminary to hermeneutical exegesis. Needless to say, such a ranking would have profound implications for the study of poiesis as well as for scripture.[17]

And what of the scriptural promise of seeing God face to face? Is this also a *visio?* Augustine says, yes, but it is an *intellectual* vision. Will the information derived from such an interchange also need an interpreter? Apparently not, for it will already be coded in signs assimilable by the intellect, namely, the symbolic sign system of language without the embedding of iconic and indexical elements. The scriptural text that he chooses to support his position comes from the Book of Numbers, chapter 12, the locus classicus for Paul's "through a glass, darkly" (1 Corinthians 13.12). When Moses' brother and sister Aaron and Miriam covertly challenge Moses' authority, Yahweh overhears them and calls Moses and them to the Tent of the Presence, where he declares:

> Listen to my words.
> If he were your prophet and nothing more,
> I would make myself known to him in a vision,
> I would speak to him in a dream.
> But my servant Moses is not such a prophet;
> he alone is faithful of all my household.
> With him I speak face to face,
> openly and not in riddles.
> He shall see the very form of the LORD.
> How do you dare speak against my servant Moses? (6–8)

The ordinary "vision" so disparagingly referred to is of course Augustine's "spiritual vision." The face-to-face view of the Direct Presence, what we might very literally call an "interview," was an intellectual vision in which Yahweh communicated to Moses the Laws of Israel and revealed to him the future of the twelve tribes. These mandates needed no further elucidation. As Yahweh says at the beginning, the faithful must listen to, that is, obey, his *words.* When he sends spiritual visions, dreams, and enigmatic apparitions, then and then alone can they consult their wise interpreters and, if he wishes, he will inspire these to interpret them aright. But when God discourses with

17. It should be noted that the life time of Augustine and the later Patristic Period coincided with the great epoch of Jewish textual editing and commentary upon scripture. The Babylonian Talmud was written between the early third and the late fifth centuries and the Jerusalem Talmud was completed c. 500. The classical Amoraic Midrashim of the early period were written between 400 and 640. For poiesis this might have been the age of "Silver Latinity," but for scriptural commentary it was indeed the Golden Age.

one "face to face" in the "intellectual vision," no interpreter is needed because *God himself is the supreme interpreter.* If to some thinkers the Supreme Being must be a geometer and to others a "Man of War," to Augustine, at his exegetical scriptorium at least, God was the Supreme Hermeneut and Heaven the place where such mysteries as the Trinity could be contemplated at last by the "eyes of the heart."

Augustine's solution to the problem of the mental image was thus to appeal to the Mosaic tradition and to the primacy of the Direct Presence, which also meant the primacy of the spokesman of the Direct Presence who could convince others that he had received the word of God from God's own lips. This principle of authority, at the very least potentially vulnerable to abuse, relegated publicly viewed indices and privately imaged icons to a lesser rank, admitting their evidence only when it could be interpreted intellectually by an authoritative interpreter. If, however, we indiscriminately regard natural phenomena as indices and poetic images as verbally coded icons, we see here the foundation of a bias against empirical inquiry and secular poetry that was to dominate Christendom until the revival of Aristotelianism and the stirrings of vernacular poetry in the thirteenth century.

Augustine's ranking of *visiones* also allowed for the fact that most people, and most were unlettered, were enamored of imagery. Dreams, fantasies, tales of miracles and monsters, pageants, plays, seasonal festivals—all these highly visual modes of communication could not be wholly suppressed, but could at last be placed within bounds. If the Bible contained second- and third-rate *visiones* that were nonetheless genuine, then villagers who witnessed miracles and mystics who had prophetic visions could be tolerated—provided the meanings of these signs could be made conformable to established doctrine. If, when the Jews required of Jesus a clear sign of his divinity, he refused them, this was only because corporeal signs are trivial and ambiguous. If even the visions of Isaiah and Ezekiel, when compared with apodictic propositions, could be declared lesser modes of communication, then the practice of visualization and the written imagery that derived from it could be submitted to the sobering discipline of interpretation and thus be ecclesiastically controlled.[18]

18. Augustine's ranking of biblical *visiones* bears a curious resemblance to the three entities that Eco declared non-cultural (see chapter 1). "Platonic entities" would correspond to Augustine's transcendent vision of God's spoken will, the *visio intellectualis.* "Psychic entities" would correspond to the *visio spiritualis* and "objectal entities" to the *visio corporalis.* Of course, Eco is concerned with a human, rather than a divine, semiosis and so the process he examines is mediated by purely human *visiones corporales* that constitute *signa corporalia.*

The Heritage of the Spoken Image

This chapter completes a brief survey of the cultural roots of iconophobia or, more precisely, of the cultural biases that have predisposed Western literary theorists either to misconstrue or to devalue the function of mental imagery.

When European literacy spread in the sixteenth and seventeenth centuries and writers in one way or another took up Plato's challenge to defend poetry, they tried to adapt their new, fully literate poiesis to the principles of Greek epistemology and Judeo-Christian ethics. To enhance the prestige of their art they strove to incorporate, or seem to incorporate, classical Hellenic and Hebraic principles into their own literary practice and theory. That this theoretical fusion proved unsatisfactory should surprise no one. The aesthetic project to reconcile the Good, the True, and the Beautiful was only one of their noble failures. The project to define the literate imagination in terms sanctified by antiquity was another, the inappropriateness of which came from the fact that the model upon which both Hellenic and Hebraic writing were based was the *agonistic style,* the oral paradigm that had deeply graven its impress upon the literacy of both these cultures.

Technology giveth and technology taketh away. A fully literate writing, a poiesis of the *lexis graphikē,* could not have explored its own unique stylistic properties until movable type made characters uniform and texts legible enough to permit fluent, silent reading (Ong, *Orality and Literacy,* 122–23). But if print literacy assisted at the birth of a new European literature, it also promoted the rebirth of older literary principles and accelerated the spread of the Classical Renaissance and what we might well call the Biblical Renaissance. Accordingly, at the very time when a literature of verbal imagery was being invented for the private, isolated reader, the influence of Plato and Aristotle was reasserted and their orally based premises misapplied to a radically literate poiesis. While this reclassicizing of the vernacular Muse was under way—again thanks to the same technology—the Bible in translation was becoming available to all readers, especially in northern Europe, and its anti-poetic, anti-image principles were being reintroduced into the imagery debate.

Modern European literature thus came of age in a culture dominated by two older, highly prestigious but mutually contentious literary traditions. Both were based on agonistic principles of style: one of these literatures was a poiesis (a "making-up") while the other was a scripture (a "writing-down"). One had made up its scripts for oral performance; the other began with an oral message and faithfully stored it in writing in order to assist readers in its oral recitation. In some respects these two traditions represented alternative stances toward reality and knowledge, but for the study of verbally evoked imagery neither was sufficiently helpful. Neither had been based on the written image, but rather upon the *spoken image.* As I argued in chapter 1, the visual presence of the speaker (the "messenger," either actor or orator) occupies the visual attention of the spectator and tends to obscure any purely mental image the words might otherwise evoke. These descriptive words are heard but the images they form instantly evanesce as they are reacted to and acted upon by the interlocutors. The words and the images they momentarily signify vanish constantly into the dynamic temporality of the actions they incite. For the spectators, the performers function as iconic representations, but the action that they iconically mime is indexically driven, for it is always responsive to verbally relayed indices. Similarly, the words of Yahweh or of the messengers who relay them to the people are always meant to transform themselves into action. The overriding function of such imagery is therefore also indexical: promises of rewards if the words are enacted and threats of punishment if they are not. To regard the biblical God's verbal commands as serving an iconic, rather than an indexical, purpose would be, for example, to contemplate the destruction of Sodom and Gomorrah for its sublimely pictorial qualities.

An important difference between these two cultural heritages lies in the role of the receiver of the word. The Greek, when not engaged in discourse, was listening to it and watching it (for oral discourse in an oral society, we must not forget, is as much a visual as an auditory performance). As a spectator (a *theatēs*), for example, of a dramatic composition, one could assume the lofty distance of the gods of the Unmanifested, unseen and all-seeing. The Hebraic counterpart, however, has no corresponding seat in the *theatron,* but is obliged to become the agonist of history, the messenger or the receiver of the message, who must convert that message directly into action. While the Greek can experience a functionally iconic mimesis of life and contemplate it in the spirit of *theoria,* the Jew or Christian is obliged to act out a traditionally scripted mimesis, a thoroughgoing *praxis,* a lifetime-long command performance before a single, unseen spectator. Job on his dunghill, blind Samson in the temple of Dagon, blind Tobit praying for the "long home" of the grave, Jesus in the dark night of Gethsemane—all these were agonists who confronted the Unmanifested of the hidden spectator who was also the omniscient author of all earthly dramas.

Humanity in the Hebraic tradition had always had works, as well as faith, enjoined upon it. Jesus had appended to his Sermon on the Mount the codicil that who ever heard his *words* and did not *do* them would be like the man who built his house on a foundation of sand, and James in his epistle stressed the same point using the same idiom: "Be ye doers of the word [*poiētai logou*], and not hearers only, deceiving your own selves" (1.22, KJV). This odd phrase, "Be poets of logos," implies a collaboration of God and humanity in a cosmic poeisis, the making actual of the meaning-of-the-oral-word, the manifesting of the design of the Unmanifested.

Writing, insofar as it serves as a channel of the oral word, could seem to preserve contact with the authorial voice of God despite the passage of time and the vicissitudes of history. As such it was a scripture, a transcription of oral encounters with and about God. But as a substitute for a face-to-face relationship of mutual presence, writing indicated absence, the separation of the sender from the addressee. As such, it was a constant subtle reminder of a loss of presence. To the extent that Judeo-Christian culture has represented a turning, albeit with great misgivings, from an oral world of presence to a literate world of absence, it has inscribed upon literacy the mark of abandonment, nostalgia, and desire.

Writing, both scripture and secular poiesis, thus became associated with solitude and a sense of emprisonment within a separated selfhood. This microcosmic self, which has come to assume the structure of the old oral universe, has become a little world of two realms, a manifested self, the conscious ego, and an unmanifested self, the storehouse of memories, impulses, and intuitions, a heaven and a hell, an elsewhere-within. Between these two realms lies the small, dimly lit antechamber, the inner sanctum where words whisper and images appear and disappear, the visionary place one enters every night in dreams, the inner stage the reader sets for the *eidōla* of writing. This microcosm has come to assume the structure of the oral universe, but who is to say that that old world view was not projected outward from the psyche in the first of many human attempts to achieve *self*-consciousness?

Whichever came first, the social agenda of every new society seems to require the subordination of microcosmic prerogatives to those of whatever macrocosm that society conceives to justify it. Christian doctrine, the civil law of the City of God, was therefore elaborated to regulate this new literate microcosm. Since literacy encouraged the autarky of the inner world, it too had to be regulated. Since the scriptures were believed to constitute the proof texts of all Christian doctrine, their interpretation was a matter of extreme social importance. The Bible was therefore the first writing subjected to interpretive regulation. Since imagery (according to the Augustinian classification, corporeal and spiritual visions) was the most problematical feature of scripture, it required the most careful interpretive effort. What this entailed was a systematic recoding of such passages in propositional terms, that is, the language of intellectual vision—the language of oral presence—the language of the teacher to the disciple that Socrates in the *Phaedrus* feared would be lost if literacy ever became dominant.

Interpretation thus becomes the revanche of the orality against writing, and its principal target becomes the written image.

EMPIRICISM AND INTERPRETIVE METHOD

It is no coincidence that in that region of the world where a phonetic alphabet was first developed, a culture came to value writing for its capacity to record the discourse of oral presence and believed that by transcribing its orally stored oracles it could transmit to later generations the phonic presence of a Divine Speaker. Before we take note of another quest for another ultimate presence and comment on the impact of that project upon the written image, we should pause for a moment to consider the implications of deriving a belief system from a privileged class of signs.

When we perceive a sign, it is present to us as an object the meaning of which is *not* present. (Peirce referred to this object as the "immediate object"). As a sign, its function is to point elsewhere. Signs (or signifiers) therefore stand as intermediary objects between us and their meanings. They are like messengers whose reports we have to take on faith alone. We are obliged to do so because we are confined by our situation in space-time—our local Manifested—and must depend on other persons and other things for the gathering, recording, and transmitting to us of information.

But we do not wholly trust such intermediaries. When information passes through a series of them, it can become distorted through forgetting, misrepresentation, and misinterpretation. And at our end we too can misinterpret it. As Eco is fond of pointing out, a signification that could not be untrue could not truly be a signification. Let us consider an example of the transmission of symbolic signs. We all know how within a community a story can spread out from a single event. Each time the story is told, it changes, and each variant prompts further variants. The more it is shared and becomes "common knowledge," the less claim it has on our credence. If the event thus transmitted is important enough to us, we would like to "get to its source." The messenger-mediated data we have received are signifiers that purport to signify that event. If we were to backtrack down the ramified structure of informants, we would eventually reach the first-hand witness of these events. Nevertheless, we would prefer to have been present, if only that had been possible, at the beginning to witness the event in person, if indeed it had happened at all.

Now suppose we imagine that, not only all variants of the same story, but *all* the stories that are told by all the narrators of our community are connected to one another as garbled variants of a single story or as scrambled words of some once-coherent utterance. This assumption, which perhaps only the wildest structural anthropologists would entertain and only at their most speculative moments, is implicit in Judeo-Christian logocentrism. The oral discourse, in its sonority and social context the immediate object present to its hearer, is always an object that points elsewhere for its meaning and, if one could trace one's way back through time, back through all the words ever spoken, one would hear the Divine Presence resonating in those first words of creation, "Let there be light." In the Johannine tradition the Word of the Divine Presence is personified and uttered in the eternity before creation as the Son of God, who later came to earth as Jesus of Nazareth.[1] According to this world view a retracing of discourse would be a search of signifiers upward through their merely human logical and poietic distortions to their Final Signified. But since this quest is for the origin of the symbolic sign-system of language, God-as-Verbal-Presence is not merely the Final Signified of all language, but also the First Signifier—the Alpha as well as the Omega.

Now, if we turn from symbolic signs to indexical and iconic signs, we find similar attempts to ground ideology upon sign function.

The perception of a sense datum becomes the perception of an indexical sign when we ask, 'Why is this as it is?' This datum is present to us as an immediate object, but as an index it points to those absent agents and events that have left their marks upon it. It is a composite of effects that points to one or several causes. Theoretical science since at least the Ionian pre-Socratics has been intent on tracing the multeity of indices back to simpler and simpler principles, which, if fully graspable, could illuminate the world,

---

1. According to early Jewish and Christian tradition Hebrew was the *Ursprache* and so when God spoke to the Patriarchs, he spoke in Hebrew. See Augustine, *City of God,* 16.11–16, 18.39. If no language preceded Hebrew, then God spoke to Adam in the very words and sounds preserved in the book of Genesis. Some have supposed that God spoke the first words of creation also in Hebrew. See also Origen, *Homily XI;* and St. Jerome, *Epistle XVIII.* This belief was later defended by scholars such as Bossuet, Bentley, Beattie, De Maistre, and Lammenais.

eliminate the last sectors of chaos, and render the cosmos predictable to man. This Promethean project, like that of logocentric religion, has had as its aim the total unveiling of the Unmanifested and a face-to-face contemplation of a cosmic Real Presence.

I will consider some of the implications of this quest for Empirical Presence in this chapter, but what about the third category of signs: is there a world view that takes as its object a hierarchy of iconic signs? Platonism comes to mind immediately with its relation of particular tokens and types to their archetypes, but those religions and philosophies, most of them non-Western, that posit a structural resemblance between the Manifested and the Unmanifested also teach that the study of visible forms can lead to a knowledge of invisible forms. This so-called Doctrine of Correspondence, according to which the Manifested is to the Unmanifested as the vehicle of a metaphor is to its tenor, has made its way into logocentric world views as a mystical way of gnosis and into scientific world views as theoretical modeling, but to the orthodox of both these systems it has never seemed wholly reliable. Images, after all, are copies, not genuine originals. They signify by their *species,* their seeming, and are therefore "specious." Images, furthermore, can be deliberately used as disguises to deceive the unwary. An iconic signifier does not necessarily reproduce with any perceptual fidelity the presence of its signified, whereas the words of a messenger are supposed to be the very words of the sender and the marks of the indexical object are trusted to preserve the effects of once-contiguous agents.

Iconic signs, furthermore, are playful. Children and artists enjoy forming images and playing roles—"making things up" and "making believe." To believers in the word, the lie is their nemesis and dark familiar; to believers of the sense datum, randomness is their dread and the finessed experiment their tempter; but to the makers of icons, belief never passes beyond the poietic play of hypothesis to the promulgation of theory and law. Iconicity is therefore a scandal to those, in Western culture at least, who yearn to decipher the world either as propositional language or as experimental data or who have upheld the primacy of one, while attempting to accommodate the other, of these two powerful gnoseologies.

We proceed now to consider one of these attempts.

The Empiricism of the Internal Senses

The Aristotelian model of the mind, revived in Baghdad and Spain in the ninth century and introduced into Paris in the thirteenth, was a biological model based on mechanical principles. When, in the *De Anima,* Aristotle inquired into the nature and functions of the psyche, he did so, he said, as a natural philosopher, a *phusikos.* He even began his survey of current opinion with the concepts of Democritus. Throughout his study we find animation explained in mechanistic terms: intrapsychic states are passive affects (*pathē*) produced by movements (*kinēseis*).[2]

Superimposed on this inertial mechanics was a rudimentary psychobiology. The human soul as a totality was thought to be composed of three animating principles, or "souls." A Vegetative Soul controls those processes that we share with all living things and specifically plants, namely reproduction, nourishment, and growth. A Sensitive Soul directs those processes that we share with animals, namely the external senses, the appetites (instinctual drives associated with pleasure and pain), and the so-called internal senses, a composite of memory and imaging functions. The Sensitive Soul, in the Platonic-Augustinian model, would be the site of "corporeal vision" (an external sense) and "spiritual vision" (an internal sense). The highest "soul" is the uniquely human Rational Soul, which forms universal ideas and applies them to practical ends (this would be the site of "intellectual vision").

The scalar verticality of Western and Middle-Eastern thought is evident in this model, as it was in Augustine's. The mental powers, or faculties, would have to be ranged from "lower" to "higher"—to picture it otherwise would be to reintroduce the primordial *tohu bohu* into God's cosmic Chain of Being. Yet Thomas Aquinas, the man most responsible for the Aristotelian revival in Europe, did not propose a unidirectional hierarchy: following the lead of Aristotle, whom he regularly referred to simply as "the Philosopher," Aquinas denied that universals are innate properties of the mind, asserting instead that the highest natural faculties of human consciousness must be supplied by the senses with raw data out of which they then construct universals. Not only is

2. Translators who choose to use words like "affections" or "passions" for *pathē* and "functions" or "impulses" for *kinēseis* blur this mechanistic model. When Aristotle says that imagination seems to be some sort of movement ("hē de phantasia kinēsis tis dokei einai," *De Anima,* 428b), that memory is the product of sensory *pathos,* and that recollection is one *kinēsis* after another, we should take him at his word: phenomena of the mind, as of the human microcosm generally, are movements through space and time just as are the phenomena of the macrocosm.

reasoning dependent on sensory experience, but reasoning is always accompanied by mental imagery (*Summa,* 1.84.7), a position derived directly from
Aristotle's *De Anima,* 449b.

Aquinas's empiricism had one aspect, however, that was peculiarly medieval:
what we might now call "extrasensory" experiences could also supply empirical data, for the internal senses were just as susceptible to direct stimulation
by external agents as were the external senses. This was still—we must not
forget—a society that believed the earth to be a battleground of superhuman
spiritual beings and that individual human souls were pawns in this five-
thousand-year war. The spectrum of sensation extended far beyond the
merely carnal range; mental acts were just as real as physical acts and, as Jesus
said concerning lustful fantasies and silent prayers, just as morally significant.
The internal senses could be induced to attend to any number of internal
displays, either devilish or angelic. Spiritual powers, though unable to present
the internal senses with an image never previously perceived by the external
senses, could easily combine parts of stored images and produce a composite
that could appear as a new sensory datum.

This process of spiritual influence resembles in several respects the process
by which readers form mental images. When, for example, an angel causes
an imaginative vision (Augustine's "spiritual vision"), it sometimes enlightens
the passive intellect of the rational soul so that the recipient of the image
understands the meaning of the image. This interpretive gloss, however,
is not always forthcoming and the recipient is often left only with the
enigmatic signifier (*Summa,* 1.111.3). This, says Aquinas, is similar to the
style of Jesus when he spoke to the people in parables, which some could
not comprehend. On the level of literary discourse it would follow that
when the signification of the image is built into the text, either conventionally implied or overtly stated, that text would be termed an allegory.
The image that would then appear in the full amplitude of the vision would
be a construct of imaginal (or visionary) details that would be fully eluci-
dated by an interpretation supplied by the intellect. The medieval preference
for allegory clearly indicates a wariness in respect to the uninterpreted
image.[3]

3. This wariness has its origins, no doubt, in the perennial response of social groups to the messages
of visionaries. Some institutional responses have been the function of the Delphic *prophētai* vis-à-vis the
mantis; Paul's concern that charismatic phenomena, if unchecked by interpretation, might get out of
hand (1 Corinthians 12–14); and Augustine's devalorization of "spiritual vision." The Medieval (and
beyond) horror of shamanistic practices—"witchcraft"—was a particularly fearful and uncompromis-
ing response.

Specifically demonic influence also has its literary implications.[4] Since evil is defined as a "defect of good" and devils are by nature unable to comprehend the Highest Good, that is, God, the images they send are copies, often bizarrely botched copies, of a divine creation that they can never fathom. Since their understanding of the material and immaterial creation is defective, their manipulation of mental images is necessarily faulty. As prototypical "mad artists" whose sound and fury signify only themselves, they incite within the human mind private imagery that cannot be rightly assimilated within the grace-enlightened cultural code of their intended victims. Devils are essentially incapable of comprehending the allegory of God's creation.

The great synthesis of medieval thought from Augustine to Aquinas involved the unstable harmonization of Hellenic *theoria* and Hebraic *praxis* — of the competing prerogatives of human logic and divine logos. Like Notre Dame de Paris which was also constructed in the thirteenth century but never finished, this amalgam formed the public consciousness of medieval and early modern Western civilization. Having delivered myself of this broad Spenglerian generalization, I might add here the suggestion that western Europe may have contributed its own element to this synthesis and that this was an empiricism of adventure, the impulse to discover for oneself the limits of reality. One of the expressions of its questing spirit was this synthesis itself, in particular the making of a model of the mind that was neither narrowly physicalistic nor narrowly mentalistic, a model that attempted to account for the reality of both sensory and mental experience, the visions both of the body's and the mind's eye.

The macrocosm described in Dante's *Commedia,* the culmination of two millennia of concern to comprehend the place of the mind in a universe comprised of a Manifested and an Unmanifested, represents a cultural concordat between the two traditions. The Ptolemaic model was acceptable just as

4. In his discussion of demonic influence on the imagination, Aquinas quotes Augustine's *City of God,* bk. 18:

Man's imagination, which, whether thinking or dreaming, takes the form of an innumerable number of things, appears to other men's senses, as it were embodied in the semblance of some animal.

Aquinas goes on to explain that this is not to be understood as a case of thought-transference, but, when this image is demonically suggested, it may appear to one person as a mental image and to another as a corporeal vision, what we would call a hallucination. Note also the belief that devils prefer to communicate to humans through bestial shapes (*Summa,* 5.147–48). See Bundy 220ff for a discussion of this matter.

long as God's angelic hierarchy was put in charge of each spherical lower heaven and God's own heaven could be situated beyond the last of them. We now think of this geocentric universe as dwarfish, but, when compared to the celestial tabernacle, this Hellenistic model had considerably greater radial depth. From the earthly vantage point, moon, sun, and planets now ranged outward in a determinate order with the fixed stars far beyond them and, from the celestial vantage point, with the perspective reversed, the earth was the deepest place of all. No longer could one easily imagine the great spirit-wind of God rushing down from his cloud-high heaven and impelling columns of fire and smoke. Mountains no longer seemed high enough to jut into the ethereal realm of gods and provide visionary places where the Unmanifested touched the Manifested. The earth was now so submerged in layers of creation that men could glimpse the Creator's own realm only by somehow rising upward out of this turbid depth.

The word *initiation,* as its roots indicate, used to mean a going inward. Temple architecture in the Middle East and Mediterranean basin with its series of enclosures reflected the conviction that humanity could *enter into* a relation with a god only through gradual entrances into darkened chambers. The new cosmology had turned this architecture inside out. Now initiatory progression was a gradual withdrawal from an inner place of darkness to an outer place of light. In typological terms, Christians viewed themselves as the new Israel destined to make their escape from Egyptian bondage to the Promised Land. The newly released from earth sing Psalm 114 "In exitu Israel de Egypto" in the second canto of the *Purgatorio.* They were also pilgrims whose progress was now no longer toward a priest-ridden temple of enclosures but to a heavenly city that, as John envisioned it, had no temple. This Christianized Ptolemaic model thus completed the destruction of the temple-idea, an objective that had for so long seemed high on the Christian agenda.

In effect, the new cosmos was one in which the Unmanifested interpenetrated with the Manifested in a differential ratio. That is, the sublunar region was more corporeal than the upper spheres but not entirely unspiritual; the upper spheres were more spiritual but not entirely incorporeal. There was no particular earthly visionary place where one could resort for special knowledge—this was condemned as sorcery and demonism—and there was no localized *skēnē.* On the other hand, the whole space between the moon and the fixed stars was a kind of *skēnē,* an immeasurably vast spirit-thronged expanse where knowledge could be found, if only one could get there. Paul spoke of "a man" (himself) who had once been snatched up to the third heaven or sphere (2 Corinthians 12.1–4) and added that God only knew if this rapture had been a corporeal teleportation or an out-of-the-body experience. Ever afterward this remark gave credibility to the notion that space travel through this cosmos was possible for the living.[5] He said he could not repeat what he heard there, but other Christians would be less reticent in their visionary narratives, whether purporting to relate actual encounters with the Unmanifested or presenting works of allegorical poiesis.

Medieval allegory was made possible (1) by the concept of spiritual vision that Augustine adapted from Plato and employed to explain biblical visions and dreams and (2) by the concept of internal sensation that Thomas Aquinas borrowed from Aristotle and defined as a natural faculty of man. If the Divine Intellect could descend into spiritual visions perceptible to the internal senses and if the simulacra perceived by the internal senses corresponded to the percepts of corporeal vision with its external senses, then the mirrored vision of God, both written and pictorial, could be presented to humankind in the similitudes of corporeal vision.

The allegorical process was of course no unfettered flight of the imagination. The reason for this was that the internal senses, upon which allegorists depended for inspiration, were receptors even more passive than the external senses, which could at least be voluntarily directed. The internal senses were like still water stirred by wind or like a mirror that was obliged to reflect the images of what passed by it. An allegory could be judged correct only by the fidelity of its spiritual vision to the intellectual vision of Church dogma: then and only then would it approximate the excellence of a vision sent by God. It was an authorized mimesis of prophetic vision, not an autonomous poiesis. Medieval psychology did not allow for self-initiated phantasia: witches, for example, did not and could not say at their trials that they only "imagined" the creatures they consorted with. Whether such beings had been perceived spiritually or corporeally, they had been real and their misshapen allegories were blasphemous abominations. The modern imagination had not yet been invented.

5. Paul, who in this epistle alludes to the "pneumatics" and their exhibitions of paranormal "powers," would have agreed with Dante that a human being alone could never successfully undertake such exploratory journeys without supernatural assistance. See *The Inferno,* cantos 26 and 29.

The Empirical Presence

The post-Ptolemaic "new Philosophy" of the seventeenth century became a system of mechanistic laws governing a *plenum* of matter in ceaseless corpuscular interaction. In social terms this corresponds to Hobbe's natural state of man, the "warre of every man against every man" (*Leviathan,* chap. 13). In psychological terms this was translated into an associationist theory according to which the mind, a repository of ideational monads, responds in a determinate manner to the input of stimuli. Finally, in terms of literature, this mechanical model led to the belief that, given the right education and the proper "Gradus ad Parnassum," any gentleman could be a poet. It led, in other words, to an exaggerated confidence in rhetoric, to a belief that the reader is an instrument to be tuned and played upon by the time-proven elements of style.

This historical evolution in theoretical and practical aesthetics was, as we see, accompanied and encouraged by developments in the philosophy of the mind, and both were inspired by models derived from the new physics. The behavior of bodies in space was like the "movement" of thoughts. The gravitational laws of attraction, when they were later promulgated, were assumed to correlate somehow with the laws of mental association: as above, so within.

If regulated mental discourse is to become thinking in the service of empiricism, then the principle of causality is an orderly indexical linkage. In a Hobbesian foreshadowing of deist concepts God is invoked not as Word, but as a First Cause, and the beginning of wisdom is not a fear of the Lord, but rather a "curiosity" concerning him:

> Curiosity, or love of the knowledge of causes, draws a man from a consideration of the effect, to seek the cause; and again the cause of that cause; till of necessity he must come to this thought at last, that there is some cause, whereof there is no former cause, but eternall. . . . [B]y the visible things of this world, and their admirable order, a man may conceive there is a cause of them, which men call God; and yet *not have an Idea, or Image of him in his mind.* (1.11, emphasis added)

The Empirical Presence of the Deity, conceived as the *fons et origo* of all indices, is as imageless as the Direct Presence of Yahweh.

Causal association "made sense." Association-by-resemblence, on the other hand, since it was the imaging of space-like analogs, tended to inhibit the time-like progression of causational thought; if one were thinking or speaking about the causal conditions and effects of, for example, an electrical storm, any description of a particular cloud formation and its resemblance to a weasel or a whale would seem irrelevant. If causation-linked discourse seems to "get us somewhere," resemblance-linked discourse seems a continual changing of the subject.

Resemblances, that is, iconic ideas, belong to the old realm of the internal senses, or imagination. If our chosen path is the indexical way of empiricism, such iconic digressions "get us nowhere." The imagination thus fares as poorly under the regime of the Empirical Presence as under that of the Oral Presence. It should have come as no surprise that in the epic struggle between scientific method and religious faith, imagination always played the role of a spear-carrier—and for both sides. As Descartes asserted in his sixth *Meditation,* the imagination is simply non-essential to humanity's essence. The empiricists disparaged the imagination, that vision of the mind's eye that St. Paul said was looking in "a glass, darkly" when compared with the oral face-to-face, but for them the invidious comparison was with the excellence of the body's eye. Hume put it this way:

> When we reflect on our past sentiments and affections, our thought is as a faithful mirror, and copies its objects truly; but the colours which it employs are faint and dull, in comparison of those in which our original perceptions were clothed. (*Enquiry,* sec. 2)

And Berkeley, ending his *Three Dialogues* with Hylas professing his conversion to the true vision of perceived objects, has him say:

> I have been a long time distrusting my senses: methought I saw things in a dim light and through false glasses. Now the glasses are removed and a new light breaks upon my understanding.

The Empirical Presence, or at least its objective traces, was everywhere manifest. One had only to cease looking into the glass or through the (eye)glasses of the imagination, darkly.

Literary Induction

At the end of the last chapter we noted how Augustine exemplified the Patristic project to convert the meanings of written images into propositional language, that is, to define the significance of iconic (visionary) and indexical (miraculous) messages recorded in the Bible. By so defining these signs, he made them conform to what he called intellectual vision, the understanding one has when, after hearing someone speak, one can say, "I see what you mean." For Augustine this of course always meant conformity to other doctrinally interpreted propositions—in short, to the Word of God, the Direct Oral Presence, the Alpha and Omega of this whole spoken universe.

Scientific empiricism had made a radical break with this interpretive tradition. It had no interest in interpreting written images, or writing in any form, for that matter. The objects of its interpretive zeal were sense data and its objective was to uncover by patient observation of cause and effect the underlying laws of the universe. Such observation would begin with the analysis of a phenomenon down to its minutest constituents, a procedure that would be followed by the compounding of these primary elements into larger and larger interpretable units until a theory could be constructed that would explain and predict the behavior of the originally selected phenomenon. Based on a faith that the world in all its variety is intelligible to the human mind, this inductive method was designed to bypass traditional knowledge with its lore of untested and perhaps untestable premises—dogmata, cultural assumptions, and class biases.

Empiricism had its own interpretive norms, for example, elegance, parsimony, and above all predictability. The welter of indexical data had to be "read" and reduced to propositional simplicity, and to this end that other symbolic system, mathematics, was enlisted and advanced. The Empirical Presence, the indexically revealed knowledge of the cosmos, would eventually find expression not in words but in formulae, not in qualitative description of percepts but in quantitative measurement. Much of what seemed to belong to percepts and their mental representations was not *there* anyway, but in the perceptual organs of the perceiver, as Locke pointed out in his distinction between primary and secondary qualities. Iconicity had a function in this, but certainly not because the Deity had drawn iconic signs in nature to remind humanity of some unmanifested supernature—the ancient "Doctrine of Correspondences" and "Signatures." Icons had a function as models and metaphors, provisional man-made constructs upon which to hang hypotheses and by which to elucidate theories and laws. As in religion, the role of iconic representation was always ancillary to other more essential activities.

Over the past two centuries the attitude of literary scholars toward empirical method has been ambivalent. Despite their objections to the manner in which data-hungry scientists have either totally ignored literary texts or used them for their own purposes, they have themselves been attracted by the empiricist ideal of universal intelligibility and the efficacy of causal reasoning. If the text is regarded as an effect, could one not argue from this effect to some particular cause, as historicists tried to do? If the text is regarded as a set of causes, could one not define the proper range of effects that might follow, as the formalists attempted? If the inductive method, as Francis Bacon outlined it, could be the *novum organon* of science, why could it not also be applied to literature and specifically to the interpretation of textual data? Why could there not be a science of philology, a *Literaturwissenschaft?*

For a better understanding of the methodological problems of literary induction, we might consider one of the fundamental models of information processing. The theory that it illustrates is one that regards cognition as a complex process in which data may either be recognized as a totality or be perceived as a set of separate features. If I engage a phenomenon first as a set of elemental features, combine them to form larger components, then ultimately construct a comprehensive concept of the total entity, I am said to follow a "bottom-up" inductive procedure. If I first recognize it as a total entity, then examine its components, I am said to follow a "top-down" deductive procedure. (In semiotic terms, a top-down procedure begins with a total recognition, an apperception, that is icon-like in its integration, its "good Gestalt." A bottom-up procedure begins with indexical details that seem to point to some possible integration.) The problem for literary empiricists is that in the arts, on the other hand, both at the productive and the receptive stage, these two procedures occur simultaneously and continuously.

This information-processing model assumes that the mind is capable of interpreting signals at various levels of integration. In reading, for example, the features that must be distinguished at the lowest level are the curves, hooks, lines, and angles that make up the Roman alphabet; then, after words, phrases, and sentences, the highest-level products are the semantic representations, namely concepts, narrative sequences, and images. Interpretation may be the result of a careful, upward quest through hierarchical levels such as these (as in the case of a cryptographer's decipherment of a secret code, for example) or a casual, downward gathering of the gist of a friend's summer vacation postcard. The more uncertain the message, the more necessary it is that the investigation begin with a rigorous feature analysis and proceed in a bottom-up series of stages. If, for example, an archaeologist discovers markings on a stone in northern Minnesota, she would do well to perform a bottom-up feature analysis to determine if the scratchings are potentially decodable human signs or simply the result of glacial detrition. Hypothesis is permitted—that, for example, these marks are crudely formed runes—but hypothesis cannot substitute for careful inductive analysis. She must prove that at no stage in the investigation has she deviated from this serial process of induction—has not, in short, taken a top-down surmise as evidential and jumped headlong to her conclusions.

That this is not the procedure we take when we approach literary texts should be obvious. The reading of a text ordinarily requires enough linguistic and literary competence on the part of the reader to perform both procedures simultaneously or in rapid alternation. Jumping to conclusions is an unavoidable hazard we accept in decoding intracultural messages. The upper-level processing of such signals as tone, situation, and genre is as much a part of literary reading as is the recognition of graphemes, phonemes, and individual words. This process is basically the same one we use when we converse with friends: we hear their words and make sense of their sentences ("bottom-up" processing) *while* we assess the pragmatic circumstances of this encounter ("top-down" processing). Reading, like the skillful reception of all cultural artifacts, is thus performed by what cognitive psychologists call a *parallel,* as distinct from a strictly *serial,* process.

The very nature of their observable data has forced upon interpreters of texts the methodological dilemma commonly known as the "hermeneutic circle."[7] They are unable to reduce their focus to simple elements—to phonemes or words or even phrases—because these elements have their definable function only in respect to the textual totality that they constitute, a totality that, in turn, can be validated only in terms of these elemental constituents. As in a conversation, we construe the pragmatic circumstances of the encounter from our understanding of our friends' words, and vice versa. Unlike spoken discourse, however, the written text comes to us totally detached from its authorial source and unglossed by its now-perhaps-unrecoverable context. Experienced readers, especially while rereading a

7. See Heidegger, *Being and Time,* H. 148–54, 311–17.

familiar text, should be able to perform both operations simultaneously, but, if they narrow their attention and introspect their own procedures, they may note a more-or-less rapid shifting from one level to the other, from an assumption of overall meaning to a reception of particular words and phrases—in other words, from the forest to the trees and back again.

There is, therefore, no way by which a theory of poetics or of hermeneutics can be constructed by the orderly method of analysis-leading-to-synthesis. As for a purely linguistic analysis of a text, Jakobson and Lévi-Strauss have conclusively demonstrated in their study of Baudelaire's "Les Chats"[8] that it results in nothing more or less than a linguistic analysis of that text. This focus on the elementary particles of a text only proves, as Michael Riffaterre was quick to point out, that the text is a whole greater than and different from the sum of its parts (Tompkins, 26–40).

One approach to this dilemma was to construct a science-*like* method wholly within the discipline of literary studies, to regard the individual "works" as constituting "phenomena to be explained in terms of a conceptual framework which criticism alone possesses" (Frye, *Anatomy of Criticism*, 15–16). By the late 1950s, said Frye, literary studies were still at the "naive induction" stage.

> Naive induction thinks of literature entirely in terms of the enumerative bibliography of literature: that is, it sees literature as a huge aggregate or miscellaneous pile of discrete "works." Clearly, if literature is nothing more than this, any systematic mental training based on it becomes impossible. (Frye, 16)

Frye's call for a critical discipline that is "scientific," one that can "build up a systematic structure of knowledge" (18), heartened many during the theoretical interregnum of the mid-60s, but if, as I have suggested, the collectible data are not susceptible to induction, the prospects for a science of textual data are about as good as for a science of basilisks and centaurs.

Some thirty years later it is apparent that literary studies have failed to attain a proper method by taking the empirical route, that an age of "naive induction" has not blossomed into an age of securely grounded theory. On the contrary, it would seem that that bedeviling tautology, the hermeneutic circle, has always been, ironically enough, the very process that constitutes the essence of cultural exchange and that it has only seemed an embarrass-

8. Roman Jakobson and Lévi-Strauss, "Les Chats de Charles Baudelaire," *L'Homme* 2 (1962):5–21.

ment to those who would prefer for aesthetic theory, and the arts generally, the analytical exactitude of the natural sciences.

Our intellectual training has led us to believe that anything can be examined more closely, that every part can be analyzed into smaller parts. Why then should a verbal "thing" resist this process of disassembly? Perhaps because a literary work comes to us already disassembled, in a very real sense analyzed into its constituent elements—graphemes, phonemes, syllables, words, phrases, and sentences. Perhaps the words of the text tabulated on the surface of the page actually constitute the ultimate irreducible analysis. If so, then any analysis beyond this point becomes an analysis of the reader's responses and of the code he or she invokes; any interpretive synthesis that follows upon this analysis is simply the signification generated by the invocation and application of that code.

Structure and Function: Two Incompatible Perspectives

An additional problem, one that affects the sciences as well, further complicates the literary-interpretive process. As we know, every phenomenon may be described in terms of its synchronically operant elements. These appear as, or as part of, a fixed network of relationships, a set of conditions or rules. We term these its structure. The actual diachronic operations of the phenomenon, the particular tranfer of energy from point A to point D through points B and C, we call its function. A writer of medieval history, for example, may choose to "freeze time" and describe the cotemporaneous political status of agricultural workers in five separate regions of Europe in the year 1250. This same historian will probably also find it necessary at some other point to present these same topics diachronically as functions of socially contingent change. Such alternate formats are as obviously necessary to historiography as anatomy, the study of organic structure, and physiology, the study of organic function, are both necessary and complementary approaches to the study of biology.

If we define "system" as the way structure functions, we have ourselves a useful concept but one that is very difficult to apply descriptively or interpretively to specific cultural phenomena. We may speak of *langue* and *parole,* but the intersubjective act of verbal communication is momentary and elusive. We may speak of code and signifier, but what of signification?—of technique and tool-use, but what of intention? Whatever it is, however, the link that bonds structure to function is evidently cognitive, mind-like, or, at the very least, telic.[9]

Though we may believe and profess that structure and function are reconcilable polarities, we do not find it any easier to abandon their use as separate methodological concepts. They seem to retain the simplicity of those erstwhile apriorities—space and time. "Space is the order of co-existing things," wrote Leibniz in 1715. "Time is the order of non-contemporaneous things." Even after twentieth-century physics has undercut its absolute basis, that distinction still seems clear and elegant. In his *La Formation de l'esprit scientifique* Gaston Bachelard indicates how misleading such formulations can be and quotes Henri Bergson:

> Notre esprit . . . a une irrésistible tendance a considérer comme plus claire l'idée qui lui sert le plus souvent

and then remarks himself that "l'idée gagne ainsi une clarté intrinsèque abusive" (15).

Though our focus is on literary studies, we must recognize that this structure-function dualism is endemic to human thought and that the methodological wrangles of structuralists and functionalists have scored the history of every intellectual discipline down through the ages. On this point the biologist and developer of General Systems Theory, Ludwig von Bertalannfy has offered what may prove to be a useful conceptual solution:

> What is described in morphology as organic forms and structures, is in reality a momentary cross-section through a spatio-temporal pattern.
>
> What are called structures are slow processes of long duration, functions are quick processes of short duration. If we say that a function such as the contraction of a muscle is performed by a structure, it means that a quick and short process wave is superimposed on a long-lasting and slowly running wave. (*Problems*, 134)

As Bertalannfy views space-time, structure and function are aspects of our world that differ from one another in degree only and not in kind. Their

9. See Roland Barthes, *Elements of Semiology,* 16.

apparent difference lies in their duration relative to the observer, structure appearing as a relatively stable set of features, function appearing as a relatively unstable set.

Let us, for a moment, imagine that we stand upon a river bank and observe the eddying flow of the stream—the sycamore leaves that twirl past, the bubbles that appear and vanish, the water-boatmen and frogs that remain at the less turbulent, shallower margins. We say that here is an image of time, of unintermitted function. Thinking back beyond this summer day, we recall that this river functions with seasonal regularity, freezing over in January and February, breaking into ice floes in March, and flooding the meadows in the thaws and the rains of spring. That, too, we say is function.

The bank we stand on is, we say, the same bank we stood on five years ago. Forty-year-old willows rise beside us. Here now we say is structure: this sloping bank, backed by a higher berm of shale and gravel and deep-rooted maples and hickories. This is the cleft that walls the river bed, the structure that constrains the functioning of this stream. Yet, having said all this, we realize at once that it is the flow of this stream that has itself not only determined its present bed but has carved and shaped from century to century the entire countryside that looms above it. If it is a "function," it is a function that has generated a "structure." If we could capture this scene in time-lapse photography, one frame for one placid August afternoon every year since 1600, we would watch as cliffs vanish like twitches, sandbars rise up like contracted muscles, shrubby banks advance and retreat as though alive—the river like a thrashing serpent, the valley like a heaving animal. We would be forced to conclude that from this spatiotemporal vantage point we can never step into the same river, nor indeed upon the same river bank, twice.

If ours was a species of which the individuals lived for several-thousand years, our perceptual systems might be equipped to view the landscape in active metamorphosis, the hills rising and falling, the trees sprouting like cornstalks, the wood and plaster of our rooms decomposing before our very eyes. Man is, in this regard at least, the measure of all things: processes that occur too slowly to be observed we regard as structures, those we observe changing we call functions. Thus we think of breathing as function and lungs as structure, a body cell as structure and nourishment as one of its several functions.

The structure-function distinction, as we have seen, is based upon a space-time distinction that is itself relative, not absolute. The universality of such distinctions is no doubt grounded in human physiology: our central nervous system has an evolved aptitude to detect movement within an otherwise stable three-dimensional environment, a distinction that has had survival value for our species. Our languages accordingly reflect this world-picture when they distinguish between noun and verb markers.

Despite its linguistic naturalization and its considerable descriptive value, however, this distinction has posed certain ideological, as well as methodological, problems that must be carefully noted. The broader cultural implications of this distinction may be seen in the conflict between the concept of history (as function) and the concept of nature (as structure). Individuals and communities must have their history, but that history is, relative to the evolution of our species, a short-term process. History, to use Bertalannfy's terms, is a "short process wave . . . superimposed on a long-lasting slowly running wave," nature. Consider Fredric Jameson's statement:

> History as ground and untranscendable horizon needs no particular theoretical justification: we may be sure that its alienating necessities will not forget us, however much we might prefer to ignore them. (*The Political Unconscious,* 102)

One might with perhaps even greater justification claim for nature this necessitous untranscendability. The word "nature," after all, simply designates that ecological system the amplitude of which encloses that system of specifically human arrangements we designate by the term "history." If time and space constitute a continuum and if function and structure differ only in wave-length, then history and nature are not antitheses but rather two aspects of the same planetary process. It would seem to follow, therefore, that any theory of human behavior and human artifacts that does not seriously take into account and attempt to correlate *both* short-term historical factors *and* long-term natural factors as phenomena within a unitary, multiphasic field will be inherently flawed.[10]

10. I realize that I have been using a term of dubious repute. I understand that "nature" has been a misapplied term that in recent years has been virtually banned from literary-theoretical discourse. I fully sympathize with Jameson when, speaking of the literary realists of the nineteenth century, he decries

their evocation of the solidity of their object of representation—the social world grasped as an organic, natural, Burkean permanence.

The human body and the aspect of the body that we call the mind did not burst into being in the late neolithic era with the division of labor. As necessary as it is to assess the effects of social institutions on human behavior, it is no less necessary to define the skills and constraints that are there to be modified by such institutions only because these traits come built into the human organism. It seems to me an unwarranted assumption that human mentation, including imagery, and the production of cultural artifacts, including human discourse in all its forms, can ever be adequately explained in terms of conventional sign-systems, subject as these are to the variations of historical circumstance.[11] It seems to me far more reasonable to assume that the interplay of conventional signifiers takes place upon a non-conventional ground, a cognitive system associated with the activity of the human brain and including processes we share with the higher mammals, and that the relation between a conventional code and this cognitive system is, like history and nature, one of a short-term process wave inscribed on a long-term process wave.

If for the moment we define poetics,[12] broadly, as the study of human artifacts and the human consciousness thereof, psychology as the study of the

---

Such a view is, as he says,

> necessarily threatened by any suggestion the world is not natural, but historical, and subject to
> radical change. (193)

I agree that the naturalization of the "social world" is intellectually and morally wrong, but I cannot agree to the wholesale historicization of what Jameson in the next breath simply terms "the world." Marxism affirms, he says, "that History is meaningful, however absurd organic life may happen to be" (261). Yet when the "absurd" constraints of organic life are least in force, the utopian ideal does not seem to materialize.

> We must ponder the anomaly that it is only in the most completely humanized environment, the
> one most fully and obviously the end product of human labor, production and transformation,
> that life becomes meaningless, and that existential despair first appears as such in direct proportion
> to the elimination of nature, the non- or antihuman, to the increasing rollback of everything that
> threatens human life and the prospect of a well-nigh limitless control over the external universe.
> (251)

This meaninglessness, it would seem to me, exists only for those who regard the nonhuman as the antihuman and the earth as an alien planet, a view that has led to the worldwide ecological crisis that now itself "threatens human life." Anomaly? There is no anomaly.

11. Here I mean to oppose those who, *unlike* Jameson, insist that signifiers refer to signifiers, not to referents beyond their code—those whose motto is: "Il n'y a pas de hors-texte." See Hayden White on Jameson in Davis, 150.

12. I will in the next chapter and throughout this book use the term "poetics" in the narrower sense of the theory of text-production and -reception, contrast it with hermeneutics, and place both within the larger field of literary theory.

human consciousness of human behavior, history as the study of human group behavior in given environments, biology as the study of organic systems, and physics as the study of the inorganic substrates of all phenomena, we see that in this list of disciplines every subsequently mentioned field is structural to its antecedent, which, conversely, is functional to it. When we arrive at physics, we come to an end of sorts, but not to some ultimate cosmic receptacle, not to anything that would satisfy our human-scale demand for a superordinate structure distinct from a set of functions. Instead we arrive at the happy recognition that structure and function are merely human fictions, as are the distinctions of space from time, and matter from energy.

Literary theory, as a subcategory of what I very broadly defined above as poetics, must alter its agenda if it discards, as I believe it must, the structure-function dichotomy. If "space" and "time" are no more than durational differences on a continuous scale of processes ranging from galactic and geologic epochs to human lifetimes, from the sudden flight of a wren to the firing of a neuron to the orbit of an electron, then the relations of such entities as author, reader, text, referent, history, and nature take on new and interdependent values.

Literary Cycles and the Performing Center

Many a literary controversy since the late eighteenth century has been aggravated by this assumed opposition of structure to function, or, as it is often styled, of space to time. In literary theory, this shifting focus on the principal topics of the field has meant that among those who argued for the primacy of the author temporal function was exalted. For them, literature was a dynamic, historical process, its production an "effect" of or a "response" to extratextual circumstances. Those who focused on the importance of the reader posited "shifts of sensibility" and taste, changing cultural codes, and the empowerment of "interpretive communities." Those who made the referent their central topic, often the same persons who objected most strongly to the inherent relativism of those functional approaches, tended to stress the atemporal, space-like character of the contemporary world, from which the author drew material, and the constant system of human values that author appealed to, values assumed to be universally possessed by all men and women in all periods and cultures. Those who hypostatized the text were similarly structuralist in that they made the self-referentiality of the text-as-object their first principle and refused to acknowledge the importance of text-production and text-reception in the constitution of the "literary work."

Meyer Abrams exemplified the latter when, in *The Mirror and the Lamp,* he placed "universe" (or referent), "artist" (or author), and "audience" (or reader) equidistant from a central point that he called "work" (or text). A focus on the text, which in his New-Critical scheme is the privileged midpoint, yields an "objective approach" to literary studies. The other approaches that have dominated the history of criticism are, he said, the expressive, the mimetic, and the pragmatic, corresponding to the assumed primacy of author, referent, and reader, respectively. His strategy in constructing this scheme obviously served his structural model—the text as a motionless hub about which the other dependent factors move and change.

But to say that a poem is a structure not a function or a function not a structure is merely to exploit the verbal artifact to demonstrate one's favorite interpretive method, a method that, as I have argued, is founded on a false dichotomy. For what we do when we point to a poem's structure is focus upon its relatively long-term aspects from a short-term vantage point. We sit down, open a book, begin reading a familiar text: though we have changed so much since we read that poem in college, the words, like the figures on Keats's urn, interact in ways that have become over the years familiar and predictable, seeming to tell the same story and thereby seeming to denote a stable world beyond themselves. The fact that authors repeat the themes, genres, and phrases of other authors impresses us also with the structure-like stability of literary resources. Conversely, when we point to its function, we view it in its short-term aspects from a vantage point that is relatively long-term. Once we posit the apparent changelessness, the institutional character of literature, we discover that on closer inspection it is alive with movement: authors write, readers re-create their writings, and nothing is really fixed or predictable. Clearly, neither approach has validity as a method-ological principle when it excludes the other, and, just as we cannot see the ground we actually stand upon, we seem not to acknowledge the very point upon which we situate ourselves to view this literary landscape. In an effort to avoid such dichotomous formulations, let us say that the activities of author and reader are short-term processes that are overlaid upon a matrix of longer-term processes, namely textuality and the world.

The controversy over the relative values of poetic narration and descrip-tion that we associate with Lessing's *Laokoon* is also based on the structure-function, or space-time, dichotomy. The written image is construed in the reader's mind as a space-like structure that iconically "stands for" a space-like structure existing elsewhere in a real or imaginary location. This same written image, given another context, may additionally "stand for" something that may be inferred from it, in which case it may be said to serve an indexical function, too. In this case the written image does not exist for itself but as a logical clue or narrative link to other subsequent images, a consecutiveness that Lessing permits to a language-art. Finally, written images can become merely nominal, that is, confined to simple unelaborated concrete nouns, when their causal function is emphasized, as in the kind of narrative poetry that Lessing extols. If, however, time and space are differences in degree but not in kind, then time-like narrative presentation and space-like pictorial presentation lie along a continuous scale of more and less accelerated movement. In the next chapter I will argue that written images logically can be kinetic as well as static.

This narrative that Lessing finds exemplified in Homer, but could also have found in the Bible, delineates actions, not actors or places, and has the consecutiveness of speech. It proposes and answers such questions as "What caused Achilles' wrath and what effects flowed from it?" Despite their obvious differences in respect to logical method, there is one striking correlation between oral narrative and scientific demonstration: each is presented as a chain of cause-and-effect. Given his background as a classically trained eighteenth-century intellectual steeped in the ideals of empiricism and primarily concerned with theater, Lessing's stance toward the written image would seem inevitable.

The written image is a space-time problem central to the problems of interpretive reading. Because it is an *image,* it is a space-like mental construct; because it is *verbal* it is a time-like unfolding. But because it is *written,* this temporality is not unidirectional as oral discourse normally is, for at any point in one's reading one can stop and go back in textual time. The spatial aspects that produce synthesis in reading are constantly deconstructed by the temporal aspects—in normal left-to-right and even more so in the bidirectional "grazing" that Roland Barthes described in *Plaisir du texte.* The resultant hermeneutic circle is an active process of building and dismantling of meaning that is most acutely experienced in the processing of written images. At the same time, however, every reader is situated within a theory of interpretive reading, a set of norms modeled either upon authorial or lectorial function or upon textual or referential structure. The hermeneutic circle, therefore, lies within this larger, more slowly orbiting circle of interpretive theory and is therefore a "short process wave superimposed on a long-lasting and slowly running wave" (Bertalannfy, 134).

The question we must now and in succeeding chapters confront is this: Is there a way of eluding these alternating phases, a center to these circles, a vantage point within the reading of poetic texts? To begin to answer this we must recognize that Bertalannfy's world of natural fact is not the world of poiesis. The empiricist seeks to formulate theoretical models that will adequately account for and reliably predict real events. But the poetic theorist must at every point confront an anarchic element unique to artworks—their sheer *imaginariness*. Authors and readers are real, the ink and paper of texts are real, historical events and natural processes are real, but literary works are fictions that we choose to believe in only temporarily. The contractual relationship of text and reader, itself a fictive statute, removes literary events altogether from the object-world that Bertalannfy's formula addresses.

Yeats's question "how can we know the dancer from the dance?" has at this point considerable import for us. Dance, we say, is a "performing art." That is clear enough. Now, if we say that the performer is the function and the dance the structural pattern, we have to admit that the dancer appears as a visible spatial object, whereas the dance keeps vanishing into the past and displays, like music, a "structure" more temporal than spatial. Shall we then conclude that the dance is a function that the dancer, as physical structure, generates? If we choose this option, we can say that the dance is a short-term process wave superimposed upon a longer process wave, namely the development, maturity, and ultimate dissolution of the dancer's body. We can, however, draw this conclusion only if we define the dancer as the person who retains the identity of "the dancer" after the dance is ended. If not—if we define the dancer restrictively as "the one who is now performing this dance"—then we must say that this person, *as dancer,* is the one who is now performing this act and that the dance itself is only a logical possibility until the dancer enacts it. We must, in other words, define dancer and dance as coterminous processes. Bertalannfy's formula had reduced the distinction between structure and function to a difference of degree, not of kind. Yeats's formula now eliminates all remaining differences of degree and presents to us an absolute spatiotemporal totality, which Bakhtin termed a "chronotope."

Like Yeats's dance, a literary work begins where it begins and ends where it ends. Tautology seems unavoidable. As a performance, the reading of the text also begins when it begins and ends when it ends. By this I do not mean that the text is self-contained and does not connect vitally with codes and contexts beyond itself, merely that the reading performance does not begin before it starts or continue after it stops. Sometimes, as Aristotle proved, the obvious needs to be established. Of tragedy, his prototype of poetic composition, all genres of which were normally performed before assembled audiences, he wrote that it is "an imitation of an action that is complete, and whole, and of a certain magnitude." Then he went on to define precisely what he meant by a "whole":

> A whole [*holon*] is that which has a beginning, a middle, and an end. A beginning [*archē*] is that which does not itself follow anything by causal necessity, but after which something naturally is or comes to be. An end [*teleutē*], on the contrary, is that which itself naturally follows some other thing, either by necessity, or as a rule, but has nothing following it. A middle [*meson*] is that which follows something as some other thing follows it. (*Poetics,* 50b 24–32, in Butcher, 30–31)

The world to which Bertalannfy's formula applies is one of different durational cycles; having no definite beginning or end, it corresponds to Aristotle's *meson.* This was the world that Aristotle acknowledged in all his works; even in the *Poetics* he recognizes that the language of poetry, the history of its conventions, and the sources of its plots derive from that unbounded continuum of action. In the *Poetics,* however, his special concern was with the *imitation* of action, and imitation he knew involves a deliberate entrance into and exit from a state of play. Like a ritual, which, as Mircea Eliade pointed out, requires participants to leave behind them profane space and time and enter a sacred space and time, an artistic performance is a sequestering act that must have its beginning and its end, its "introibo ad altare Dei" and its "ite, missa est." For the solitary reader this is not an entrance into a public theater, but rather into a private viewing room, a visionary place, a *skēnē* within the microcosmic self.

As the performer is indistinguishable from the performance, the performed work as *holon* is coterminous with itself. The work imitates the real world, the *meson*-realm of contingent events, by the overlap of process waves that characterize its own fictive *meson.* Thus plots enclose subplots; narrations enclose dialogs; structure-like patterns, scenic descriptions, and themes enclose function-like decisions and events. Nevertheless, since all that "happens" in the work is make-believe and is bounded, as the real world is not, by a beginning and an end, these overlapping elements with their structures and function-like aspects are thereby also bounded and contained. This containment requires of the receiver a unique mode of processing, one that does not need to pass through exclusive phases of analysis and generalizing synthesis. This artifice of the *holon* calls for a peculiarly altered mode of consciousness that, being both diffuse and attentive, allows for the awareness of both structural and functional aspects *simultaneously*.

There is yet another way to view the cycling of literary factors. If we agree that literature is an activity of some sort and try to isolate its necessary constituents, we might borrow the paradigm of those early grammarians who distinguished three kinds of verb-generated nouns, namely, *nomina agentis, nomina acti,* and *nomina actionis*–nouns of the doer, of the thing done, and of the process of doing. (Cf. the Latin series *dator, datum, datio,* based on the verb *dare,* "to give.")

When this paradigm is applied to human communication, it becomes more complicated. The *agens* category bifurcates into sender and addressee and the *actum* bifurcates into signifier and signified. The four literary factors thus derive from a doubling of the human subject and of the object of exchange. That is, the two *agentes* become author and reader; the two *acta* become text and referent. The *actio* that brings these four together is also doubled and becomes the processes of encoding and decoding. But as the founding principle of their participation—their reason for being—*actio* has a privileged status, the status of performative construction, both that of the author and that of the reader. As such, it is the special purview of poetics.

The vantage point we must assume in the experience of any aesthetic *actio* must be the spatiotemporal center, the here-and-now in which the performer performs and the receiver performs the action of skillful reception. But to cognize action, this here-and-now must itself be an action, a moving center, a medial line that intersects all the process waves imitated in the work and enacted by the receiver in his or her efforts to comprehend the work. The central vantage point is the conscious mind, the system that encompasses sensation, perception, memory, thought, and speech. This is the center about which every horizon, real and fictive, is drawn. Decentered as it may appear to be from a vantage point outside it, the mind at the performing center is unitary and comprehensive.

To call literature a performing art and liken it to dance or music may in some respects be misleading. In these other arts there seems to be a gap between performer and spectator. The performer is responsible for the performance: she can outdo herself or have a mediocre evening, she can improvise or stick closely to the choreographic or musical notation. The spectator is there to make the most of the spectacle, to respond visually, kinesthetically, auditorily, and, at higher levels of cognitive integration, aesthetically, but if we ask, How can we know the dancer from the spectator? we would have to say the obvious—the spectator is sitting in the darkened hall, the dancer is gyrating on the lit stage. Taking more thought, we might add: the dancer is the object of the spectator's consciousness and therefore partly constitutes his consciousness while he watches. Despite their obvious differences, the overt performer and the silently reading performer, as Umberto Eco has said, "can be seen as different manifestations of the same aesthetic attitude. Every 'reading,' 'contemplation,' or 'enjoyment' of a work of art represents a tacit or private form of 'performance' " (*The Role of the Reader,* 65 n. 1).

Yet even when we say this and believe it, we find it difficult to put our belief into practice. The gap persists. The spectator imaginatively participates in the play of the mind and body of the performer, but does not actually initiate this enactment. This person is not responsible for the skill of the production, only for his or her own alertness and skillful reception. The spectator may think about an appointment calendar or even doze off, but these distractions do not affect the performance. Only the performer is truly situated at the "performing center."

Verbal artworks, too, were once performances reenacted before spectators. The memorizer—the rhapsode, the bard, the scop—was the skilled living repository of the verbally encoded lore of the community. A poetics of oral performance was, like Aristotle's, a theory of the public enactment of verbal art. A gap lay between the viewers in the *theatron* and the speakers upon the *logeion.* But with writing all this changed. Once translated into graphic signs and transformed into the small, mute, portable scroll—later the codex, and then even later the printed book—the story, the lyric, the epic, and even the drama became the property and responsibility of the possessor. This meant that the solitary reader had to incorporate both performer and audience and was obliged to practice, aloud or silently, the ancient art of the reciter. The reader, using the external memory of the written text, enacts a performance in which he or she, like the dancer, is central and coterminous with the action. "How can we know the reader from the reading?" is the question we must now consider.

INTERPRETATION AND THE POETICS OF PERFORMANCE

The silent, solitary reader is a microcosm in which any written image can appear. Mediated by language, these images depend upon two arbitrary sign-systems for their *parousia,* a graphic code that encodes a phonetic code. Thus derived, these images are not the word made flesh, but the word made spirit. As such they are present only to the reader; to non-readers they are invisible and unvisualizable. Even when other persons read this same writing, they will not imagine exactly the same images. This has inevitably led theorists to conclude that these entities are not true phenomena, but mere epiphenomena.

To its characteristic of *unaccountable difference* we can trace the hostile treatment the written image has in the past received at the hands of both religion and science. To those who on doctrinal grounds have demanded that words signify univocally, written images lead to "vain imaginings" and foster private interpretation. If words can evoke different images and if images are signifiers, then their signifieds multiply and words can "mean anything." To those who on empirical grounds have demanded that every difference render a strict account of itself, written images are unverifiable non-data unworthy of serious attention. Needless to say, one does not have to be consciously committed to a scripture-based religion or to scientific method to regard the written image as a mischievous seed of chaos let loose in an otherwise-lawful universe of discourse and to call it into, or rule it out of, order by a magisterial act of interpretation.

Despite all attempts, however, to convert them into non-images through paraphrase and exegesis, these images have continued to spring up in the microcosm of the literate mind. Having come into existence through linguistic encoding and having been liberated through decoding, they resist being rounded up and marched back into the prisonhouse of language to be reprocessed into logical propositions. The attempt to police imagery and an alternative to this attempt are the two main topics of this chapter.

Enactive and Critical Interpretation

Interpretation is the transference of information across different codes. An interpreter is a person who first construes the meanings of a message and then restates these meanings in a code accessible to another party. As such, the interpreter is at first an addressee who faces, as it were, an addresser (a speaker or a written text), comprehends the message—that is, directly converts verbal signs into concepts—then turns 180 degrees to face another addressee and, selecting signifiers from the code of this addressee equivalent to those of the first addresser's message, recodes its concepts for the benefit of this interested party. Both poles of this transaction are, strictly speaking, "interpretations." This go-between is alternately addressee and addresser—as addressee, interpreting (making sense out of) the words of the source, and as addresser, interpreting (or more properly *re*interpreting) this message for the sake of a person unable to interpret it directly in its original encoded form.

When we read a text the code of which is not wholly familiar to us, we find ourselves performing both interpretive acts. If, for example, we find ourselves reading a foreign language that we have not mastered to the point of "thinking in it," we find that in order to follow the drift of the argument we have to stop and translate words and idiomatic phrases into English. If the unfamiliar language is French and we read the phrase *il ne s'agit pas de,* we might first try out "he does not act upon himself from," but we will soon conclude that this makes no sense in this sentence. If we look it up in our Larousse, we find it means "it is not a question of." The next time we encounter this phrase, we may substitute the equivalent English idiom, but if we encounter it often enough we will eventually so learn to identify *il ne s'agit pas de* with the rhetorical gesture of dismissal, which is its speech-act function, that it will immediately signify this gesture. Reading these words will henceforth prompt us to enact this conceptual gesture or imagine someone else doing so.

When we read a poem, even one written in our own language, we confront an analogous situation, for it is an idiomatic, that is, stylized, utterance that may be estranged from us in its historical moment, class context, and cultural reference, not to mention the idiosyncrasies of its author. We do not immediately achieve fluency in this idiom. We shuffle at an irregular pace through its lines. We backtrack. We start again haltingly. We straighten out grammatical inversions. We even translate difficult tropes. It is not until we have stored a smooth set of responses to its anticipated verbal cues that we can read this text with any fluency. This achievement permits us to perform the text in what I will call *enactive interpretation.*

It is for the sake of this reading experience that we are attracted to poetry. It was for most of us, I would venture to guess, the reason why we undertook our study of this art form. But the *study* of poems, we discovered, called into question the very concept of fluency. Instead of being esteemed as hard-won achievements, these skillfully produced silent performances of particular texts were lumped together with initial readings and random, uninformed browsings and were termed "impressionistic," "prereflective," "partial," "naive," and "aesthetic" (as in "mere aesthetic"). The only stance toward the poem that seemed to have professional respectability was one that problematized its idiom and therefore required its continual retranslation. *Dont il s'agissait* was now "what it was about," then "what was questioned," then "what was at stake" and the nuances of these variant renderings were compared and interminably argued by warring hermeneutical sects.

The problem with internal text-cued performances, we were told, was that they could not in themselves be evaluated. How could her fourth-grade teacher know that little Jennifer had read her assigned poem carefully if she did not quiz her? The little paragraph report that gave her teacher some evidence of Jennifer's ability to construe this poem is in later years replaced by other longer and more sophisticated critical responses. In graduate school, and even beyond, her literary competence continues to be measured by her ability to do *critical interpretation,* that is, to produce statements and texts that not only reflect the quality of her prior encounters with literary texts, but take on a value superior to such encounters.

To observe that critical interpretation has dominated the study of literature is to state the obvious. No one would take exception to that statement. But to argue, as I do, that this has created an unbalanced stress on one pole of the interpretive exchange and a corresponding neglect of the other pole is likely to raise hermeneutical hackles and provoke misinterpretation. I am not denying the value of critical interpretation as a public activity indispensible to a society that needs to know—and know through interrogation—what it means. Nor am I saying that enactive interpretation should proceed under the aegis of blissful ignorance and inspired whimsy. What I am saying is that "interpretation" is an activity that encompasses two distinct but interdependent procedures, immediate construal and mediate exegesis. A critical interpretation is only as informative as its enactive interpretation was skillful. The converse, I hasten to add, is equally true: an enactive interpretation is only as skillful as its critical interpretation was informed.

Critical detachment is an absolutely necessary procedure in the understanding of literary texts, but rather in the sense that medicine and automotive repair are necessary aids to a healthy human body and an efficient car. When these latter show signs of dysfunction, we call upon expert remediators. If, for example, one breaks an arm, he or she goes to a person trained to reset the bone, a person to whom the arm is a known *object*. For us, too, what had been an *instrument* of our will, a limb that did a myriad of nimble maneuvers for us, is now also an object, albeit not an object of knowledge, but an aching object attached uselessly to our shoulder. A poem that we cannot read with fluency and smoothly enact upon the inner stage of our mind is similarly a painful, problematical object that we are obliged to scrutinize.

The proliferation of written texts and the rapid development of diverse global literatures has made it unlikely that we will be able to do without expert critical interpreters in the foreseeable future. Yet our need for critical interpretation seems to exceed any practical need we have to improve our understanding of texts. This guild of explicators seems to serve some additional function in society. The makers of literature have often expressed their suspicions concerning some hidden agenda, some cabal of critics. Those poets, novelists, and playwrights who have scorned critics as meddling, uncreative parasites, accused them of perpetrating an institutional hoax on an insecure middle class, and responded to their demand for explanation with quizzical mockery—these critics of this critical clerisy neglect to question how deeply this impulse to extract and decode poetic meaning and to consume these recoded transcripts is rooted in our culture. This impulse is implicated, I would suggest, in the problem of the mental image.

Like the image one forms in response to a verbal cue, the construal one makes of a poetic text is in itself unobservable, not subject to public or institutional surveillance. The written image, as I noted in chapter 3, presented a special threat to those who felt empowered to direct social discourse. The written image was the most polysemous factor in the written text, which itself was open to multiple, potentially subversive construals. Critical interpretation was a professional discipline that thus served a managerial need. However, the need of individual readers to aggregate in "interpretive communities" was, and still is, probably just as great. This need expresses itself in the wish to corroborate one's reading experience with that of others and thereby intersubjectivize one's subjective construals. Beneath this fear of being alone with an opinion unshared by others lurks, I suspect, a more primordial iconophobia—the ineradicable dread of unbidden images and the invasion of alien selves.

If, as I suggest, there exists in us a deep reluctance to trust our own and others' private realizations of poetic scripts and if that wariness is founded on a fear of falling prey in isolation to the self-estranging processes of our own mind, it would follow that we suppose ourselves helpless before the mesmeric influence of the alien text—helpless until, that is, we call upon critical powers, ours or others', to objectify the text. This procedure is a Cartesian ritual of exorcism. The text, according to this supposition, is eager to possess the reader, to exchange its object-hood for the reader's subject-hood. The reader for his or her part must be a subject powerful enough to drive the text back into object-hood. Unless that reader succeeds in doing so, the text will arrogate to itself the status of the subject, and the mind of the reader, having lost control of this erstwhile object of its consciousness, ends by losing control of itself and drifting off among its own random fragments of association. Thereupon, what dreams might come once it has shuffled off its Cartesian dualism must give it pause.

But, as I proposed earlier, there is an alternative to this model, this subject-object contest for supremacy. For there is a kind of object that allies itself with the subject. It is an object that obliges the subject to submit to it to the extent of learning its skillful use, but then permits the skillful user to wield it and extend outward through it to the world of other objects. This kind of object we call an instrument.

Instruments and Objects

Instruments—tools, utensils, machines, equipment, gear, furniture, these constructions that we place about us—are all prosthetic devices, extensions of ourselves that are meant to help us act more efficiently. The oar is a lengthened arm; the classroom pointer a lengthened index finger; the hammer is an extended, rigidified fist. The telescope and microscope extend the powers of the eye; the camera extends the capacity of the visual memory; and electronic communication networks serve, as Marshall McLuhan said, to extend our entire central nervous system. When we take up an instrument, we situate ourself at what we might call the "performing center" and from that point extend into and interact with our environment.[1]

Now, if we make a slight effort to reflect on our state of mind while we are extending ourself from this center, we note that our attention is curiously divided and differentiated. We are aware, for example, of the hammer in our right hand: we know, we *must* know how to grip it, raise it, and direct it without smashing the fingers of the left hand that hold the nail. Our use of it cannot be "innocent" or "prereflective." Yet our focus is not on the hammer but on that narrow nail. It is the object of our attention, while our instrument, which we wield with such complicated efficiency, receives only subliminal attention. We conclude that to have a skill simply means being able to assume that a tool shall obey our will just as smoothly as does the limb or organ to which it is temporarily attached. This assurance allows us to focus our attention on the place where the tool engages the non-tool object-world — the image to which the pointer points, the nail head that the hammer strikes and the hole into which we drive the nail shaft, the planet or microbe which the optical instrument captures, the word that forms under the squiggling tip of the pen, the familiar voice at the other end of the telephone line — these are the true objects of our attention. "Talk into the phone," we tell our two-year-old who stares mutely at the little black holes looking for a person; but when we take hold of the receiver we talk directly to "Grandma."

As these examples illustrate, when we use a tool skillfully, our attention operates in two distinct but simultaneous modes: *peripheral awareness,* in which we virtually merge with the tool and manipulate it on a subliminal level, and *focal awareness,* in which we objectify the thing that is to undergo immediate change.

The term "peripheral" sometimes connotes "unimportant" and "super-numerary." This is not my meaning. I derive this term from the psychology of visual perception, where it designates the wide-angled, almost hemispheric, field that registers a multitude of objects and maintains them in simultaneous awareness. Any system that can respond to a complex input with this degree of complexity would certainly seem to serve an important function.[2] Indeed, without such a capability the rapid, parallel processing of information

1. See Heidegger, H.67–89. See also Donald G. Marshall, "The Ontology of Literary Signs: Notes toward a Heideggerian Revision of Semiology," in *Martin Heidegger and the Question of Literature: Toward a Postmodern Literary Hermeneutics,* ed. William V. Spans (Bloomington: Indiana University Press, 1979).

2. The term "peripheral consciousness" was, according to Graham Wallas in *The Art of Thought*

would not be possible and we would have to perform every task in a laborious serial fashion. To paraphrase the saying, we would have to chew our gum first, then do our walking.

The term "focal" designates that narrow, but sharply defined, sector within the peripheral field. While peripheral awareness can process many signals at once, focal awareness must devote itself to one event at a time. Familiar things we can efficiently maintain in peripheral awareness (cf. "top-down" synthetic processing), but strange things we must focalize serially (cf. "bottom-up" analytic processing). In the performance of a skill, we presumably use familiar tools and operate them in peripheral awareness; wherever these tools encounter a non-tool, that object is recognized as potentially problematic and therefore an object of focal awareness. We cannot be quite sure of the nail, for example. It may go straight in or it may hit the slant of the grain and bend. At every stroke we must keep our eye on it.

Besides tool and object, a third element in a skillful performance is its intended outcome, its *idea.* During the productive performance, the *poiesis* of a work, we hold its idea in peripheral awareness. Of course, we may have objectified the idea by sketching out our project in advance. If, for example, we intend to build a bookcase, we probably have outlined the measurements on paper and visualized the finished product set in place and filled with books and boxes of filecards. This is the completed structure, the entelechy, to which our carpentry functions lead; while we are sawing, nailing, gluing, and painting, the idea is not suppressed or forgotten, any more than is the hammer or the paintbrush. The idea of the bookcase hovers in the peripheral background while each tool we use lies in the peripheral foreground; the object occupies the middle distance and claims our focal awareness. If at any point we choose to consult the plans and revise our measurements, we stop our work, stand outside it, and critique it. We stop the constructive performance and perform another learned skill, mathematical measurement.

Before returning to the topic of poetry, we must consider two further implications. The first is the concept that there can be instrumentality without tools (in the sense of artificial appendages); the second, which follows from that, is the concept that language can function instrumentally.

(publ. 1926), often resorted to by early-twentieth-century psychologists when explaining the functions of the preconscious. Wallas specifically contrasts this with "foveal" awareness, i.e., sharply focused attention. Harold Rugg, in his useful study *Imagination,* called it "off-consciousness" ("off" as in "off-center"). The term "focal awareness" I take from Michael Polanyi's *Personal Knowledge.* His correlative term, "subsidiary awareness," I have changed to "peripheral" because I wish to apply a visual-perceptual model to consciousness in general and to imaging specifically.

Once we note that tools, as extensions of our organism, facilitate its actions, we also note that our organs also function like tools (in Greek, *organon* was the common word for "tool"). Our built-in equipment—the physical and mental aspects of our organism—are the instruments that we extend by means of specific tools.[3] When I push a tack into the wall with my thumb, I use my hand, my arm, and, to a degree, my whole body instrumentally in respect to the object. I do not worry about my ability to perform such basic tasks and so can afford to shift my focal attention from my organic self ("organic" now in the double sense of biotic and instrumental) to my external object. Similarly, we speak of a singer's "instrument" as the diaphragm, vocal chords, and so forth and of a dancer's "instrument" as the motor reflexes, musculature, and so on.

Speech is also an act performed by organic instruments. If our speech is skillful, that is, fluent, we produce it without worrying about grammar or pronunciation. When we are speaking fluently, we also "know" what we wish to say; we are aware, again peripherally, of our idea, the gist, or tenor, of our emergent discourse. Our object, when we choose to focus on it, may be the person or group that is receiving and reacting to our message,[4] or it may be the referent, the absent world that our own words imaginatively make present.

It would follow that potentially the most efficient of all human instruments is the signifier. Heidegger calls signs "equipment for indicating."[5] If the definition of a sign is a signifier linked to its appropriate signified, then to identify the sign-function of a particular item is to be instantaneously aware of its signified. This signifier-signified recognition appears based on the instrument-object relation. Viewed from this perspective, semiosis becomes an evolutionary spin-off of the opposable thumb.

What occurs when we experience the tenor, or overall significance, of a discourse? In everyday conversation we "gather" the import of another's words and adjust our verbal responses accordingly, a recognition and adjustment that, though it may often involve many conflicting impulses and

3. I will not speculate here concerning the "we" that are extended by such intrinsic equipment except to observe that this "self" is no homunculus hidden away like the Great Oz behind his pulleys and levers. The notion of instrumental extension humanizes the tools and thereby enlarges the subject as Dasein. In the next chapter I will again take up this question of the "extended self."

4. The early anthropological account of the Bubis of Fernando Po in which a speaker asked his friends to come closer to the fire so that he could see what he was saying may illustrate this need to use addressees as objects.

5. This is much catchier in Hoch-Heideggerisch: *Zeig-zeug* (H.79).

judgments, ordinarily takes only a second or two to perform. The speed with which we can process a variety of input signals, compute their relations and relative values, then generate a message that can be grasped by both sender and receiver in a single moment of focal awareness is truly remarkable.

> As you listen to an address, phonemes disappear into words and words into sentences and sentences disappear into what they are trying to say, into meaning. (Jaynes, 27)

Since by definition a skill is a developed ability to perform an operation with ease, focal awareness when it occurs *within* a performance can be a quick, easy, and momentary narrowing of attention achieved without wholly relinquishing the broad, alert overview of peripheral awareness.

The literary text is the instrument that permits these momentary glimpses and formulations, but to be of use to us as an instrument it must be held in peripheral awareness. The poet, as Lessing observed,

> wishes . . . to make the ideas awakened by him within us so vivid [*lebhaft*] that for the moment we believe we are receiving the true sensuous impressions of the objects he describes, and cease in this moment of illusion to be conscious of the means he uses—namely, his words. (*Laokoon,* xvii)

If, however, we choose by a deliberate shift of attention to become "conscious of the means," we instantly disable both tool and performer.

Ortega y Gasset compared this situation to looking at a garden through a window:

> The clearer the glass, the less we will see of it. But then, with an effort, we can disengage ourselves from the garden and, retracting our visual beam, fixate it upon the glass. Then the garden vanishes from our eyes and all we see are confused masses of color that seem stuck to the glass. Thus, seeing the garden and seeing the window-pane are incompatible operations: the one excludes the other and each requires a different ocular accommodation. (8–9)

To serve its instrumental purpose, the windowpane must be the transparent foreground through which we observe the scene beyond. Similarly we say a person's words are "clear" only when we see *through* them to their meaning.

It follows then that all critical theories that define the text as an object can only be aimed at clarifying the instrument, a clarification that, while it is being made, obscures and subverts the actual purpose of the instrument, the performance of signification.

The Instrument as Object

Fluency implies, for both sender and receiver, the transparency of language. In fluent discourse, a word becomes an opaque object of attention only when a syntectol occurs, and principally at that syntectolic spot in the discourse. I choose the term "syntectol" advisedly, because as far as I know there is no such word in the English language. If what I had been proposing up to that point had been at all clear, my discourse became suddenly opaque when I introduced that word. Having an uncertain semantic function, this word drew attention to itself. It lost its instrumental character and became an object. We can always know the dancer from the dance when the dancer slips and falls, but then for that moment he or she is not *the dancer* but rather the embarrassed person up there, who has been shown to be as subject to the forces of inertial motion and gravity as the rest of us.

If, as I proposed in the first chapter, the text *as words* is already irreducibly analyzed, then the simple act of shifting focal awareness from their developing meaning to the words themselves is to initiate an act of analysis, that is, a critical interpretation, and to render the text unavailable to the reader as a semantic instrument. It matters little, moreover, whether the text is approached as an exquisite *objet d'art* or as a botched or broken tool: it is dismantled all the same and examined piece by piece with an emphasis on the function of the separate parts rather than on their ensemble coordination. That the results of enactive and critical interpretation should be radically dissimilar should surprise no one. As Einstein once remarked, the chemical analysis of a cup of soup should never be expected to have quite the same taste as the soup.

Analysis has its proper uses. I do not want to overstate the case for enactive interpretation, but only to question the assumption that only critical interpretation has worth, the pedagogical tradition that has it that the unexamined poem is not worth reading. This was the attitude that Susan Sontag questioned in her acutely pointed polemic "Against Interpretation." Generation after generation of the uninitiated also question this attitude. The teacher delivers a brilliant exegesis of a difficult Donne text, pauses, looks about the room, and asks, "Are there any questions?" After another pause a student in the back asks, "Professor, I just have this one question—why do we always have to tear apart every poem we read?" Suddenly the teacher yearns to see this reprobate transferred to that classroom in hell where the intellectually slothful are made to caper uncontrollably and everlastingly under a fiery hail of logical disputations. And yet there may be some justice in that often-voiced complaint. An unexamined habit is not worth having and the objectifying of the textual instrument has become just such a habit. Despite all their other differences, the practitioners of traditional methods of literary study have collaborated in reenforcing the value of this activity. In the last chapter I suggested that the inductive method of the natural sciences has had a great formative impact on the development of modern critical theory and method. Two older, more directly related traditions, which we examined in earlier chapters, should also be mentioned here in passing: classical rhetoric and biblical hermeneutics.

This habit of objectifying the tools of communication has come down to us, in part, through twenty-five centuries of the teaching of rhetoric—of reading student themes with an eye to the typical obstacles set in one's path by novice writers—twenty-five centuries of reading literary texts, not for their intrinsic merits, but as models of technical excellence. The propositions "Something must be wrong here, so let's take a closer look" and "Something must be working well here, so let's take a closer look" both effect the same result: whatever might have been working in the reading performance stops working, and another skill, that of close critical scrutiny, takes over. Usually, "Let's take a closer look" seems all that needs to be announced, as though that were a self-justifying activity.

This rhetorical tradition, even when it seemed most concerned with understanding the immediate processes of text-reception, has actually promoted critical interpretation. In her essay "The Reader in History: The Changing Shape of Literary Response" (*Reader-Response Criticism,* 201–32), Jane Tompkins speaks of the reader's performance as a perennial concern of Western literary studies from the Greeks through the nineteenth century. This was the case, she says, until the formalists of the twentieth century took hold of the text and changed the agenda so decisively that even in the 1980s the "text remains an object rather than an instrument, an occasion for the elaboration of meaning rather than a force exerted upon the world" (225).

While I agree entirely with Tompkins's analysis of formalism, I fail to find in the past the same consistent reader-response orientation that she finds. Interest in the reader has indeed surfaced over and over again, but in the past the motive was almost exclusively the manipulation of the reader's judgment and emotions. For orator, preacher, writer, and aspiring courtier alike, the principal question was not "How does the audience use the text?" but "How can the text use the audience?" The author's seeming tool was the art of rhetoric; his real tool was his audience. Toward such ends, the literary classics were down through the ages dismantled block by block to build *gradus ad Parnassum*, or, if not to Parnassus, at least to a moderately comfortable station in life.

Biblical hermeneutics, by asserting the unavailability of the textual tool to the uninitiated reader, also served to validate the work of critical interpretation. Since biblical texts were thought to be cunning webs of symbols and types, they had to be carefully unfolded and translated into the mental, no less than the linguistic, vernacular of the lay folk. Here indeed was a lofty model for the literary explicator. When, in the wake of Romanticism and the Higher Criticism, literature began to assume quasi-scriptural status, the literary professional, till then the mere sacristan in charge of the vestments of rhetoric, found himself at last promoted to the very priesthood of Culture.

Literary studies have always placed a special emphasis on the text-as-object. Though rhetoric flourished, as Tomkins rightly asserts, in eras of readerly interest, the text nonetheless was made the object of focal awareness in the grammarians' schoolrooms. While hermeneutics, on the other hand, flourished in eras when the author, divine or merely human, was viewed as the mysterious sender of messages, it was the text again that was dismantled. Referent and text have also had their day of seeming primacy, but with similar results. When the referent was extolled, then literary works were deemed access-routes, more or less direct, to knowledge or moral enlightenment or were valued for their help in adjusting readers to their stations in society and improving their efficiency once they arrived there.[6] True, in these eras when texts were quarried for commonplace books, centoes, and elegant allusions, they were not so often subjected to the concentrated light of analysis, but neither were they taken very seriously as instruments of performance. The text always tended to be objectified, but in those eras when it was declared to be the one exclusive focus, this tendency was unrestrained, and in the hands of the literary specialist the verbal specimen was opened up and explored with a zest that sometimes verged on the manic and the obscene.

Literary scholarship, I think it is fair to conclude, has consistently pre-

6. See Terry Eagleton's brilliant chapter on the beginnings of English literary education in the late nineteenth century in his *Literary Theory*.

ferred to approach the text as an object rather than as an instrument. From the Greek and Roman grammarians to the patristic exegetes, from the scholiasts of the Renaissance with their glosses and emendations to the philologists of the eighteenth and nineteenth centuries with their Longinian passages and Arnoldian touchstones, from the close-readers of the mid-twentieth century to the deconstructionists of our own generation, literary commentary has always seemed more comfortable with the tool in pieces than with the tool in action. The reason for this is all too obvious. The tool in action presupposes a user, a performer, a living human mind. If one is unready or unwilling to come to grips with the functions of the tool-using mind, one's only option is to isolate and objectify the tool the mind uses. Once one adopts that methodological stance, the results are predictable: the logically separable aspects of the tool, many of which operate simultaneously in use, are now spread out on the dissecting table and reconnected consecutively in linear prose discourse. Units and aspects that in one's actual reading may be apprehended at once in peripheral awareness—instrumental aspects like tone, prosody, genre, imagery, and to some extent even narrated events—these are now parsed out and serially scrutinized with an exclusively focal awareness.

At this point something else very interesting happens: the traditional rift between "form" and "content" emerges like a natural fact. What had been the instrumental aspects of the text are now flushed out of hiding and designated as its "form," while whatever remains after the formal devices have been thoroughly laid bare is called its "content." How very distinct these two now appear! The form becomes the totality of devices deployed to produce the content, the content, the paraphrasable "core meaning" of the work; the form is extracted through analysis and induction, the content through synthetic generalization and deduction; the form is the "nuts and bolts" of the mechanism, the content the one, grand, overarching blurb. Objectification of the tool thus ends in the trivialization of its purpose. And the hermeneutical circle makes a full turn.

Having proposed an instrumental theory of poetics, one that characterizes the text as a virtual extension of the mind of the reader, a transparent lens by means of which the hitherto unknown is envisioned, I must confront an obvious problem: the commonly experienced fact that texts do not always appear as transparent lenses or "user-friendly" tools.

If we had come to the conclusion that critical interpretation is an unnecessary procedure and that poetic texts need only to be read to be fully effective, we would have been ignoring the obvious fact that poetry is a specialized form of discourse, one that regularly draws attention to its own function.

Though, as I have argued, a poetic text is meant to be a tool like any other piece of human equipment, it is often a puzzling tool at first, a tool that fairly invites its own objectification. Here is a serious contradiction that we must ponder carefully.

All literary theorists have at some point attempted to account for this "syntectolic" peculiarity of literature. Contrary to the position I have tried to maintain, many have held that some texts, far from being transparent instruments, are by nature opaque verbal objects that must be cracked and probed like walnuts. Sartre, for example, in his monograph *What Is Literature?*, after contrasting the language of lyric poetry with that of prose fiction, concludes that poets obstinately refuse to use language as the "certain kind of instrument" that it naturally is. Poets, unlike novelists, have "chosen the attitude which considers words as things not as signs." Like the novelist, the ordinary speaker of words

> maneuvers them from within; he feels them as if they were his body; he is surrounded by a verbal body which he is hardly aware of and which extends his action upon the world. (6)

Discourse is a tool by which such speakers extend into the world and into one another. Not so the poet:

> The poet is outside language. He sees words inside out as if he did not share the human condition, and as if he were first meeting the word as a barrier as he comes toward man. (6)[7]

How shall we deal with this concept of the verbal "barrier"? Does poetic language bar the author from communicating with a world, real or imaginary, beyond words? Is it, as many have come to believe, an entrance into the resonating chamber of language and textuality? How might we account for this perverse recalcitrance of what I have tried to characterize as a purposefully designed instrument?

We cannot deny it: poems are curiously wrought verbal artifacts. As Michael Riffaterre declares on the very first page of his *Semiotics of Poetry*,

---

7. Sartre's contrast of engaged novelist and private poet exploits a loose generic distinction. Literature written in verse form is generally more concentrated and therefore more "difficult" than that written in prose. As a generalization this is correct, but no theoretical principle can be based on this distinction of genres.

"Poetry expresses concepts and things by indirection. To put it simply, a poem says one thing and means another." This peculiar norm of deviance would seem to relegate the textual instrument to the state of objecthood. Like tools that stubbornly insist on expressing their individuality by deviating from the operations outlines in the owner's manual or that come to us with no manual at all, poetic texts either never start up or, when they do, seem to break down so often that they regularly require some licensed expert to dismantle and inspect them. The very fact that literary criticism and pedagogy continue to be done at all is at least *prima facie* evidence that something is oddly problematic about this art form.

Many have tried to reason out a cause for this difficulty. Throughout the nineteenth century theorists struggled with the question of what function, if any, is served by the peculiarities of poetic form and the elliptical procedures of poetic discourse. The solution that the Russian Formalists proposed in the 1920s was particularly ingenious—that the principal use of poetry lies in its revolutionary potential to defamiliarize the world and deautomatize the reader. This theory began with the assumption that the reader *should* be unprepared for the truly new text, that the possession of what we have come to call linguistic and literary competence should not guarantee an effortless reading of the work. The reader's mind is *supposed* to snag on a strange image or pause vertiginously at an abrupt gap or become lost in the devilish toils of a periodic sentence. This was the stylistic theory that was to inspire Stanley Fish early in his career, before he abandoned stylistics altogether for the "authority of interpretive communities."[8]

The concept that poetry conveys a knowledge inaccessible by other linguistic means has in recent years fallen out of favor among the dominant schools of theory of Europe and America. Yet, if I might hazard a guess, it is still implicitly believed by most poets, who, even if they do not speak of inspiration or see themselves as bards or visionaries, would affirm that in the process of writing they seek to formulate that that cannot otherwise be revealed. Few, at any rate, would tell us that engaging in intertextual dialog

8. Fish's later position on ordinary and deviant language, viz. that this distinction is false and merely trivializes literature, is necessitated by his belief in the Orwellian power of institutions to control interpretive opinion. Yet he seems to leave us with one (institutionally authorized) free choice: "What characterizes literature then is not formal properties, but an attitude—always within our power to assume—toward properties that belong by constitutive right to language." "How Ordinary is Ordinary Language?" in *Is There a Text in This Class?,* 108–9. If it is in our power, not that of the text, to make discourse specifically *literary* discourse, so be it: deviance is in the eye of the beholder. For further discussion of these matters see Lentricchia, 151.

with their literary predecessors was ever a major motivation. Of course, one may argue that poets, like critics, are members of interpretive communities, that they share the same zest for one-upmanship, but are insufficiently self-critical to acknowledge their textual debts and too burdened with *mauvaise foi* to own up to their meaner-spirited anxieties.

One may so argue, yet the evidence for such a judgment would have to come from an objectification of the text in the act of critical interpretation, that is, from a close reading of the dismantled verbal instrument. Since this procedure only leads to the hermeneutical circle, none but the most obvious borrowings can be proven. After all, if words are conventional, why are not phrases also? Even the most far-ranging *bricoleur* is constrained by the limits of his salvage. Yet it is what one does with a tool, borrowed or homemade, that really matters. What I am suggesting is that the text-as-tool, when it is anomalous, is so not because it is a cento or palimpsest of other texts, but because it is constructed to perform a task that has never been done before. Its analyzable materials will always, therefore, be less important than the use to which they are put. Whitman made this point in one of the small poems he used to introduce the 1881 edition of *Leaves of Grass:*

> Shut not your doors to me proud libraries,
> For that which was lacking on all your well-fill'd shelves,
>   yet needed most, I bring,
> Forth from the war emerging, a book I have made,
> *The words of my book nothing, the drift of it everything,*
> A book separate, not link'd with the rest nor felt by the
>   intellect,
> But you ye untold latencies will thrill to every page.
>   "Shut not Your Doors" (emphasis added)

The end product of the words—the "drift"—constitutes the defamiliarization by representing to the reader a new and unique conception of the world. It is a transcendence by means of language of the reader's habitual, language-mediated universe. "*The limits of my language* mean the limits of my world," declared Wittgenstein (*Tractatus,* 5.6), but in fact the frontiers of this "world" are constantly being probed and crossed by the verbal instrumentality of poetry as well as by the extra-linguistic means at the disposal of the non-verbal arts and the empirical sciences.

The transcendence of the habitual is not, however, an easy matter. If it were, the habitual would not be the habitual. All of us necessarily use language to define our world and use the instrumentality of verbal artifacts to extend those provisional limits. But familiar texts tend to refamiliarize this world and so habituate us to their own instrumental peculiarities that we may well resist learning to use an unfamiliar text. There are risks involved: we cannot know what it does until we learn how it works, and how can we be sure we really want to find this out, because whatever it does it has to do *to us.*

In terms of interpretation, the text-as-anomalous-tool is not written in a familiar code, and so we need the help of a critical interpreter. What is it saying? we ask. The critical interpreter may then translate it into a familiar idiom. But this will not suffice: no paraphrase, as such, will enable us to read that text, that is, use it as an instrument of knowledge, if we cannot master its peculiar idiom. To that end, textual analysis can be helpful. Like an unknown language, the structure of an unfamiliar text must be extrapolated from its apparent functions. Again the critical interpreter can help us, or we can easily learn to assume this role ourselves. Standard literary training, if it teaches little else, teaches us to analyze the verbal tool into its effective components. Critical interpretation—both the activity of translation and the completed translation—has its proper uses, but, as I have tried to demonstrate, these uses lead from and to that other interpretive mode, for the validity and purpose of critical interpretation are grounded in enactive interpretation.

The Poem as Performance

Having distinguished the enactive from the critical interpretation and the text as instrument from the text as object, I wish to draw one final distinction that underlies the preceding two—the distinction between the poem and the text. The *text,* as I have used this term, is the set of words as they appear on the printed page or as they are regularly recalled by the oral reciter. The *poem* is the active engagement of a skilled mind with these words. It is the performance of an act of making, of a *poiesis.* "Poem," therefore, denotes for me an action not an object. In this action, author and reader, though they do not merge, become correlative.[9]

9. These particular distinctions, as far as I have been able to determine, were first articulated in 1937 by Louise Rosenblatt when she distinguished "*the text,* the sequence of printed or voiced

It seems to me that we can truly regard reading as an art and not mean by that merely the art of oral interpretation. I want to avoid hyperbole here. I do not mean to flatter the reader or use a superficial resemblance to assert the twinship of author and reader. Let me begin by proposing that the art of reading is an art that recapitulates the art of writing. The final act in the order of text-production occurs when the author reads the text and makes no further changes: the work of revision, Horace's *labor limae,* has come to an end; critical interpretation has, for the writer, been completed, and the creator is allowed the joy of enactive interpretation. The first act in the order of text-reception is the reader's initial reading, but subsequent acts may well involve critical revisions that ultimately lead to the comprehensive performance of enactive interpretation, a performance that is operationally similar to the author's first reading after the final revision. The poem is the performance that correlates both author and reader as enactive interpreters insofar as both use the text instrumentally. The author in the activity of composition uses the evolving text as a web (a *textum*) in which to catch and hold the sensations, memories, emotions, ideas, and options for action that constitute that unresolved complexity we call a "mood" (Empson's "feeling [,] . . . an elaborate structure of related meanings," 57). The reader uses the completed text as a means of discovering that complexity in oneself. The undeniable fact that the author's experience of meaning in the text is not identical with the reader's does not contradict the reciprocity of their relationship: no two readers decode texts identically, nor does any reader decode a text in the same way each time he or she reads it.

There are yet more interesting factors involved in the variability of performance. These involve the dynamic interrelations of focal and peripheral awareness. In a response to an analysis by Roman Jakobson of Shakespeare's Sonnet 129, Louise Rosenblatt cautioned: "The fact of 'selective attention' must again be recalled" (*The Reader, the Text, the Poem,* 168). The fact that, when confronted with a broad array of items, we rapidly *and selectively* scan them is beyond dispute. That this process occurs legitimately in the act of reading and that reading "involves many—one is tempted to say all—levels of the organism" (173) need to be among the first principles of any humane study of literature. The yearning for the Superreader or for any other compendious beast bundled with the brains of variorums bespeaks a desper-

---

symbols . . . [from] *the literary work (the poem, the novel,* etc.), which results from the conjunction of a reader and a text" (*Literature as Exploration,* 113). See also Rosenblatt's later theoretical statements in *The Reader, the Text, the Poem,* particularly the early chapters.

ate desire for what Keats might have called Positive Capability. Worse than that, it indicates a failure to respect the exquisite alertness and liberty of the human mind. Since an enactive interpretation, that is, a performed poem, is the parallel processing of a text, a reader will hold in peripheral awareness a number of textual components simultaneously but will not necessarily retain a given component at the same level of salience from one reading to the next. Thus, for example, a reader might find that in every performance of Eliot's "The Love Song of J. Alfred Prufrock" certain components are recognized and encountered—a miasmic atmosphere, autonomous body parts, extratextual allusions, and the involuted arguments of the speaker—but in every reading these components appear in different degrees or levels of salience and in different permutations. Peripheral awareness, though it does not narrow itself to exclusive and sustained focuses, never presents a perfectly homogenous attentional field: its scope is wide-angled and filled with many potential points of interest. Psychology has documented what poets and philosophers have always known: consciousness, as Wilhelm Stekel put it, is a "polyphony of thought" (1–21). A text directs this chorus but can never reduce it to a monophonic lecture.[10]

We understand that a degree of variability, of interpretive emphasis, is a necessary element in the performing arts. We say that a certain actor "interprets" a particular role, that a musician brings to a work a particular "interpretation." Without revision or improvisation, they construe the script or the score and produce from these coded jottings a unique realization of the text. We may say that a musician, playing Bach, is "making" music, but we are not accustomed to say that a reader, reading Shelley, is "making" poetry. The reason is obvious. Because we cannot see and hear the performance of the silent reader, we are hesitant to allow that reader the latitude of an interpretive performance. We cannot monitor this performance, so how can we be sure it

---

10. "If one asks the question 'how many ideas or things can we attend to at once,' that is, 'how many entirely disconnected systems or processes of conception can go on simultaneously, the answer is, *not easily more than one, unless the processes are very habitual; but then two, or even three,* without very much oscillation of attention" William James, *Principles of Psychology,* 1.409). James's statement does not specify degrees of awareness: presumably, if the processes are *very* habitual they will not require a high intensity of attention. Norman (65) asserts that the "level of training" rather than the nature of the task is the determining factor, that when a skill "has been practiced for years and years . . . it becomes automated." And what about the habitual performance of such overlearned tasks? Are they "automated" and thereby precisely replicated? Not if the stimulus pattern is altered, according to A. N. Sokolov, "Neuronal Models in the Orienting Reflex," in Brazier. The possible implications of his findings for literary studies is this: novel textual input, as Shklovsky long ago maintained, can successfully deautomatize, or subtly "deprogram," even the most habituated reader.

is not as harebrained as those of I. A. Richards's students recorded in his *Practical Criticism* or as self-involved as those recorded by Norman Holland in his *Poems in Persons?*[11]

Of course we cannot be sure, and for that reason we require that student readers "validate" their enactive interpretations by producing critical interpretations. But in training them in this, we promote a skill that, as I have pointed out, is radically different from the skill of reading. That it serves a real, though limited, pedagogical purpose, I readily concede. It has, however, two major drawbacks. First, as we have seen, the results of textual analysis are always invalidated by the hermeneutic circle, so that the absolute significance of a text is, as the deconstructionists say, "undecidable." "Validity in interpretation" is at best a rough approximation, at worst the consensus of a self-appointed establishment. The second drawback of critical response is its effect on the literary experience itself. The special esteem that it has always enjoyed in literate societies has tended to make reading-as-performance seem a trivial preliminary, a sort of limbering up before the main event. Yet the fact that the performance of enactive interpretation cannot be institutionally monitored should not cause it to be depreciated, for the ultimate value of any artifact, verbal or otherwise, is its performance value, not its susceptibility to analysis.

The habit of analysis is exceedingly strong and not caused entirely by our pedagogical system. In every art form, every performing art especially, there are two necessary phases, practice and performance. Practice involves a breaking down of acquired bad habits and a laborious building up of more effective ones. In most performing arts the practice and the performance phases are clearly distinguished. In singing practice, for example, one may wear blue jeans and sneakers and spend two hours at Madame So-and-so's apartment doing gamuts, trills, and parts of a Mozart concert aria. At a performance one may be dressed in a floor-length gown, have a silent and solemn accompanist, and present a scrupulously selected program of songs before an audience of hundreds. One may be nervous. One may momentarily falter and focus on an inappropriate vibrato. But one knows one is there to perform, not to practice.

Such is not the case with the poetic performance, because both performance and analysis have the very same setting—the reader silently confronting the printed text. How easily we shift from one mode of interpretation

---

11. Kintgen's *The Perception of Poetry* uses a similar approach but is more rigorous than Richards and less tendentious than Holland.

to the other! All it takes is a moment of inadvertance and we stop and move our gaze back to a preceding line or ponder the meaning of a particular image within the context of that author's work. Our rapid shiftings from peripheral to focal awareness of the text are made possible by the fact that these two operations are not readily distinguishable; and breakdowns in the poetic performance occur because these operations are *mutually inter-ferent.*

Interference is a crucial concept in the psychology of learning. It may be defined as "a conflict of competing associations in learning or memory" (Chaplin), a situation in which one learned skill is not sufficiently distinguished from another and thereby inhibits it. Two procedures that use different sensory and motor channels are simultaneously performable. "Walking and chewing gum" are supposed to be non-interferent activities, but over-hearing music from another room and making music oneself may well occupy the same channel and be interferent. The performance and the analysis of a text may be fundamentally distinct, but often they do not *seem* so. We do not distinguish the two interpretive procedures by their setting or by any change in our appearance. The silent, solitary performance seems indistinguishable from the silent, solitary analysis. It is little wonder that, when we read a text, we confound the two.

It has been argued, by those who still hold out the possibility of interpretive certitude, that analysis could be subtly contaminated by performance and that the resultant explication would thereby be flawed by impressionism. Analysis, itself intrinsically problematic, has not much to fear, I would say, from the interference of the performance mode. The focal awareness that analysis exerts on a text is a relatively easy procedure: the text is, after all, already a linear series of lexical signs.

In this interference situation it is not critical analysis but performance that clearly runs the greatest risk of contamination, both for the reasons already proposed and by the simple fact that the peripheral awareness of a text is technically quite difficult to achieve. The reader-as-artist must apply to this serial medium a parallel process, convert a linear input into a quasi-three-dimensional representation, and retain at various levels of con-sciousness a large number of components—rhythmic, conceptual, imaginal, and affective—all to realize that complexity to which we assign the general label "mood." This knowledge that the performance produces is the "drift" that Whitman declared to be "every thing," compared to which his words were "nothing."

Enacted Imagery

Enactive interpretation—the Greeks had not one, but two, words for it. One word was *energeia*. As with all their rhetorical terms, its normative context was oral-mimetic. Literally the term meant the condition of being *energos*, that is, "at work" (*ergon*), or "in operation." In the art of oratory it appears to have meant the ability of a speaker to foreground himself as perceptual image and his referents as mental images and to have included a number of features: declamatory vigor involving gestures, vocal effects, and certain dramatic techniques that help express the speaker's feeling and imitate ("act out") his referents. Aristotle variously refers to it as a power of endowing objects with human characteristics and of describing humans in animal terms, as when Isocrates likened Philip to a free-ranging animal (*Rhetoric*, 1411b). It does not appear to have been considered a separate figure, like simile, metaphor, metonymy, and allegory, but a way of investing images, figurative and non-figurative alike, with intense immediacy. Was this word a catch-all term for all those devices that make for a rousing speech, or is its specificity to be found rather in its purpose than in its means? Aristotle suggests the latter when he tells us that its purpose was that of "placing things before the eyes" of an audience. In the *Rhetoric,* after using this latter expression some half-a-dozen times, he stops and says:

> We must now explain the meaning of "before the eyes" [*pro ommatōn*] and what must be done to produce it. By this term I mean placing things before the eyes in such a way that they signify things actually occurring. (1411b)

The Romans called this *actio,* the technique of an *actor,* one who enacts a given role. The "eyes" in question are in part the body's eyes, in part the mind's eyes: while the audience for such a speech would actually see the physical movements of the speaker and hear his voice modulate, they would be imagining the objects that his words led them to believe he was at that moment imagining. His gestures were therefore indexical signs, while his words were symbolic signs that generated iconic representations in the minds of his auditors (cf. the player's speech in *Hamlet,* 2.2).[12]

During the long historical transition during which orality shared with

---

12. *Energeia* involved an extralinguistic code, kinesic in respect to gesture and paralinguistic in respect to phonation. See Birdwhistle and Crystal.

literacy the public task of teaching, exhorting, and pleasing with words, *energeia* had with it a less public companion, *enargeia,* which had as its primary meaning the condition of being *enarges,* that is, "in brightness" (*argos* = bright, white). Like twin wheel ruts that mark some ancient road, their progress and direction can still be traced, though now and again only one of them is visible or both seem to have faded into the eroded terrain.

One reason why they are difficult to trace, besides their similarity of sound and spelling that made them near-homonyms and subject to scribal error, is that even Greek and Latin rhetoricians were themselves unsure of their precise definitional difference.[13] Aristotle's *Rhetoric,* our earliest extant source, does not clearly differentiate the two, leading one to suspect that their contamination had begun among the earlier Sophists. Quintilian confessed his uncertainty. This confusion continued through the Renaissance.[14] Gradually, through the sixteenth century we note a fading of *energeia* as a rhetorical term and its emergence as a term of mechanics; since *enargeia* had been so long confounded with *energeia,* it too faded. Over the next four centuries these terms are referred to less and less, but their core meanings survived under different names and guises.

Despite the obscurities with which their history is wrapped, we can assume that some rhetorical principle once marked their specific difference. To hypothesize this principle, we will need to draw several lexical inferences. At the start we find ourselves on solid ground when we assign "forcefulness" and "motion" to *energeia,* for Aristotle could not have used this term without understanding it as "act" as opposed to "potency" (*dunamis;* see *Metaphysics,* 1043a20, 1048a26). If act is necessarily preceded by a state of potency, does *enargeia* correspond in some way to the state of potency that precedes action? If we regard foresight, or "deliberative phantasy," as a visualization of potency in which we place some proposed action "before the [mind's] eyes" (*De Memoria,* 431b), then *enargeia* appears to be the vivid envisioning of the

---

13. See Quintilian, *Institutio Oratoria,* 4.2.63–64.

14. A perusal of early dictionaries is instructive. Thomas Elyot's *Dictionary* (1538) included only "energia," but defined it in the alphabetical place where one would expect "enargia," then conflated the two in a definition that had "energia" as a description that is such "that it seemeth to the reder or herer, that he beholdeth it [standard definition of *enargeia*], as it were in doinge [standard definition of *energeia*]." This was later amended by Thomas Cooper in 1548 in the revised *Biblioteca Eliotae,* which printed separate definitions of the two words. "Energia" now takes on the general meaning of "an efficacie or operation," a meaning broad enough to apply equally well to rhetoric and mechanics. Jean Cousin concludes that "Les textes des rhéteurs grecs ne sont pas sûrs et les éditeurs modernes ont confondu assez fréquemment" these two terms. *Études sur Quintilien,* vol 2 (Paris: Boivier, 1936), 75.

not-yet-enacted. To justify this inference and apply it to *poiēsis* we might turn to the *Poetics* (1455a22–26):

> In constructing the plot and working it out [*synapergazesthai*] with proper diction, the poet should place the scene, as far as possible, before his eyes [*pro ommatōn*]. In this way, seeing [*horōn*] everything with the utmost vividness [*enargestata*], as if he were a spectator of the action, he will discover what is in keeping with it, and be most unlikely to overlook inconsistencies. (Butcher's translation)

The eyes before which the speaker's meaning is to be eventually dramatized are the outer eyes of the audience, but in these passages from the *De Memoria* and the *Poetics* it is clear that the eyes are those of the mind. The dramatist is instructed to visualize a scene, and, since this scene is not actualized before it is acted on stage, this vivid visualization represents to him his *potential* scene. A fully actualized drama, Aristotle in a later passage asserts, will produce in a spectator the most vivid pleasures (*hedonai . . . enargestata*), but this piece of writing will have "vividness of impression [*to enarges*] in reading as well as in representation [*epi tōn ergōn*]" (1462a16–18). This adds the suggestion that the dramatic text, read as a closet drama, evokes mental imagery, that is, *enargeia*, by written signs alone, just as an epic does when it is perused by a reader. Keeping to his oral-mimetic aesthetic preferences, Aristotle notes that such effects have a less vivid impact than those of perception, but have *to enarges* nonetheless.

At this point let me attempt a definition of these two terms as they may originally have applied to addressers and addressees in the oral situation:

> *energeia:* the persuasive assertion by a speaker that he is presently imaging something, that he has been roused to action (has become *energos*) by a situation that the objective indices of gestures, intonations, and words demonstrate that he is now contemplating.

> *enargeia:* the subjective act of imaging, the receptive state of potency that precedes the active (energic) response.

Whenever and wherever the transition between oral and literate discourse took place over the two millennia from the fourth century B.C. to the sixteenth century A.D., an *energeia* proper to writing had to be devised. Many a writer, knowing that his text was destined to be read by solitary readers more often than it would be publicly recited, felt the need to maintain some illusion of oral presence. In Aristotelian terms this meant somehow incorporating the agonistic style within the graphic style. In a strictly literate genre, speakers (authors and their characters) cannot be seen physically reacting to mental imagery, as for example we can observe the face and hand of the actor who, as Macbeth, hallucinates the dagger. The energic outer behavior, no less than the enargic inner events that prompt this behavior, must now be displayed through the reader's *enargeia.* The reader must therefore be able to enact upon the inner stage of the mind two kinds of fictive imagery: (1) the imagery of objective human behavior and (2) the imagery of subjective human images. In this purely literate circumstance the old distinction between perceptual and mental imagery had to erode and *energeia* and *enargeia* came to seem a distinction without a difference.

At this point another shift may have occurred, one in which the referents of the discourse, rather than the participants, became classified in energic and enargic terms. Another lexical peculiarity of Greek may have reenforced this later development. The adjective *energos* (also *energes*), meaning "active" or "at work," had as its original opposite *aergos* (*a*-privative + *ergon*). This Homeric word in time lost its epsilon through syncope and became *argos,* and so the Greek word for "inactive" ("out of work," "idle," "at leisure," "quiescent," etc.) became homonymous with the word for "bright." Quintilian seems to have this connotation in mind when, after deriving *energeia* from the philosophical concept of act, adds that its "proper virtue" is "not to be idle [*otiosa*]" (*Institutio Oratoria,* 8.3.89). If *energeia* is actualization in the form of perceptible motion, can we infer that *enargeia* is the potency of a visualized object prior to act once its state of rest is exchanged for one of movement? Do we have here a distinction that applies to the verbal description of static, as opposed to kinetic, objects and therefore to the visual artifacts verbalized in *ekphrasis?* The evidence is admittedly inconclusive but nonetheless suggestive. If we note that the verb commonly used to describe the senses at rest is *argeo* and that the *phantasia* of the internal senses was known to be facilitated by the inactivity of the external senses (in reverie, dream, meditation, and in the absorbing concentration of reading), we find this *energeia-enargeia* opposition shifting from addresser and addressee to referent. *Energeia* mimetically suggests the actualization, perceived motion, and sensory presence of a speaker's verbal referents. *Enargeia* connotes potency, stasis, and imaginative vision—effects associated with the graphic arts and descriptive writing.

The inherent, functional similarity between these two terms lies in their imaginal evocation of absent persons, places, and things: *energeia* through indexical gesture and voice (*hupokrisis,* or acting technique), *enargeia* directly through symbolic (verbal) signs. *Energeia* is heightened mimesis; *enargeia* is heightened diegesis. The evocation that results from either, or both in combination, is mental imagery, that is, iconic signs. The energic image is the object, invisible to all but the speaker, the imaginary object to which his words refer and to which they may be addressed in apostrophe. The activity of *energeia* is provoked by the activity of its quasi-hallucinated object, which, if it would only stop moving and changing, could be calmly described in mere words. The enargic image, on the other hand, is at rest and may be scrutinized and described detail by detail. *Enargeia* is therefore the process by which ekphrasis is produced.

Keep in mind that the above speculation in the archaeology of rhetoric applies only to the context of oral discourse. *Energeia* can only be understood in such a context; *enargeia* must also be understood in this context, though it seems to have been easily adapted to writing. Writing, however, eroded these distinctions. As early as the dialogues of Plato, the speaker's oral presence of visual gesture and vocal tone and dynamics (*energeia*) and the imagery of his referents (*enargeia*) are writing-mediated and must be imagined. Since only the page of written characters is directly available to the receiver of such a message, what once was *energeia* is now difficult to distinguish from *enargeia:* with oral presence no longer a perceptual factor and words alone generating iconic signs, the written image of speaker and referents wholly occupies the mind's visual attention.

The older, orally based distinction did not, however, wholly vanish when its primary usefulness was over. Like exploded planets whose asteroid chunks loop close to our orbit, they have persisted to exert their subtle force on the theory and practice of imagination. What they have left behind as a distinction still valid in writing is the distinction between *kinetic* and *static* imagery. Kinetic imagery, the imagery associated with narrative action, appears to be the literate descendant of *energeia,* specifically of the "diegetic mimesis" of oral reciters. Static imagery, associated with the inscription of iconic signs and with ekphrasis, appears to be derived from *enargeia.*

Writers and theorists who in the past have felt drawn to the static image with its *copia* of copresent details have always found attractive the saying of Simonides, that, while a picture is a mute poem, a poem is a speaking picture. And reading it out of context, they have taken Horace's *ut pictura poesis* as their motto. Those on the other hand who, like Lessing, felt that an unbridgeable gulf separated *pictura* from *poesis* and that the true qualities of language were energic and kinetic, argued that static imagery has no place in literature. The values that Lessing accumulates about these two poles is worth considering. W. J. T. Mitchell has suggested that *Laokoon* is built about a set of "oppositions that regulate Lessing's discourse," not only poetry vs. painting and time vs. space, but masculine vs. feminine.

> Paintings, like women, are ideally silent, beautiful creatures designed for the gratification of the eye, in contrast to the sublime eloquence proper to the manly art of poetry. (*Iconology,* 110)

Mitchell's main concern here is to point out the relation of gender roles to the aesthetics of space and time, that the cultural coding of sexuality may have been a powerful, unspoken motive behind Lessing's iconophobia. My reconstruction of the meanings of *enargeia* would then place it clearly in the "feminine" category of pictorial image, totally, albeit momentarily, revealed and present to the mind of the reader. According to this dominant cultural code, *energeia,* with its implications of productive force, of active response and causative effect, corresponds to the "masculine" category of oral expression—and to drama, the genre to which Lessing was most committed.

The genealogy of Lessing's picture-poetry opposition with its underlying sexual polarity might well be traced back to Hebraic, rather than Hellenic, sources. The Word of God was nothing if not masculine, energic, and effective—his *sermo operatorius.* Pictorial representation was hemmed about by taboo and more often than not associated with the worship of visualizable divinities, whose graven images were regularly derided for their inability to move and act. The *eidōla* that appeared in dreams and visions to the devotee after the ritual contemplation of icons were enargic and considered passive, seductive images of the same order as erotic mental images, which from a male point of view were predominantly female and of which Lilith was the demonic prototype. While it is true that Hellenic culture privileged *logos,* it did not do so with quite the same patriarchal intensity as Hebraic culture. There is a little less Hellenism and perhaps more than a little Protestant Hebraism in Lessing's anti-imagery position.

In a purely literate context, and again in terms of imaged objects, every verbally cued mental image might be placed on a continuum between the ideal poles of absolute kinesis and absolute stasis. That is, images may appear in metamorphosis, in motion relative to a static viewpoint and to other objects, at rest relative to a moving viewpoint, or at rest as viewed by a motionless viewer. Thus, as the *energeia-enargeia* polarity becomes a time-space polarity, or spectrum, the reading performance is called upon to be flexible and fine-tuned enough to contemplate a noun phrase *ut pictura,* able to speed up and move about it as about statuary or within architectural space, and able to accelerate to the speed of verbs whenever energy propels nouns through the space-time of narration.

In 1934, looking back on his break with the early Imagists, Ezra Pound cited this polarity as an aesthetic issue:

> The defeat of earlier imagist propaganda was not in misstatement but in incomplete statement. The diluters took the handiest and easiest meaning, and thought only of the STATIONARY image. If you can't think of imagism or phanopoeia as including the moving image, you will have to make a really needless division of fixed image and praxis or action. (Pound, 52)

This "really needless division," which in critical interpretation has generated the opposition of structuralist and functionalist theories, is based on the false dichotomy of absolute space and absolute time. The written imagery that the reader performs in enactive interpretation need not be limited to pictorial description. If written imagery is the symbolically coded representation of visual perception and if we actually perceive motion and change, there is no reason to suppose that writing cannot evoke it. True, when we anatomize a passage of narrative action into its grammatical constituents, its kinetic action ceases. But then again if we anatomized a cheetah, it too would be immobilized. Unlike critical interpretation, which objectifies the text, enactive interpretation uses it as an instrument and performs it in such a way that its images seem to move at the indicated pace or remain at rest for the indicated interval. If including narrative movement as one of the potential aspects of imagery requires an enlarged concept of "image," it may be worth our while to undertake this enlargement.

Contemporaneous with Pound's reappraisal of the "moving image" was the work of the Prague Linguistic Circle. When Garvin began translating the writings of the Prague Structuralists into English (*A Prague School Reader on Esthetics, Literary Structure and Style,* 1958) he encountered the Czech word *aktualisace*[15] (actualization) and understood it to mean the capacity of discourse to draw attention to itself by deviating from expected linguistic or literary usage, to "become strange," as the Russian Formalists had phrased it.

---

15. Willie Van Peer, *Stylistics and Psychology: Investigations of Foregrounding,* 6.

The rhetorical, as well as the metaphysical, meanings of *energeia* are suggested by the Structuralists' uses of "actualization." Not only addressers, addressees, and referents, but the coded medium of language itself passes from potency to act when it passes from an ordinary to an extraordinary stylistic state. It realizes its semiotic potential only when—through linguistic means alone—it defamiliarizes its referents and forces its deautomatized reader to reperceive the world.

The fact that this re-vision of the world is one of the principal effects of poetic actualization may have influenced Garvin to choose a visual term to translate *aktualisace*—"foregrounding." This old pictorial term with its more recent Gestalt connotations implied a figure, having closure and partly occluding its background, that appears to the viewer to step forth from that less defined ground. Verbal foregrounding was not, however, limited to imagery: it could as easily take the form of paradox or catachresis. We have here, it seems, an attempt to treat the Modernist poetic text, that ultimate literate artifact, as the locus of *energeia,* rather than any real or imagined speaker, and as the locus of *enargeia* as well, rather than any real or possible reader.

This dyad that has operated together down through the centuries as the communication of excitement through verbally cued mental imagery has assumed different functions and forms. In a purely oral setting *energeia* was the dominant of the two, because it was only in and through the speaker that mental images could be represented. As literacy began to prevail, so also did *enargeia,* becoming the reader's imaginative activity of reconstructing the energic activities of fictional speakers and narrated events. As this pair of correlatives did not end in Athens or Rome, it did not end in Prague. We have observed its traces—like those of an ancient highway that fade off, abandoned perhaps and outworn, or covered over by history, but only to reappear miles further along—rebuilt by other hands with new materials to serve altered needs.

THE POETIC FOCUS

We have seen how methodological assumptions have a way of determining the data selected for interrogation as well as the first questions that are asked. The inductive approach to critical validity revealed upon examination the unavoidable circularity of its logic, a basic flaw attributable to its false dichotomy of structural and functional aspects. We have also examined the consequences of these approaches to the experience of reading, namely, that the text shifts from instrument to object when it is critically analyzed and that this shift radically alters its ontological status.

Since literary method cannot be centered on the author or the reader as separate operatives nor upon the text or the referent as separate fields of data, I have proposed that it be centered on the action that brings into play and integrates all these four factors. Only a performance model, I submit, is an adequate paradigm for the grounding of a method.

We now come to the question, *What* in the performance should we question? Having rejected the text-as-object, we must find another "object" from which to select relevant data, from which, in turn, valid propositions may be formed. This means that, without inducing theory directly from textual data, we must attempt to induce it from performance data. We must turn our attention from the text as semantic indicators to the poem as a cognitive performance. Wallace Stevens began one of his statements on poetics ("Of Modern Poetry") with the enigmatic noun phrase: "The poem of the mind in the act of finding what will suffice." What will suffice? Words addressed to the "delicatest ear of the mind," where an "invisible audience listens," not to the performance on an outer stage "but to itself."

The "object" of poetics is not an object or a hypostasis but an act of the mind. The poem (the *poēma,* the thing made) is the act (the *energeia*) of the mind that actualizes it. What the mind finds sufficient is a focus that, as

Stevens suggests, performs the imitation of a performance. The "visionary grot where spirits gat them home" of "Sunday Morning" is now found within the literate microcosm.

Exploration and Labor

Before we can begin to speak of conscious imitative activity, we need to speak of cognitive activity in more general terms. Piaget's distinction between *accommodation* and *assimilation* provides us with a good starting point.

Accommodation is the process by which we adapt our concepts of the world to events as they present themselves. We flexibly "accommodate," or adjust to, what we are forced to accept as reality. It is characterized by what has been termed "exploratory behavior," an instinctual activity based on the need to orient oneself and discover one's environment, an impulse that is driven by an even more basic requirement, the need for sensory stimulation and cognitive challenge. Among mammals, all but the very largest predators need to be constantly alert. We smaller predators, ourselves potential prey of other species as well as of our own, find we must keep perceptually alert even when we do not feel potentially threatened. Even when we are not actually obliged to reconnoitre our territory, we take walks or vacation trips or travel imaginatively through the reading of books. Even when we do not need to learn the ways and habitats of animals and plants for purposes of survival, we can still have a disinterested fascination in natural history. This innate need for stimulation and reality-testing also includes a need to test ourselves: hence the largely *self*-exploratory activities like running, rock-climbing, and so forth.[1]

Exploratory behavior is accommodative activity and as such is spontaneous and unselfconscious.[2] The agent is so intent on discovering "what is there" that he or she extends outward in, or through, bodily organs and

1. Roger Caillois in *Les Jeux et les hommes* elaborates a four-fold classification of play behavior: risk-taking, games of chance, mimicry, and competition. They all may involve skill and rules but the first two would seem more closely related to exploratory behavior, the more primordial sort of *jeu libre*, and the latter two, in their more formal literary and sport manifestations, seem to exhibit a qualitatively higher order of organization. See also Wolfgang Iser, *Prospecting*, 254–58.

2. See Hebb (1958) and Berlyne (1966). As I suggested earlier, the sharp contrast we make between structures and functions, space and time, is one of our survival mechanisms. We may understand this discrimination now in terms of exploratory behavior and accommodative strategies.

extrinsic tools toward the objects of awareness. In this act of peripheral awareness and parallel processing of information there are simply no channels left by which to contemplate the self-reflexive "I." The "joy of adventure" for the anxiety-ridden burgher, when it does occur, lies in a cognitive overload of this experience—an immediate construing of the meaning of objects, an intuition, an enactive interpretation. Exploratory behavior is a trait that we share with all mammals, particularly of course with our primate ancestors. All young mammals explore themselves and their habitat by risk- and chance-taking, but only the higher species prolong this behavior into adulthood.[3]

Assimilation, as distinguished from accommodation, is the imposition upon events of preformulated schemata, paradigms designed to help one recognize, classify, and utilize objects. The ability to assimilate an experience implies a prior familiarity with it and a presumed ability to predict its outcome. It implies, in other words, a culturally enhanced mastery of one's environment.

If exploratory behavior is an instinctive accommodative response to unfamiliar input, *labor* is a learned assimilative response to familiar input. Since the conditions of labor are relatively controlled and the objects familiar, the activity can be repeated indefinitely without risking undue interference or resistance: the sickle will not turn on the harvester, nor will the grain wriggle out of the mortar and attack the grinder. If exploratory behavior is characterized first by a wide-angled peripheral awareness, then by a focal awareness of selected objects of interest, labor is characterized first by a focal awareness of the task at hand, then by a more diffuse peripheral awareness. As the body of the laborer becomes fixed in its routine, the mind wanders off in search of its requisite level of stimulation. It may wander off into song or into irrelevant fantasy, or it may oversee the self-in-the-action. Labor, as an effort to assimilate raw materials into culturally defined products, cannot tolerate or coexist with exploratory behavior. Improvisation has no place in a totally familiar, totally routinized activity. When the accommodative drive is thus inhibited,

3. To use the word "play" to describe this behavior is, I think, to overwork "play." Exploratory behavior is our most critical survival asset. It is pleasurable and engrossing like play, but then again most activities that are "hard-wired" in the genetic code of a species have their hedonic pay-off. To call exploratory behavior "play" is to devalue that important term by overgeneralization. In his book *The Play of the World* James Hans argues that play is the basis of all cultural activity, including production, though he acknowledges that he creates problems for himself when he makes such terms "too global in conception" (49). This, I believe, is what he has done throughout what is nevertheless a very stimulating study of the philosophical, linguistic, literary, and socioeconomic aspects of play-related activities.

the laborer has the leisure and the option to objectify the self, the tool, the technique, the raw materials, and the ultimate goal. In this segmentation of action we see the origin of critical interpretation.

In exploration and labor we thus have two basic stances toward activity, one wholly absorbed in an action, the other detached and self-reflexive. Though we may associate exploratory behavior with paleolithic hunting and gathering societies and labor with the development of primitive agriculture, we cannot say that humankind has evolved beyond the need for the former skill. Likewise, though we can associate accommodation with Piaget's preverbal sensorimotor stage and assimilation with the later operational stage, we cannot say that individuals outgrow their need continually to rediscover themselves and their environment. We must, I believe, think of these two stances as copresent, alternative levels of cognitive response and consider ourselves equipped with a sort of toggle switch that turns off one to turn on the other.

I would go further and suggest that these two stances are built-in pro-grams that can be "customized" into two distinct activity modes, each able to generate an infinite number of uniquely patterned procedures. These modes and procedures can be transmitted culturally through imitation, that evolu-tionary trait common to all warm-blooded animals but possessed in different degrees by different species: the higher the species, the less dependent are offspring on instinct and the more dependent on observing their elders. Imitation enhances exploratory behavior in all higher animals, and, to the degree a species has the capability, it also enhances the effectiveness of repetitive labor. Labor, when it assumes technical complexity, let us call "imitative work" (or simply "work"), and exploratory behavior, when it is formalized, let us call "imitative play" (or simply "play").

Imitative Work

Imitation, when it enhances labor to the level of "work," raises human behavior to a new plateau. Put simply, the distinction I wish to make between labor and imitative work is that between unskilled and skilled production. The former is quickly learned and needs little alertness in its operation, the latter is only gradually mastered and in its operation needs both alertness and adaptability. The one requires repetition, the other a sequence of different actions and the acquisition of rules to govern that sequence.

Work, as distinct from mere labor, entails both assimilative strategies (in that it is a rule-governed activity) and accommodative strategies (in that the circumstances and materials it deals with may be novel and must always be carefully construed). In varying degrees, the carpenter, the cook, and the physician, for example, must regularly confront the unexpected and rely on "instinct" and tacit knowledge.

Much of this tacit knowledge has to be learned through imitation, not simply instruction. By "instruction" I mean a narrowly focused transmission of information, one that often takes the linear form of "now you do this and then you do that and after that. . . . " Imitation may include such sequences, but it does so by including much more, permitting the learner to observe and absorb even those skills that the master is incapable of verbalizing. Instruction is characterized by what has been termed "intentional learning," whereas imitation is a learning process that is enhanced by what is called "incidental learning." Needless to say, this latter transmission of knowledge is most necessary for the learning of complexly coordinated skills.[4]

Apprenticeship is a holistic learning process based on the impersonation of the technician. We must not, however, assume that this sharing of knowledge is a purely benign transfer of skills. Since it purports to furnish the apprentice with mastery, it will allow that person to compete on equal terms with the master and in the absence of adequate social sanctions would lead to what René Girard has called "conflictual mimesis," the ability to appropriate the same objects with the same degree of skill, resulting in a sequence of violence, vengeance, and scapegoating ("unanimous victimage").[5] Technological discoveries have through human history been guarded as state secrets more often than they were offered as boons to humankind. Military and industrial espionage is not an innovation of the modern nation-state. From metallurgy to computer software, know-how has been appropriated and jealously guarded. The ambiguity of copyright lies at the heart of this problematical exchange: the innate imitative impulse confers on all of us the inalienable right to copy, a right forever in conflict with the skill-owner's right to conceal this skill from the copyist. In circumstances of real or falsely

4. See George Mandler's "Organization and Memory" in K. W. Spence and J. T. Spence, Eds., *The Psychology of Learning and Motivation,* vol. 1 (New York: Academic Press, 1967).

5. See his *To Double Business Bound,* particularly the introduction and "Interview" (chap. 10). also *Des Choses cachées depuis la fondation du monde,* bks 1 and 3.

perceived scarcity, imitation has always assumed a threatening character; universal education, to cite one example, has always seemed to some a subversive goal, and a little more knowledge a very dangerous thing indeed.

Imitation, this profoundly hominizing act, has two principal meanings: to duplicate another's behavior and to duplicate a product. We can therefore divide imitative work into two categories: (1) *self-shaping,* the effort to become the persona of the master in order to absorb the master's powers, and (2) *other-shaping,* the effort to apply those powers to the object-world in order to produce copies. Each of these may be further divided.

Self-shaping may be either private or collective. *Ego-formation* is its private form, a constructive activity that young people constantly engage in at various levels of consciousness. Perhaps all of us, to the extent that we feel the want of a desired power, engage in tacit or overt role-playing. This basically imaginative procedure is essential, as we have seen, to the apprenticeship stage of learning.

Collective self-shaping may be termed *social function,* the work of collective role-playing. This subcategory includes professional and class-identifications, political and religious allegiances—in short, all patterned activity performed in public and in concert with others. As a demonstration of collective identity, it may include participation in an activity that has within it a strong element of symbolic drama, for example, electoral politics, war, and religious ritual.[6] According to Girard's mimetic hypothesis, the goal of these public activities is to mitigate the hostility aroused by appropriative imitation and, when necessary, direct it toward a sacrificial victim whose death and ultimate divinization reconciles the community—a god, hero, or group that then becomes the object of collective identification, that is, a self-shaping on a collective level. "Imitative work" would degenerate into utter mayhem without these ceremonial restraints on appropriative mimesis.

Other-shaping, finally, may be divided into *production* and *use.* By production I mean the making of instruments by means of which human will is extended into the environment, and by use I mean the active wielding of those instruments to alter the environment. To learn such work through imitation entails technical training and practice.

Let me recapitulate this outline of "imitative work" by applying it to literary training and production.

6. "Social function" is characterized, says Goffman, by a " 'we rationale' . . . , that is, a sense of the single thing that *we* are doing together at the time. Ceremonies of entrance and departure are also likely to be employed, as are signs acknowledging the initiation and termination of the encounter or focused gathering as a unit" (*Encounters,* 18).

Ego-formation is that personal kind of self-shaping that begins with the aspiration to "be someone," to be someone who has been acknowledged by the community to possess certain powers and privileges. Of the four literary factors, the only one that qualifies for this role-model is the author. When a person thinks, "I want to be like ——," or simply, "I want to be an author," that person is conceptualizing a particular object of imitation who is assumed to have particular, desirable attributes. In that moment of admiration—in that one moment at least—the aspirant sees all of literature concentrated in the person of the master, real or ideal. The literary theorist who similarly centers literature in the biography, psyche, or *oeuvre* of an author thus resembles the writing-workshop student with the crush on the famous instructor.

Imitative work may be inspired by a particular ego-ideal, but, if one is ever to play that role credibly enough to be recognized by others and publicly certified as that persona, one must learn the rules of the craft—not only how to use the basic materials, but also how to use them in ways acceptable to the community. In other words, one has to learn style, one has to know and respect the professional conventions of one's community.[7] Stylistic tradition closely resembles ritual: both are publicly repeated patterns of behavior that reenforce cultural identity. Literature has its culturally specific stylistic patterns that the apprentice writer must learn in order to qualify as an author within a given community. This constitutes the world as verbally mediated, that is, the referent. It also involves a skillful appropriation, again through imitation, of the skills of the masters. Recent attention to the "anxiety of influence" and to intertextuality has highlighted the ambiguous relationship of disciple and master. The theorist who regards this category of imitative work as paramount will examine the human values—those stated outright and those concealed within conventions—and will ground this examination on a more-or-less explicit axiology and theory of literary signs. Implicit in such a theory will also be answers to the questions, Why do people write texts, and why do others read them?—questions that can be illuminated but not fully explained in terms of cultural conditioning.

Production happens at the moment that a suitable product appears, a Heideggerian *Zeug,* an instrument by which the human community extends itself and its purposes. When a writer produces a text, a *Zeig-zeug* (or indicator-instrument), this product (like this philosopher's compound noun)

---

7. This is even more true for the traditional "performing arts" and those who work in "service industries." Their performance is their "product." See Goffman, *Presentation of Self,* 75–76.

is a neologism, but an exceedingly complex one. The theorist who decides that this manifestation of imitative work deserves to be the exclusive object of literary study will seek within the verbal materials and architectonics of the text the causative principles of the literary experience. Writer, referent, and reader will either be ignored or somehow subsumed within this mysterious construct, an artifact that loses its substantiality the closer it is examined and that must be hypostatized to preserve its theoretical objectness.

Use, the final category of imitative work, is the ability to wield such products, an activity that may constitute an end in itself or a fashioning of other instruments. Theorists who focus their study upon text-reception view the product in terms of the user, the spatial artifact in terms of its temporal realization. But since the performance of this skill cannot be monitored directly, they must rely on informants' reports or on the supposition that particular stylistic devices produce particular reader-responses. To support their claims they must, in other words, ground them in a particular theory of signs and of style.

This survey of imitative work, with special attention to its literary applications, further clarifies the interdependence of writer, reader, referent, and text, which now appear not as actually separate entities at all but simply as theoretically distinguished subcategories of imitative work. Like the phases of inductive analysis, these four aspects of poiesis are circular because imitative work is circular. To say one is an author is to say one has learned certain acceptable routines by which a textual tool can be made that can be used to justify one's claim to authorship, which is to say, one's worthiness to be imitated as a possessor of culturally valued routines that produce imitable tools, the uses of which are implicit in their construction.

If we could once and for all separate text-production from text-reception, we could perhaps list the procedures necessary to compose a poem and those necessary to extract its meanings. If we could, we could teach one skill to young writers and the other to young critics and expect them to learn these methods through the discipline of imitative work. The reason why this cheerful pedagogical project has always been doomed to failure is that every writer must be a reader and every reader a writer. That is, production needs at every revisionary instance the feedback loop of reception, which needs the hermeneutical circle of construction. This circularity has always existed to bind the poet and the community, but literacy—reading-and-writing—has bound them both in a yet-profounder intimacy.

Again, the center of this circle, of all these circles, is performance and in the case of verbal poiesis to place oneself in the center is to view the circle of work transformed into a circle of play.

Imitative Play

Play, like work, is meant to be a skillful performance. Unskillful play is as tedious an exercise for the performer as it is for the spectator. Most play, again like work, is best learned through imitation and, like work, requires mental alertness and, often, physical effort. The similarity between play and work does not stop there: play behavior exhibits themes and patterns that seem to derive directly from the earnest undertakings of work. This is a commonplace observation: Eskimo children play with miniature harpoons, American children with dump trucks; all children "play house," mimicking the serious, usually merely work-weary, expressions of their elders; older children play team sports that resemble the competitive social rituals of corporations, sects, and nation-states. The division between play and work can become blurred in some play activities, such as professional sports, but the value of play lies always in its perceived *metaphorical* relation to work. That is, it is understood as both different from and similar to work behavior.

The essential difference between the two lies in the attitude that Coleridge defined as preconditional to the reading of literature. This attitude, he declared, is "that willing suspension of disbelief for the moment [that] constitutes poetic faith" (*Biographia Literaria*, xiv). Play is a deliberate act, but this "willing" act is extraordinary: it is a voluntary decision to suspend the customary norms by which we assess our reality. Once we disentangle Coleridge's double negative, we can interpret "suspension of disbelief" as "invitation to believe": play therefore is initiated as an "as if" activity, a game of "pretend." It is surrounded by what Gregory Bateson called a "play frame," a clear signal that the signals to be communicated within this spatiotemporal frame will not mean what they mean outside the frame.[8]

This suspension of disbelief is similar to the religious confession of faith and the scientific hypothesis, but with these important differences: play is

---

8. "A Theory of Play and Fantasy," in his *Steps to an Ecology of Mind*, 177–193. This "metacommunicative" capacity, he says, is a mammalian trait. Kittens and cats must be able to frame their "war games" in such a way that a nip denotes a bite without conveying the sort of violent escalation that a bite would denote.

premised upon its own untruth, its purely conventional fictiveness, and its temporariness. This latter trait is quite important for, as a secession from the ordinary world of consensual reality, its excursion into its own ad hoc consensual reality would be madness if it were not bounded by a beginning and an end (the *archē* and *teleutē* that open and close the Aristotelian *holon*). Imitative play, the category that subsumes all the arts, is licensed to exhibit its *furor ludicrus* — the obsessive behavior of the chess player, the catatonic rigidity of the billiard player, the berserk frenzy of the football player. The subcategory of ludic madness that governs verbal play is called *furor poeticus.*

Imitative work, on the other hand, cannot be regarded as a willing suspension of the assumed rules of reality. Its social functions may be rife with Barthesian mythologies, but, if they are behavior patterns based in belief or embedded in the episteme of a community, they are naturalized and unrecognized as fictions. Work is not an "as if" performance: the student of electrical engineering, her shop instructor at her side, does not wire her first wall saying, "Now I will pretend to be an electrician." She had better say to herself, "Now I am an electrician." Nor does the student-teacher enter his first classroom saying to himself, "Now let's pretend that I am a real teacher," or the airline pilot don a uniform and say, "Now let's pretend I know how to fly this plane," but the child says this while throwing a balsa model into the wind. Finally, imitative work is not a temporally bounded activity, though we interrupt its continuum to insert a holiday, a weekend, a vacation. Work is activity for the sake of ulterior ends. Its meaningfulness lies beyond itself. As play is metaphoric to work, work is metonymic to itself. As an activity that leads into other productive activities, it therefore extends indefinitely beyond the moment of actual performance. Human time, and with it human history, begins by conceiving long-term projects and deferring immediate gratification: agriculture produces the solar year, irrigation projects extend through lifetimes, wall-building for the storage and defense of surplus goods constructs royal dynasties. Work, like its unskilled form, labor, has the nature of a *meson,* a middle preceded by something and followed by something else — and that something is more of the same. It is "extrinsically motivated," as Berlyne put it. Play, being temporally bounded, has the nature of a *holon* and is "intrinsically motivated."[9]

Work creates human time — unidirectional, linear time — by allowing the separation of worker, tool, activity, and idea. The overseer procures the

9. See Berlyne (1968), 840–41. See also Hans, 42ff., where it is clear that what he generalizes here as "play" I have been discussing as exploratory behavior.

worker, the worker procures the tool, accomplishes the work, and views, or only visualizes, the completed project. Between the readying of the tool and the realization of the idea stretches the long intermediate process of work, including within it innumerable other, briefer works and being itself included within the worker's lifetime of work and that of the community. Work may absorb the mind of the worker into a meditation on the moment of the performance, but, providing the worker with a potentially long temporal perspective, work permits the worker the time to stop and objectify the tool and the idea, as well as him- or herself—to stop work and, in effect, to slip out of the performance mode altogether and to contemplate the work disjunctively in terms of the four categories: of ego-formation (What is my self-image in this role?), social function (How do my peers judge my competence?), product (What am I producing and why am I doing it?), and use (How does this tool work and how will this product work when it is finished?). These sample questions may well lead to improvements in working conditions and technique, but such divagations more often than not lead to mere inadvertance, to pleasurable or anxiety-toned daydreaming, and to a necessarily deferred desire for the stimulation of exploratory behavior and its cultural formalization, play.

The unity, and the unifying power, of play is what differentiates it from work. To enter play, and art, is to enter a *technē* that is pared down to essential rules and patterns and that constitutes a happening with a beginning and an end. It is an activity that, as Horace prescribed, is *simplex et unum*. To participate in it as a performer, actual or vicarious, is to enter a fulfilled interval of time, one in which neither self nor role nor idea nor instrument is separable from the act itself.[10]

These are the differences; The similarities are equally important. Work is learned through imitating workers; play is learned through imitating players. All cultural transmissions of practical information, that is, skills, require parallel processing, and this sort of processing is best imitated. Our discussion of work and play has already suggested, however, another similarity: that play is an imitation of work, or, to apply Plato's phrase unplatonically, play is the imitation of an imitation. Its significant context is the work, or work values, it imitates. A player may undergo a rigorous apprenticeship to be publicly certified as a player. This is obviously imitative work. But it is work preliminary to the playful imitation of work.

10. "Play itself does not focus specifically on either a subject or an object; it is an activity in which the activity itself is focused on. . . . Play is an experiential mode of confirming or denying the connections we make with our world (Hans, 11–12).

Play is forever set apart from the work-process; artists and athletes, even when they derive their livelihood from their play, are set apart from the quotidian world of work. Their "work" is specialized and valued for its metaphorical relation to the "work of the world." The imitation of the apprentice is inspired by a desire to become the imitated object, for example, to become the master, but the imitation that is embodied in play is prompted by a desire to *know* the imitated object—to epitomize it, to heighten its features, to enhance its intensity, to question its principles, to reveal its poignant contradictions, and, by offering alternative values, to transcend it. If, as René Girard has proposed, imitative work has within it the seeds of intraspecific murder and of creation, imitative play may be the Ariadne's thread that has always been there to lead the consigned victims out of the dedalian deathhouse.

Now let me offer a breakdown of categories of imitative work and, as their mirror-image, the categories of imitative play (Diagram 3). The frame that encloses the play categories represents Bateson's "play frame," the basic understanding that these activities may look like the work of life-and-death struggles, but that they are not such. The difference is that between map and territory, between representation and its referent.[11]

The diagram is not meant to be read as a flow chart, but as an abstract classification. As "imitative work" should be understood as including all its binary subcategories, so also "imitative play" must be understood as incorporating all its mirror-imaged subcategories. "Self-reshaping" corresponds to "self-shaping," but as an objective of play it involves the temporary assumption of a role, a feat that is possible only through a suspension of disbelief and by the agreement to be bound by a certain set of rules. Self-reshaping is the temporary, rule-governed assumption of a mask, a costume, a "position" in a team sport, or an alternative persona. It is a self-metamorphosis designed to play out the behavioral values of a particular work-world action. It is an imitation of action, of human praxis; as Aristotle said of scripted play, it is a *praxeos mimēsis.*

In the tenth book of *The Republic* Plato attacks artistic imitation for being at once not good enough and too good at what it does. The artist (a painter, for example, or a tragedian) mimics a knowledge he does not actually possess—like horsemanship or kingship—and so is an expert only in a "kind

---

11. See Korzybski, *Science and Sanity.* Bateson neatly summarizes the metaphorical function of play and celebrates its superior sanity when he says, "In primary process, map and territory are equated; in secondary process, they can be discriminated. In play they are both equated and discriminated" (185).

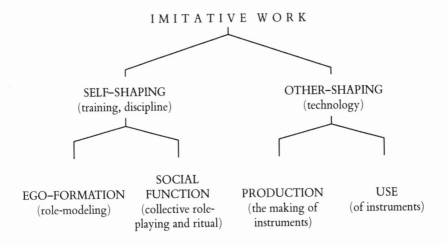

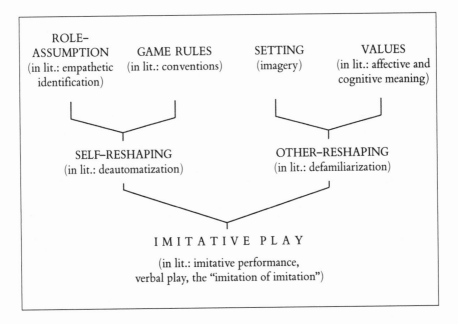

Diagram 3

of play or sport." At the same time, this poor imitation of a skill often inspires onlookers to imitate *it,* not the skill it unskillfully imitates. Plato is concerned that most citizens will not recognize the play frame inscribed about the imitation and will leave a tragedy in an unmanly state of self-pity or contract from a comedy an annoying case of domestic buffoonery. He fears, in short, that imitative work would imitate imitative play—that life would imitate art.

However one may judge Plato's motives and conclusions, he seems to have recognized the power of imitative play to affect the course of imitative work and its institutions, to serve, as we might say, the function of a feedback loop. For in imitating social reality, play reveals the imitative character of that reality: the conventional aspects of selfhood, the play-acting and mythological scripts that a culture ordinarily conceals from its members. Its function in respect to subjectivity is, therefore, one of self-reshaping through deautomatization. Its function in respect to objectivity is one of other-reshaping through defamiliarization.

The Poem as Verbal Play

The expression "work of art" is paradoxical. It is like "the darkness of light" or "the up of down." No one can ignore the fact that the production of art involves an imitative technique, a careful study of the masters with or without the apprenticeship experience of formal "workshops." Art*work* is the lifelong dedication to one's skill. The "work of art" is another matter altogether. To attempt to define, for example, "the mode of existence of a literary work of art," as Wellek and Warren attempted in their *Theory of Literature* (chap. 12), is like trying to define a tennis racket: as a product, a *Kunstwerk,* it can be described and evaluated, but, unless it is discussed as an instrument of play and unless that play is described in detail, little is accomplished. Even if that little were accomplished and the rules of this object's use were outlined, so what? The meaning of a structured play, or game, is not to be found in its equipment or its rulebook, though these are important elements in its performance. As a piece of equipment, a literary "work of art" effaces itself when it is used. Georges Poulet described this phenomenon as "the disappearance of the 'object' ":

> Where is the book I held in my hands? It is still there, and at the same time it is there no longer, it is nowhere. That object wholly object, that thing made of paper, as there are things made of metal or

porcelain, that object is no more, or at least it is as if it no longer existed, as long as I read the book. For the book is no longer a material reality. It has become a series of words, of images, of ideas which in their turn begin to exist. And where is this new existence? Surely not in the paper object. Nor surely in external space. There is only one place left for this new existence: my innermost self. (Davis, 351)

If the "work of art" becomes itself only when it is transformed into the "play of art," we must seek to discover the elusive objects of play, of imitative play, *as action*. When we make this attempt, we discover that the objects it presents are in such continuous transformation that our experience becomes one of fugitive glimpses. We discover ourselves engaged in exploratory behavior, but within a rule-governed play frame. The field so framed we hold in peripheral awareness and scan by selective attention. We return through play to the primordial world of exploratory behavior, to our never-forgotten childhood and to the childhood of our species. But, even when we do so, the accommodative strategies by which we explore the field of a text are modified and guided by the assimilative strategies, the "shapings" of reality that are implicit in this set of cues, specific shapings that we recognize as having themselves been shaped by the conventions of poetry and of language.

Some have believed that language was our first poetry. If we define our species as a "symbolical animal," however, we may be sure that language was among our very first products, a tool used in the making of all other tools, an auditory/articulatory system capable of generating an ongoing series of speech-acts. These speech-acts, in turn, indicate all other human acts, those concurrently performed and those remembered or projected. Capable of reference, of forming veridical propositions, language could thus seem to subserve the world of sense experience and imitative work; but as a representational medium, that is, a symbolic mimesis of the world, it could play the trickster god as well. The capacity to lie, essential to human sign-systems, is also the capacity of language to quit the duties of imitative work, to stand beyond the work-world and the language therein employed. Verbal play to the extent that it comments upon the shortcomings and abuses of verbal work, to the extent that it defines the limitations of a product that is spent so unwisely, spilled out upon the air, dissipated, lost forever—to the extent that verbal play thus stands to the side of ordinary language it is metalinguistic.

As a medium of imitative play, language can be used to produce texts with beginnings and ends (*holons*) that comment on that seemingly unbeginning and unending work (the *meson*). The limitations and concealments of words have always been the reason for the making of poetry. Whitman, for example, made it a major theme of his work:

> The lack of any words, I say again, is as historical as the existence of words. As for me, I feel a hundred realities clearly determined in me, that words are not yet formed to represent. (Pearce, xxiv)

Edward Sapir described this verbal poiesis when he said of a new concept that it enters a culture only after it is embodied in language, but before this occurs this concept must be grappled with and "foreshadowed by a more or less strained or extended use of old linguistic material" (17).

A "strained or extended use of old linguistic material"—this provocative phrase accords well with the Russian Formalists' definitions of poetic style. According to this general view, the individual words and syntactical forms of a language are the bearers of the dominant cultural paradigms. The allegiance of such words to the status quo is implicit. Having become thoroughly coopted, they can be made to articulate alternate views of reality only if they are returned to the crucible of reference to alchemize new compounds better capable of grasping the complexity of human experience. These compounds are the scripts of verbal play. Neologism is the terminological method of science and philosophy; structural complexification is the method of poetry.

A poetic text, then, is an extended locution used to indicate an entity or state of affairs for which as yet no single word exists. "There's a certain slant of light / Winter afternoons" initiates a series of objective correlatives to a state of mind for which Dickinson had no single word. Presumably, if she had had a word accurate enough to specify that "internal difference / Where the meanings are," that one word would have sufficed and no such extraordinary measure as formulating a poem-as-extended-word would have been necessary. Of course we have designations that have some descriptive precision within strict nosiological contexts, but to compare "depression" or "melancholia" with this text is to demonstrate how crude the terms are that we apply to complex states of mind. The poet, whose business regularly takes her or him to the frontiers of language, knows that extraordinary means are often necessary. Hart Crane echoed Mallarmé when he wrote:

It is as though the poem gave the reader as he left it a single, new *word,* never before spoken and impossible to actually enunciate, but self-evident as an active principle in the reader's consciousness hereafter. ("General Aims and Theories," 78)

Suppose I term the poem-as-extended-word the *mega-word.* A book of poems, as a collection of mega-words, is a list of "words" that simultaneously reveal and define heretofore unverbalized entities. Each mega-word is a complex signifier that indicates as its signified an entity or set of significances unknowable by any other verbal formulation.

This concept of the poetic text as a new word has been current for some time. It was recognized by the New Critics, who spoke of the interreferentiality of elements within the text. Murray Krieger, perhaps the last of that lineage, speaks of "forces" within the poem

> reduced to a new word (defined in and through the poem itself) in the poet's and his culture's vocabulary, which has now enlarged its capacity to speak. (*Theory of Criticism,* 202)

More recently, some semioticians have come to similar conclusions. Umberto Eco, for example, regards the aesthetic text as "self-focusing," a whole greater than the sum of its parts (*Theory of Semiotics,* 264). "The disengaged words, which we analyze," he writes, "have *ipso facto* lost, or at least diminished, their value as signs" (264). For Michael Riffaterre, ordinary language has "meaning" insofar as it represents the world beyond the text, but the text creates "significance" by the indirect path poetic language regularly pursues:

> From the standpoint of meaning the text is a string of information units. From the standpoint of significance the text is one semantic unit. . . . [W]hereas units of meaning may be words or phrases or sentences, *the unit of significance is the text. (Semiotics of Poetry,* 3, 6)

So far we have seen that an imitative play, or "game," is meant to be a *holon,* that the script of a verbal game is a text, and that a text constitutes a "unit of significance." This unit is composed of, or segmented into, a "string of information units"—that is, words—and, by assimilating those constituents into itself, becomes "one semantic unit," the mega-word that, as soon as it is uttered, brings into consciousness a new *scibile.* The individual words are demoted to the status, as it were, of phonemes and morphemes within this sesquipedalian creation. But if we suppose that at this point we may ground critical interpretation on a linguistic model, establishing a "megalinguistics" to govern the behavior of mega-words, we immediately come up against another problem. If the mega-word is, as it seems, absolutely unique, then, as Roland Posner points out,

> the aesthetic process of decoding can at best be compared to the deciphering of a secret code present only in a single text of which only some conditions of its use are known. (Chatman, 694)

Here is a "word" that is not differentially situated within a known lexicon. As a unique, extended locution it is a *parole* independent of a *langue*. Even if "some conditions of its use are known," these do not constitute anything so systematic as a syntax. Instead, the text as mega-word is a *parole* that seems to constitute its own *langue*. What Posner terms the "linguistic fallacy in poetics" is the act of reducing this mega-word to the status of an utterance within the linguistic system of its constituent verbal elements. If this one-of-a-kind text is irreducible and if, as Dilthey liked to say, *individuum est ineffabile,* then it is an unspeakable thing, an instrument that always arrives with inadequate instructions on how to use it, a unique signifier that points mutely to an ineffable signified.

We have come to an impasse of sorts. If the verbal text of a poem is an instrument and the idea is the *telos* of that instrument, that *telos* very definitely lies beyond language, just as the entity denoted by the word "elephant" is ontologically and conceptually distinct from and beyond its verbal signifier. No amount of graphemic or syllabic analysis of that word will help a six-year-old construe its meaning if the child has no sensory image to correlate with this lexeme. Likewise, the verbal analysis produced in critical interpretation will be of only limited value to the reader. It will be about as useful to the reader who wishes to understand it as it would be useful for the child to be urged to "pronounce it syllable by syllable — 'el-e-phant.'" The problem with learning or teaching others to read mega-words is simply that these "words" do not belong to a publicly available lexicon, and so we can never assure ourselves or others concerning their semantic content.

That the poetics of poetry must establish itself ultimately on some non-linguistic basis should come as no surprise. Every art — music, painting, sculpture, dance, architecture, even calligraphy — is an exercise in non-linguistic modes of consciousness. This is true not for the obvious reason that the media of these arts are non-linguistic. A medium is only the instrumental means by which an art realizes its objectives. In general terms, the objective of every art is the formation in the receiving mind of sense-mediated patterns. Accordingly, the medium of poetry—language—is the means by which mental events are performed that are just as wordless as those performed in the presence of sculpture or dance.

We ought not to reify the concept of the mega-word or assume that we cognize it as one, particular, complex signifier each and every time we read a given text. Frye speaks to this point when he defines his use of the Aristotelian term *dianoia* (understanding, thought, theme):

> We *listen* to the poem as it moves from beginning to end, but as soon as the whole of it is in our minds at once we "see" what it means. More exactly, this response is not simply to *the* whole *of* it, but to *a* whole *in* it: we have a vision or *dianoia* whenever any simultaneous apprehension is possible. (*Anatomy,* 77–78)

In enactive interpretation the *holon* is knowable only as "*a* whole *in*" the whole text-facilitated performance. It is selectively construed by the reader, and the complexity of meaning that it appears to embody is formulated by the poetic focus.

If we agree that poetry, and literature generally, depends for its realization on the reader's power to convert words into affectively charged imagery— landscapes, rooms, faces, physical movement—and through such imagery to form complex conceptual structures, we have no recourse but to look beyond language for a valid poetic. This will mean looking beyond not only traditional literary studies, but beyond linguistics and beyond semiotic and poetic theories modeled along linguistic lines. We will have to look to psychology.

Focusing Within the Intermediate Area

Having found ourselves, inevitably it seemed, requiring a performance model of the literary experience, we have found it difficult to locate a field of objects to which a method of inquiry might be addressed. Poetic data were objects of consciousness and, as intentional objects, indistinguishable from intentional acts: in literary performance the text became simply an act of the mind, and the objects of that act were the focuses performed by the mind, the virtually unconscious decisions a reader makes to focalize a concept, affect, or sensory image.

In chapter 5 I sketched out a phenomenological model of what in this chapter I have called "imitative work": the carpenter building the bookcase, his or her body and its inorganic extension, the hammer, both lying in a foreground perceived in unfocused peripheral awareness, the idea of the finished product hovering in the peripheral background, and only the small nail head held firmly and focally in the middle distance. That nail for that moment represents the one focal object of the carpenter's consciousness.

When we turn from the performance of work to the performance of play, we find that in many play formats (or games) this model also applies. Countless games require keeping one's "eye on the ball" or on some other perceptual object, while one keeps ends and means securely in peripheral awareness. To that extent these games preserve the operational character of work. Literary play also has its equipment, is scripted within a play frame, and permits its participants certain possibilities of pay-off, but, as imitative play, it displays this special difference: its focal "objects" are the incommunicable creations of its individual players. These focalizations may be recoded in the idioms of critical interpretation, of course, but they themselves cannot be shared as we might share as onlookers in the intersubjective perception of a struck nail or a flying baseball.[12]

In order to arrive finally at a concept of the "poetic focus," we might do well to consider the developmental model of Donald Woods Winnicott as put forth in his last book *Playing and Reality*. In brief, Winnicott's therapeutic encounters with both children and adults revealed to him the importance of what he called "transitional objects," objects that infants between four- and twelve-months old fixate upon and invest with symbolic powers (4). These objects, for example, blankets and dolls, occupy an "intermediate area" between the "inner or personal psychic reality" and the "actual world with the individual living in it" (102). They are perceived by the child as partly incorporated into him- or herself and partly belonging to the unincorporated world; and as such they allow for a successful transition from the autoerotic stage, in which the mother is regarded as an extension of the self, to the stage in which the mother is granted the independent status of an "other." These

---

12. While it is true that the carpenter's hammer-stroke and the outfielder's self-positionings to catch the ball may be for each of them and for each spectator a unique experience, their focuses are upon non-unique objects, entities that are certainly not of their own ad hoc making.

play objects, which an individual may hold precious all through childhood and retain a sentimental attachment to even into adulthood, are usually by puberty decathected, their usefulness completed. But at the point at which their magical powers begin to decline, another sort of magic begins to appear, the magic of metaphor. Having experienced the disinvestment of meaning, the child learns the lesson that meaning may also be reinvested, that objects can be consciously used as instruments of meaning. "Transitional phenomena . . . become diffused." The term "intermediate area" Winnicott now refers to as the

> territory between "inner psychic reality" and "the external world as perceived by two persons in common," that is to say, over the whole cultural field. (5)

Thus "culture" becomes the ultimate intermediate area between the self and the other and is "the derivative of play" (102).[13]

Here, it seems to me, we have an opening of the microcosm to the human universe of society. The privacy of the self that literacy has fostered cannot be absolute—as Aristotle said, only a beast or a god could sustain that sort of solitude. Imagination in all its various modes of play is not an isolating exercise, even when the intermediate area is found within the silent, solitary self. Winnicott's wording, provocative though it is, cannot be stretched as, for example, Jean Duvignaud, has done in his *Le Jeu du jeu,* when he remarks on Winnicott's "electrifying" insight that

> play appears inseparable from the imaginary [*l'imaginaire*] and from every creation of form and seems also inseparable from man's very being, that distance being unbridgeable that separates him from a universe he will never attain to. The fictions aroused by play fill this "intermediate area," extending between us and things, and, all questions of utility and effect aside, seem to be so many efforts to conquer a reality [*un réel*] forever in flight. (48–49)

The pathos of a Cartesian Tantalus condemned to create fictions to assuage the pain of separation from "un univers qu'il n'atteindra jamais" seems an

13. For an energetic conflation of Lacan's and Winnicott's thinking, especially as it applies to the reading of texts, see Gabriele Schwab's "Genesis of the Subject, Imaginary Functions, and Poetic Language," *New Literary History* 15, no. 3 (Spring 1984): 453–74.

unnecessarily strained response to Winnicott's thesis, as though being down to earth among Sartre's nauseatingly coiled tree roots and at the same time lost in Pascal's terrifying universe of infinite space were not both equally the human condition. This notion of a sharply delineated boundary between self and other is patently mistaken. Even if it were a boundary, it would simply be a place where a unity that had once been cleaved continues, as parts, to cleave together at a common surface. But rather than imagine it as a membrane or an interface, I think we might more usefully regard it as a vast, expansible region—the intermediate area of which Winnicott spoke—a field traversed by sensory signals, an extension of consciousness beyond the integument. This intermediate area is "culture," but culture defined as the humanly known world, the world that communicates itself to us as sensory signals, predominantly through sound- and light-waves. This is hardly a boundary line or no-man's-land: it is the lived world that, by stretching from the unknown within us to the unknown beyond us, bonds those two unknowns.[14]

Winnicott's "intermediate area" of culture has to include fictions, that is, the artifacts of verbal play, but I would suggest that it also includes other imitative activities, which are no less "cultural." It is interesting to note, for example, that as the "transitional object" gradually loses its cathexis and symbolic skills become consciously available, the child's improved physical coordination allow her to become increasingly adept in using tools. As the dolls spend more and more time with their tea set under the bed, the child is spending more and more time riding her bicycle or learning to use a fishing pole or a pencil. She is beginning to extend her will outward toward the other by using tools to reach for what she wishes, tools that she incorporates and learns to wield using peripheral awareness. Growing up is coming to inhabit, with the help of tools, the intermediate area between self and world.

The intermediate area is the area of focal awareness. It is what I have earlier called the middle distance between the incorporated tool and the final goal. For the child the stuffed toy is the symbolic focalized object that lies between the vaguely constituted self and the shadowy powers of the grown-up world. If we regard literature as symbolic play on a higher level than a snuggle with a velveteen rabbit, it seems to me we must understand: (1) that it is an instrumental performance that imitates both the procedures and the

---

14. To those interested in further readings on this topic I would recommend J. J. Gibson, *The Senses Considered as Perceptual Systems,* 100–101, 187–208; George Matoré, *L'Espace humain;* and E. T. Hall, *The Hidden Dimension,* 1–4, 109.

values of work and (2) that in this imitative performance the intermediate area is the mind of the performer. It is a place, which is not a place, where objects, which are not objects, seem to appear and disappear. On this flickering stage of the mind, upon which the whole universe can be deployed, it is the imaginary, not the real, as Duvignaud maintained, that is "toujours en fuite."

This stage is not the page. The process by which our eyes scan the words in a left-to-right series of saccades is not really the focal awareness of fluent reading. In this process the ocular scanning is an instrumental act, peripherally executed, the text being the tool that, by the instrumentality of the eyes, is grasped and wielded by the reader's mind. The mouth "does" the talking, the ears "do" the listening, the hand "does" the writing, the eyes "do" the reading, but it is the mind that cognizes language. The surface organs, with or without extrinsic *organa,* perform under the peripheral supervision of the mind while the mind itself, that is, the centers of consciousness in the neocortex, focuses on the direction of this process. Literary theorists who visualize this process as a transaction between text (or author-behind-the-text) and reader are describing the critical interpretive task, not the enactive act of construing meaning. No less an astute theorist than Wolfgang Iser betrays this false orientation when, in a reply to Wayne Booth in 1980, he confesses that

> the event that takes place between text and reader is a peculiarly difficult region to chart.[15]

This concept of a text-reader transaction has become a conventional reader-response perspective, and such phrasing has become familiar and naturalized—which is all the more reason for its implications to be scrutinized. In reading, the poem is not performed as a tennis match is played. It is not a two-sided give and take, not if the text is connected to the poem player as securely as the racket is connected to the tennis player. Moreover, we might note that an "event" is indeed difficult to chart when it is spatialized as a "region." Here again, the language is casual, we "think we know what it means," and it is not easy to expurgate all spatialist and temporalist terms from literary discourse. Yet in this sentence, the clash of time and space perspectives—plus the polarity of text and reader—constitutes the very difficulty that Iser strives to address.

Before concluding this chapter, I need to clarify my position further. My

---

15. *Diacritics* (Summer 1980):69.

concept of an intermediate area within which a play frame is inscribed, within which, in turn, certain scripted actions are performed, needs to be carefully differentiated from two theoretical models to which it may bear some superficial resemblance.

One of these is the spatialist model, the perennial similitude of the poem and the visual artifact.[16] The other—I hesitate to call it a model—is deconstruction. When I speak of verbal play, I do not speak of it in deconstructionist terms. Deconstruction is hermeneutical play—negative hermeneutics, perhaps, but hermeneutics all the same. It is the play of the critical mind with what the reader once confidently wielded as a familiar instrument. The "play of signifiers" is itself a playful formulation, a vision out of Hoffmann or the Brothers Grimm of tools on their own, working by themselves late at night, coupling and generating new tools. A universe in which signifiers play would be a universe in which baseballs throw themselves at bats that swing themselves. This formulation has meaning in our universe only if we believe that human consciousness is totally determined by the differential structure of language. Any study of mental imagery necessarily calls this assumption into question.

These two views, as I have argued in chapter 4, are grounded on a false dichotomy of space and time, structure and function, and represent two ways of doing critical interpretation. There is indeed more than one way to skin a cat. To live with a cat requires quite other skills.

The focus of the eyes on the text is not the poetic focus. The printed words are instruments that, like optical lenses, facilitate another kind of

16. The statement of Simonides, quoted by Plutarch, that poetry is a speaking picture and painting a mute poetry has no doubt caused a great deal of mischief, especially for aestheticians. Greeks commonly lumped the two arts together: Plato did so in *The Republic.* That jaunty phrase of Horace "ut pictura poesis" echoes that tradition. His epistle to the Pisones, the "Ars Poetica," is indeed premised on this similitude, but the purpose of his treatise is to teach the rhetorical uses of poetry not to define *the poem.* A poem is like a painting not because of the intrinsic similarities of the media or the art forms, but because they must both be cognized by a human mind, a mind that requires consistency and coherence: "denique sit quidvis simplex dumtaxat et unum"—"in short, do what you want but make sure it's more or less homogeneous and unified." Since the eighteenth century the cause of poetic spatialism has been supported and attacked by countless theorists as diverse as Addison, Lessing, Babbitt, and more recently, Joseph Frank. Such is the nature of this topic that no matter how judiciously one qualifies one's position, it is quickly distorted by both admirers and detractors. The problem seems to have been that the very mention of painting and space in relation to poetry conjures up a rigid stasis, a textual architectonics of timeless, simultaneous presence that seems to elicit as a rhetorical retort the equally exaggerated claims of pure temporality, the infinite play of signifiers. For Frank's "Spatial Form in Modern Literature," see *Sewanee Review* 53 (Spring, Summer, Autumn 1945); revised version in *The Widening Gyre* (Bloomington: Indiana University Press, 1968), 3–62. For a more recent appraisal of this controversy see *Critical Inquiry* 4, no. 2 (Winter 1977).

focus—one that scans restlessly an unfamiliar territory beyond the organs of vision, beyond the instruments of words, beyond language itself. As Sartre put it:

> The literary object, though realized *through* language, is never given *in* language. On the contrary, it is by nature a silence and an opponent of the word. In addition, the hundred thousand words aligned in a book can be read one by one so that the meaning of the work does not emerge. Nothing is accomplished if the reader does not put himself from the very beginning and almost without a guide at the height of this silence; if, in short, he does not invent it and does not then place there, and hold on to, the words and sentences which he awakens. (*What Is Literature?* 27)

The author's own silence, which Sartre states had been "anterior to language," becomes particularized by language and thereafter becomes the object of the reader's attention. The "inner speech," without which, according to Vygotsky, thought would be impossible, is furnished to the reader by the text, permitting the reader also to enter that silence anterior to language. But this silent world is not simply "there" as words are present on the page: the reader must actively reproduce it.

> And at the very interior of this object there are more silences—which the author does not tell. It is a question of silences which are so particular that they could not retain any meaning outside the object which the reading causes to appear. (27)

The silence of language, the silence produced by language, the silence concerning which the proponents of a language-delimited reality have contrived to be silent: this is the silence that poetry compels language to utter, the world that "reading causes to appear." We must now find words to describe and account for such speechless apparitions.

The empowerment of the reader that has transferred the visionary place from the macrocosm and the collectively tended shrine to the microcosmic self has not absolutized this self, this frail ego with its even frailer imaginings. Literacy has moved the visionary center to the interior sanctum, but cultural codes are no less binding than they were in an oral society. The visionary center is a private place, but one in which the signs exhibited are public signs. For readers of literature, the intermediate area of Winnicott reveals itself in enactive interpretation as a mediating center, a meeting place of the Unmanifested and the Manifested, a threshold over which the unknown emerges as the known. The intermediate area exists in its externalized forms, but it *plays* only within the conscious performer. As he suggested, culture and psyche are homologues.

POETIC FAITH
AND THE WRITTEN IMAGE

In his study of Christian mysticism, *The Ascent to Truth,* Thomas Merton wrote:

> Faith, in the broadest sense, is the acceptance of truth on the evidence of another. The essence of all faith is the submission of our judgment to the authority of someone else, on whose word we accept a truth that is not intrinsically evident to our own minds. Human or *natural faith* is the acceptance of truths on the authority of other men. *Supernatural faith* is the belief in truths revealed by God, on the testimony of God, and because of the authority of God Who reveals these truths to us. (30)

If "faith" is the belief in the truth of a message derived from a belief in the truthfulness of the messenger, the all-too-human intermediary whom Merton tactically omits in his account of supernatural faith, what we have here is no simple problem in pragmatics. Every semiotic act is premised by a tacit faith in the lawfulness, and therefore the intelligibility, of a conventional code, but not in the veracity of the messenger. Faith in the truth of any statement must be premised on an act of faith in its messenger and in every prior messenger who transmitted it in serial relay. At any rate, with or without infinite regress, faith must deny the possibility that falsehood, distortion, or fiction has crept into the transmission of this message somewhere along the way. Every affirmation of faith must therefore begin with a "willing suspension of disbelief."

The difference between poetic faith on the one hand and natural and supernatural faith on the other is temporal. The kinds of faith Merton defines are temporally unlimited: no one who possesses either of them says, "I believe this statement now, but in a short while I will disbelieve it." Yet the possessor of poetic faith implicitly says just this; as Coleridge put it, the willing suspension of disbelief is only "for the moment." Poetic faith is play faith and poietic activity is a make-believe that generates a made belief. If verbal semiosis is social play at the level of the word, poiesis is social play at the level of the mega-word. Its statements, as I. A. Richards said, are "pseudo-statements," but in the same sense that singing is pseudo-talking, dancing pseudo-walking, and chess pseudo-warfare.

Concerned as ever with the relation between literary structures and readers' responses, Michael Riffaterre in *Fictional Truth* has examined closely the truth-like values of narrative discourse, that is, its appeal to the reader's credence. Choosing his examples from realist novels, he has concluded that fictional truth is based on purely verbally generated verisimilitude, not on any appeal to actual, shared experience. Fiction (poiesis) does not require that the reader verify an assertion: on the contrary, it requires that the reader *not* attempt to do so. "An apodeictic statement . . . deprives the reader of any ground to question the statement" (126). The reader has no evidence except that furnished by the text itself, which produces its own frame of reference by means of a network of metaphors and metonyms. Such a system of images, Riffaterre maintains, is a purely semiotic construct not necessarily dependent on, or even related to, the reader's extratextual experience of factuality (28). This image-mediated truth that the reader is thus induced to believe is therefore

> a linguistic phenomenon; since it is experienced through enactment by reading, it is a performative event in which participation on the reader's part can only serve to hammer the text's plausibility into his experience. . . . [F]iction emphasizes the fact of the fictionality of a story at the same time it states that the story is true. Furthermore, verisimilitude is an artifact, since it is a verbal representation of reality rather than reality itself: verisimilitude itself, therefore, entails fictionality. (xiv–xv)

But what is this enactment, this performance, this construal of verisimilitude? Riffaterre refers at several points in his book to the reader's "presuppositions" but does not directly consider them. He focuses on the stylistic factors that induce the reader to attribute verisimilitude to the text but neglects to examine the "participation on the reader's part" that must proceed according to the rules of verisimilitude as a kind of veri-simulation.

To conclude this study I will suggest several of these presuppositions, then argue the crucial importance of verbal imagery to this play theory of poetic faith, and finally offer a schematic model of the written image.

Re-oralizing the Sender

Like any communicative act, verbal poiesis involves a sender, an addressee, and a message. In respect to each of these three elements, Coleridge's "poetic faith" enjoins upon the reader a particular kind of suspension of disbelief.

First of all, while reading a written text, we must choose to regard, that is, pretend to regard, the sender as credible. In an oral performance the reciters must support our feigned credulity by their perceptible presence and technique—their *energeia*—but in the case of writing, the text must facilitate *our* performance, which to some extent entails our re-oralizing it and our reconstituting the oral presence of its narrator and its narrated speakers. Not all texts seem to require the same degree of re-oralization. Oral poetry, for example, an epic or a ballad, has a rather distanced tone when read from a written text, though in oral performance this impersonality is somewhat offset by the immediate presence of the performer. Some narratives can offer a detached, quasi-omniscient sender or "camera's eye" point of view, but any diegetic "voice," even an unanimated or mechanical one, can be imaginatively reproduced in the mind of the reader. Narrative dialog, of course, usually calls for more expressive re-oralization, as do polemical, persuasive, and lyric writings.

What I have called "re-oralization" is somewhat better known as "inner speech," or "endophasia." According to the research summarized by A. N. Sokolov in *Inner Speech and Thought,* thought is mediated by subvocal speech.[1] That is, groups of the over-one-hundred muscles that are selectively used in overt speech are activated in precise sequences, but at low levels of innervation, whenever we engage either in private thought, in the comprehension of another's speech, or in reading. In these processes we use this motoric miming of articulation to back up our auditory memory. Every item

1. This concept of inner speech has come to be associated with the work of Lev Vygotzky. See especially his *Thought and Language,* 43, 47, 131, 139–49. For an updated theory, see Barry H. Cohen's "The Motor Theory of Voluntary Thinking," in Davidson et al., eds., *Consciousness and Self-Regulation: Advances in Research and Theory,* vol. 4 (New York: Plenum Press, 1986).

of verbally mediated thought is normally rehearsed for a split second by being re-heard and re-said, or "re-oralized." This research into inner speech processes has not, however, proven that all cognitive judgments are speech-mediated and sequential. There is considerable evidence of "spatial thinking" and parallel (or as some prefer to term it, "right-brain") processing.

This preconscious process of inner speech by which we re-oralize a text induces in us a tacit consciousness of prosodic and syntactic patterns. We assess their linguistic appropriateness and the "tone" with which they imbue the semantic content of the text. We do this in peripheral awareness. Only when an articulation seems strange or otherwise salient do we shift our attention from enactive to critical interpretation and focus our attention on some phonological or syntactical detail of the text. Ordinarily, however, we try to keep "poetic faith" with the text by assuming a correlation between the meaning of the speaker and the oralized experience of the textualized *energeia* of the speech.

This application of Coleridge's "poetic faith" to the sender of the message is a logical extension of a theory of imitative play to poetic imagination. If we choose to believe in a message, we must believe in its messenger; if we pretend to have faith in this speaker, we pretend that he keeps faith with us. We will therefore pretend to believe that *the way he speaks* reflects *the way he means,* that is, his feelings and attitudes toward himself, toward his referents, and toward his utterance itself. We assume, in short, a correspondence between form and content.[2] Even when the fit is approximate, we wish to believe it natural and necessary. We like to assume that a given rhythm or assonant effect imitates a movement or represents a sensory effect or that a type of syntactical pattern perfectly expresses a feeling and is absolutely "right." But when we discover through linguistic analysis that another passage uses the same means to achieve quite different, perhaps even opposite, effects, we are tempted to throw up our hands and throw out our stylistics altogether. If the correlation is not natural, is it then conventional or genre-based? When even these supports prove unreliable, we may become bewildered, then skeptical. We sense there is something too Panglossian about the stylistician's assumption that, in every canonical work, form correlates with content in the best of all possible match-ups. And then there is the stylistician's fallback strategy—to argue that, when a match-up cannot be asserted, the correlation

2. I am indebted to Professor Suzanne Hoover of Sarah Lawrence College for this insight, though I have taken it in somewhat different directions. It will be found discussed in her forthcoming study *Unified Reading.*

is one of tension, antagonism, counterpoint, and so forth. This formalist's attempt to have it both ways makes us reluctant to let him have it any way.

Even if we end up concluding that stylistics has about as much to tell us about poetics as phrenology has to tell us about neurobiology, we need to account for the fact that stylistics has enjoyed centuries of scholarly plausibility. If there has indeed been so little to recommend it, why do we still consider it worth writing about, even disparagingly? To paraphrase Voltaire, if form-content correlations did not exist, we would have to invent them. This, I submit, is exactly what we as readers do: we accept the harmony of formal means with contained meaning as section *A* of Article 1 of poetic faith (of which there is no Article 2), in other words, we accept it as a proto-convention of poiesis. Does the harmony truly exist? Yes, but only within the play frame of poetry. Outside that specific play frame, or set of game rules, there may also exist potential correlations of form and content, correlations based on natural factors and on conventions. Within this play frame of poetry, however, a higher convention authorizes the match-up.

The main implication of this "proto-convention" is that poetic texts can be, indeed *ought* to be, experienced in such a way that the incidental aspects of speech (the prosodic patterns of the natural language, conventionalized patterns, and syntactic arrangements) *seem* to signify what the semantic elements of the sentence *seem* to signify.[3] Since the semantic elements determine how the formal aspects are enactively interpreted, one's construal of the denotative and connotative meanings of the statements will seem to finesse the form into conformance with them. The lengths to which a reader will go to extend this convention of verbal play to a given text are remarkable. If one conventionally associates a given verse form with a given topic— triplets with light, amatory subjects, for example—then there is a perfect congruence when form and anticipated content correspond. But there is also a sort of congruence, an "ironic counterpoint," when they do not match up

---

3. Cf. "Nevertheless our final view, implicit in our whole narrative and in whatever moments of argument we may have allowed ourselves, has been that 'form' in fact embraces and penetrates 'message' in a way that constitutes a deeper and more substantial meaning than either abstract message or separable ornament. In both the scientific or abstract dimension there *is* both message and the means of conveying message, but the poetic dimension is just that dramatically unified meaning which is coterminous with form." Wimsatt and Brooks, *Literary Criticism*, 748. Their "deeper and more substantial . . . dramatically unified meaning," which they suggest is an experience, not an object, could only be realized in the sequential reading performance of what I have called "enactive interpretation," an approach that Wimsatt had definitely implicated in the "Affective Fallacy." This "final view" seems at variance with New Critical practice. Ideologue though he was, perhaps Wimsatt was, as de Man remarked, simply "too sensitive an aesthetician to distort things altogether." *Blindness and Insight,* 24.

as anticipated, when, as in Empson's "Missing Dates," the triplets bear a grimly anaphroditic message. If the opposition is somewhat less than diametrical, some other linkage needs to be made in order to demonstrate the optimal suitability of form to content. In short, the reader aware of section *A* of Article 1 of the rules of poetic faith will be disposed to play along with the poet to the extent that this text, this made belief, is personally useful. Evaluation seldom begins with a form-content discrimination and with a judgment on the poet's formal choices, though it usually ends by adducing such factors. At the beginning and during every enactive interpretation, the reader is willfully blind to incongruences, choosing to believe in the form-content wholeness of the poem until belief becomes untenable on other grounds. We will consider these other grounds in the following two sections.

Becoming the Addressee

A reader, as research into the processes of inner speech has shown, interiorizes and resonates with the writer's words and, by virtue of the role-playing imagination, becomes the speaker. This identification is phonologically mediated, that is, the reader becomes an other by experiencing the semblance of articulation, the "feel" of the words. But when one encounters difficulties in comprehending their meanings, one steps back from this identification, recognizing oneself as the receiver, not the initiator, of this communication, the member of the audience, not the actor on the stage. This is the *crisis,* the discrimination, that when focused upon develops into critical interpretation, a crisis that poetic faith must overcome if it is to continue the play of enactive interpretation.

Before we consider the ways we have to mitigate this separation, we must understand its function in verbal play. We must understand that, if no tacit knowledge of separation existed, poiesis would not be play; it would be delusion.[4] But to be conscious of oneself as a reader of a text and to be aware of a distinction between reader and text, is not necessarily to become preoccupied with this distinction.

4. The reader's "I," when it becomes the "I" of the fictive speaker, becomes a "me," an object of which another "I" is tacitly aware. Georges Poulet in his much anthologized essay "The Phenomenology of Reading," *New Literary History: A Journal of Theory and Interpretation,* trans. Richard Macksey, vol. 1, no. 1 (October 1969), has carefully drawn the line between illusion and delusion.

The particular strategy of poetic faith in this instance requires that the reader pretend to be the intended addressee of this text, the person attuned to the sender, and able to re-oralize that sender's delegated intratextual speakers. Even if a speaker seems to be thinking to him- or herself, as is typical in lyric poetry, the reader is not to question the right to be privy to those thoughts and indeed to appropriate them. But of course to decide consciously that one is or is not an appropriate addressee or implied reader of a text is already to stand a distance from it, to objectify it and to subjectify oneself—in other words, to assume a stance of critical, rather than enactive, interpretation. I have done just this by deciding to speak of the addressee, or pronominal "second person," as separate from the "first person" sender of the "third person" message. In the performance of enactive interpretation, however, the three "persons" appear and disappear behind one another's masks and their separateness is not a matter of conscious concern. Since play always involves this double consciousness—that one is and that one is not what one imitates— the reader is of two minds, one tacitly recognizing the separation, the other pretending to believe that this separation is irrelevant. Insofar as the performer is conscious of a self in this performance, it is the re-oralized self of the sender's text, while the habitual self of the reader is relegated to peripheral awareness.

The complex act of faith required of the reader is that he or she pretend to be both the intended addressee and the speaker, for only by that latter identification can one participate in the generation of the message. Plato's Socrates spoke of this in the *Ion* as a sort of magnetizing of one person by another, a sharing of a god-inspired visionary state beyond the bounds of reason. It might be likened to a *folie à deux*. But to share in this text-induced altered state of consciousness, a reader must decide to share in it completely and, if this make-believe is not total, at least to try to ignore those aspects that do not reenforce empathy and belief in the statements of the text.

This becomes a problem, of course, when an obscurity of phrasing trans- forms the textual instrument into a puzzling object (see chapter 5). In addition, proper nouns can sometimes bewilder the enactive interpreter. Common nouns are supposed to be entries in a common lexicon and, if concrete, to evoke generic images, but proper nouns presume in us an acquaintance with particular persons, places, and things. In oral dialog we lose some of the meaning when our interlocutor drops a name we do not recognize. We feel momentarily excluded and, if it seems important, we stop and ask whom or what that word refers to. In reading, if we have no first- or second-hand acquaintance with the referent of a proper noun, what enactive imagery can we possibly produce to that cue? How do we keep faith and not feel barred from this verbal play? What does the reader evoke in response to Villon's "Berthe au grand pied" or "Alys" ("Ballade des Dames du Temps Jadis," 1.19), Milton's references to Moloch's land "in Rabba and her wat'ry plain, / In Argob and in Basan, to the stream / Of utmost Arnon" (*Paradise Lost,* 1.397–99), or when Eliot in "Gerontion" whirls "De Bailhache, Fresca, Mrs. Cammel . . . / Beyond the circuit of the shuddering Bear / In fractured atoms" (69–71). Even if historical scholarship should prove that Villon had never laid eyes on Berthe or Alys, that Milton had not the least notion of what Argob looked like, and that Eliot took his names from a telephone directory, the reader of these proper nouns must still treat them as though they designated very real, very unique percepts.

The reader may stop and research these names, may be satisfied with the second-hand knowledge thus derived or with the assurance that this or that proper noun is fictitious or generic or relatively unimportant, but the question remains: must the reader who holds to poetic faith respond to unfamiliar proper nouns with a sense of bafflement and exclusion from this verbal play? Or cannot the game rules that have one pretend to be the addressee of the text have one pretend also to have known Alys and Mrs. Cammel and to have visited Argob, even though the recollection of these referents may be somewhat dim?

The convention that authorizes a reader to enter into this *folie à deux* with the speaker in the text and to pretend to know the referents of the proper nouns has on the broader cultural plane a correlate in the collective possession and transmission of the onomastics of a people. Here we find proper nouns that display the imaginal characteristics of remembered percepts, yet derive from the personal experience neither of the speaker nor of the addressee. Included in this common inheritance of *proper* nouns *common* to a community of speakers are the nouns of story and myth, that is, collectively preserved and transmitted narrative. The distinction I have in mind between story and myth is this: by *story* I mean a simple narrative text purporting to be based on the narrator's experience; by *myth* I mean a narrative that has come to be accepted as having broad relevance to a community and possessing definite etiological or cosmological implications. These two forms of narrative differ in degree only, not in kind; their distinction is useful only because it establishes the extremes on the scale of experiential discourse. Not only do these categories meet on a continuum, but individual texts from opposite categories have a way of blending into one another: personal stories become universalized and mythic archetypes reveal themselves as the substructures of life experiences.

When one thinks of story and myth one thinks first of proper nouns. Common nouns are grammatically indispensable, needless to say, but their importance usually lies in their connection with some special person or place or unique and specially named implement. To qualify for story or myth such proper nouns must be meaningful to persons who have never directly encountered them. Whether or not we believe in their factuality, we can discourse about a myriad of episodes: the falls of Icarus and Adam, for example, Alexander cutting the Gordian knot, Washington throwing the silver dollar across the Potomac, the journey of the Magi, the Lady of the Lake presenting Excalibur to Arthur, the Haymarket Riot, Snow White meeting the Seven Dwarfs, or the Siege of Stalingrad. We have here, in effect, a conventional, intersubjective, experiential memory store that we draw upon to supplement our personal experience. Belief systems, folklore, historical narrative, and literary texts all contribute to the list of names that constitutes this collective experiential lexicon. Winnicott's intermediate area of culture may be regarded as a playing field of names and human images portrayed in action.

The unique power of these names is the power to define a community and to naturalize speaker and addressee within that community. One of the functions of genealogical lists, like Homer's Catalog of Ships in the *Iliad* or the generations of the patriarchs in the Bible, seems to have been to instill a collective experiential store in a nation in need of cultural coherence. Tedious as such texts may be for contemporary readers, they undoubtedly served once to memorialize an ideal of social unity for readers who had come to know only the effects of social disintegration.

In the ancient world, besides the communities of family, tribe, polis, and amphictyony, there was another community, based on this other, less powerfully integrative but yet significant, form of participation. This was the community of *fame*. When, for example, the Sirens meet Odysseus, they lose no time informing him that they know all that has come to pass in Troy, thus demonstrating that they are, after their fashion, proper Hellenes after all; Dido boasts a similar knowledge when she meets Aeneas; and *Beowulf* begins with the presumptive declaration:

> Lo, we have heard of the glory of the Spear-Danes' kings of old, how the princes of that people did mighty deeds.
> Oft Scyld son of Scef snatched mead-benches away from hostile

bands, from many a tribe, frightening their nobles, though he began as a helpless foundling.

These are not merely instances of idle name-dropping: they establish a frame of reference within which a specific community is circumscribed and defined. Allusion, whether it occurs as in direct reference, literary echo, or formal imitation, is the signal that the collective experiential memory is being addressed. This *participation mystique,* this pretense of shared experience, is the convention that underlies all myth.[5]

Gary Snyder's "Myths & Texts (Burning)," number 17, is an interesting example of how private memory, once it is collectivized as poetic discourse, becomes story and myth. The poem is divided into two sections entitled "the text" and "the myth." The "text" is a matter-of-fact account of an episode in which Snyder, then a twenty-two-year-old forest ranger in Washington State, is called to help put out a fire "up Thunder Creek, high on a ridge." He and others worked through the afternoon and night subduing the blaze. Their job was not finished until the morning star appeared before dawn. What he calls the "text" constitutes the "story," or personal narrative. The "myth" section is evidently a reconceptualization of this event as a set of literary and cosmological archetypes that include the burning of Troy, the cooling of the molten earth over geological epochs, and the Buddhistic concept of the void. It concludes with a verbal allusion to the coming age of illumination forecast by Thoreau at the end of *Walden,* "the sun is but a morning star."

The "myth" section ostensibly serves to absorb the "text" episode into the public domain of collective memory. Yet the contents of the "text," merely by being text, have in a sense already been transferred from private to collective knowledge. Literary publication ipso facto deprivatizes experience. Once made public, the text enters into the possession of the collective memory of a certain public and for a certain period of time, where it is stored as a cultural artifact and, whenever needed, retrieved. Intertextuality, which allows one to quote Snyder quoting Thoreau, is thus a function of this collectivized memory.

Let us observe exactly how the reader pretends to be included in the intended audience even of a story. When Snyder tells me that

---

5. Horace acknowledges this when he says of the epic writer that he "rushes his auditor into the middle of things *as though these circumstances were already known* [*in medias res / non secus ac notas auditorem rapit*]." "Epistle to the Pisones," or "Ars Poetica," 11.148–49.

Sourdough Mountain called a fire in:
Up Thunder Creek, high on a ridge

I do not judge the poet to be perversely obscure. Of course, most of his readers, like me, will have no familiarity with these locations, but I do not demand that he be more generic and write: "a lookout on a nearby mountain called a fire in, saying it was up a creek high on a ridge." Because the poet familiarly mentions it, I, too, casually assume familiarity with it and fictively I too become part of that community of speakers that employs those proper names.

In literate cultures poetic texts continually force the reader to assume a non-empirical familiarity with the world, to accept the unfamiliar as though it were familiar. In an isolated tribal community, nothing the poet uttered would be wholly unfamiliar, but, for a heterogeneous readership, the new and unfamiliar must perpetually be assimilated into the collective store. For readers of a world language, a lingua franca like English, defamiliarization has become over the past three centuries an unavoidable literary experience. This second proto-convention of poetic faith, the reader's play belief that he or she belongs within the text-defined community of knowers, has always been available to mitigate the potentially alienating shock of the unfamiliar.

Playing the Message

The formal aspects of the speaker's words and the reader's ability to construe their significance, though they underlie the performance of the message and make it possible, remain nevertheless peripheral to it in enactive interpretation. The message, the third element implicitly included within Coleridge's "first article of poetic faith," is the focal object of poetic attention. It is this imagined world that so fixes our attention that, as we allow ourselves to be absorbed in reading, we are drawn away from questions of how the author has created the text and how the trained reader recreates it. We are drawn into the unquestioning act of participation in the making of an imaginary world.

Critical interpretation, on the other hand, presuming the appropriateness of systematic doubt in respect to the speaker's means and the reader's reception, always commences with a questioning of form (as distinct from content) and content (as distinct from form). By contrast, enactive interpretation, governed as it is by poetic faith, puts in question neither the speaker's means nor the reader's reception. Faith, the as-if faith of poiesis, is simply contrary to doubt. By making this observation I am by no means advocating true credulity, but legitimizing its simulation.

To consider the difference between these two interpretive stances we might reconsider the differences between work and play. In the last chapter I spoke of imitative play as an imitation of work, which was itself learned through imitating others' work. Recreational exercises thus borrow their form from productive and goal-oriented activities, and the more rule-governed and stylized games are usually patterned on endeavors of considerably more consequence. Many individual and team sports, for example, feature actions that mimic flight and pursuit, concealment and ambush, attack and defense. Even in the non-exertive playing space of board games the spirit of the predator lurks never far below the surface.

Now, if we say that verbal poiesis is a play that imitates a work, what do we mean, and what is that work? Language as a system of symbolic signs can imitate anything that it can name. It can therefore imitate all other imitative activities, but though all human skills can be verbally represented, most skills need to be learned through observation and practice. As Plato noted, this imitative function of language is not a reliable way to learn a work skill. It is a kind of play in which mental imagery substitutes for reality.

But language is not learned because of its potential use as play. Its primary function—its own proper *work*—is considerably more narrowly motivated. The work of language, which children learn through imitation, is that of negotiating with others to satisfy needs. Using speech acts, by which they manipulate the signs of absent objects, children learn to bargain with adults and with one another. In this way they learn to avert stressful situations and potentially violent conflicts. Imitating the ways language can be used to serve the speaker's self-interest, they learn how to divert blame from themselves and to seem to deserve approval. If they are skillful, they learn how to interpret a situation to their best advantage, to persuade others of the correctness of that interpretation—in short, to make themselves believed. The world in which they eventually assume their roles as adults is also organized verbally in belief systems that maintain themselves through information management, for example, teaching, promotional advertising, propaganda, and public (mis)information. Of course by the time they are old enough to become models for others' imitation, most children are unaware that the work of the language they have learned to use has as its main purpose the concealment, rather than the communication, of intentions. As Voltaire put it, "ils ne se servent de la pensée que pour autoriser leurs injustices, et emploient les paroles que pour déguiser leurs pensées" (*Dialogue XIV,* "Le Capon et la Poularde"). They will also probably believe in the magniloquent ideals of those who use the same language to use them that they themselves use to use others. This is a work of faith.

Poiesis imitates this same rhetoric-honed linguistic activity, but in such a way as to transform dissimulative work into simulative play. This distinction is crucial: dissimulation is the representation of something as other than it is in order to deceive others; simulation is the representation of something that is openly declared to be the mere semblance of what it signifies. Critical interpretation at its best is an attempt to raise to conscious awareness the covert motivation of linguistic work generally, that is, speech and writing, and of particular poetic texts once these are removed from performance and laid out as objects. Critical interpretation is an activity that, as de Man and others have amply demonstrated, can never be wholly innocent of dissimulation, for despite its ideal of fail-safe rigor it remains a variety of linguistic *work* and bears the burden of the original sin of such work, mendacity.

Enactive interpretation, as the relation of reader to text that acknowledges the play of poiesis, knows that, in Sidney's words, the poet "nothing affirmeth, and therefore naught lieth," but it makes believe that poetry does affirm and does not lie. When Paul Eluard writes:

> La terre est bleue comme une orange
> Jamais une erreur les mots ne mentent pas,[6]

the enactive interpreter agrees—yes, the earth *is* blue as an orange, (and that) that was no mistake, (because) the words (of poetry) do not lie. They "naught lieth" because they deceive no one. They play at lying and the reader plays at swallowing that lie, but to play at lying after all is to deny implicitly the intention to mislead and to play at believing a lie is to remain undeceived. Poetic faith can never be abused because, in the act of reading, the sender and the addressee of the message are dual personae of the performer. For, since the reader is occupied with the articulation, subvocal or spoken, of the author's words, it is the reader who initiates the play of deception in

6. Paul Eluard, *L'Amour la poésie. Premièrement,* vol. 1, 232, 1405. See Riffaterre's discussion of this (*Semiotics,* 61).

which he or she also plays the willing dupe—for the Coleridgean "moment." We knowingly tell ourself a lie that we knowingly believe.

Jamais une erreur.

The Image in the Message

In this study I have tried to disentangle the written image from the perceptual image and from the image orally delivered by a messenger that is also a perceptual image. I have argued that the objectified image, exhibited for theatrical, mnemonic, or religious purposes, has generated specific, historically contextualized patterns of response that have, unavoidably perhaps, skewed our understanding of the purely literary image and its function. While drama (theatrical and liturgical) and the visual arts directly present to the senses what they represent to the understanding of their receivers, writing does not, and so its imagery is operationally different. Failure to appreciate the importance of these differences is a principal symptom, it seems to me, of an iconophobic bias that has tended either to discredit, ignore, or dismantle through interpretive analysis the images that writers with unrepentant exuberance have gone on constructing century after century.

I began chapter 1 with a consideration of the "image of the messenger," the perceptual image that in an oral society is always interposed between the addressee and the speaker's referents. With the currency of written texts, the messenger became a letter-carrier, a newsstand operator, a bookstore clerk—an employee of the word, but no longer its accessible embodiment. Has the messenger simply vanished away like some obsolete technology? I have proposed that the messenger has not gone away, but only gone within, that the play of reading is the re-oralizing of written texts, and that the reader in the act of construing the graphic signs and covertly articulating them in inner speech now incorporates the persona of the messenger. The oral messenger is therefore not absent at all but most intimately present within the central nervous system of the reader. Since the messenger is now present *in,* rather than present *to,* the receiver and since the reader's responsibility is now *to deliver and to receive* the message, its imagery is unobstructed by a mediating other. It is fitting therefore that this concluding chapter should itself conclude with a close look at the "image in the message."

If the messenger, as function at least, has persisted, so has the oral play frame. In earlier chapters I sketched out a model of the "visionary place" and proposed that both the Greek theater and the ancient shrine (oracle, temple, church) were built upon a division between the Manifested and the Unmanifested and that only a door or veiled entrance separated the two worlds. The link that literate poets have often asserted between their compositions and the utterances of prophets and visionaries should not be altogether dismissed as professional hyperbole. As with the messenger, this place of revelation has also been transposed within.

Reading is an activity that reinstates a ritual showing place, a place of agonistic combat, of sacrifice, of offerings, and of witnesses to the powers that rule our lives. The settings and images that we are asked to construct while reading a literary text we construct, we say, "in our minds." Without relying on any "pictures-in-the-head" explanation we must nevertheless acknowledge that somehow we form mental images in response to verbal cues. When one reads, in other words, one's mind rearranges itself as an interior "seeing place," a *theatron*. What it forms before it is a foreground, a middle distance, and a background (in the terminology of the Greek model: an *orchestra*, a *proskēnion*, and a *skēnē* wall). What it does not "see," and cannot anticipate unless it knows the script, are the events and personae that have not yet been introduced, that wait in, as it were, the darkness of the *skēnē*, that sanctum of the Unmanifested.

Writers, as well as readers, have their *skēnai*. They often describe composition as a process of coaxing images out of a darkness, which before the twentieth century was regarded as a storage place of memories and is now more often spoken of as the unconscious. But whether this interior place is understood in associationist or psychoanalytical terms, its resemblances to the exteriorized visionary places of the ancient, preliterate world seem too striking to be ignored. This Unmanifested continues to be the place out of which events inject themselves serially into the Manifested and thereby generate narrative time. For the reader of the writer's text these incursions are encountered in the left-to-right construal of the graphic signs and in the images that such construal fashions. The reader may not have the experience of struggling to wrest clarity from the darkness of the writer's *skēnē*, but that same darkness is never further away than the next sentence.

We would be well advised, however, not to overstate this theatrical analogy. Literature with its specifically written images is not constrained by the fixity of seated spectator and frontally oriented actor. Sudden leaps in space and time, awkward, if not forbidden, in drama, were regular features of epic; later, in Hellenistic and Roman times, as texts were written as much to be perused in solitude as to be recited in public, such exercises of the imagination became unexceptional. Greek romance especially unfixed the reader's point-of-view and added fantastic and exotic description. The popularity of *ekphrasis* marked an interesting complication in written imagery — words that do not represent a referent but represent instead a representation of a referent.[7]

Of all the early genres that exploit the emancipation of the mental image from the constraints of the perceptual image, the described from the displayed, *closet drama* has perhaps the most to tell us of the empowerment of the written image. In the earlier chapters of this study I have been concerned with the roots of iconophobia, the historical impediments to the practice and theory of the written image, but any history of the positive rise of the literate imagination would find useful evidence in Senecan tragedy, Milton's *Samson Agonistes,* and the dramatic works of Shelley, Byron, Yeats, and Eliot. Insofar as Shakespeare can be read successfully in private — that is, insofar as he invites a reader to direct a cast and place them in a rapid succession of settings — he too can be regarded as having extended the range of the written image, at the expense of the dramatic unities of place and time.

A positive history of the rise of the image in the literate message would trace its struggle to survive in centuries dominated by scriptural faith and empirical method and observe its gradual emancipation from the constraints of dogmatism and factuality. But such a history would also have to acknowledge the gradual marginalization of imaginative literature as a social force. One way we might try to account for this diminished status would be to review the kinds of images we have already examined and apply to them the criteria of credibility.

The perceptual image displayed in drama and liturgy is a representation of a meaningful action, a reenactment that plays upon the credence we give to ocular evidence. The spectators, saturated with sensory information, suspend disbelief long enough to entertain the belief that the significance of what they witness is real because its representation is actual. *Seeing is believing,* at least for the duration of the spectacle. The verbally mediated oral image within such a spectacle or as part of a recitation is accompanied by the more or less persuasive tone and gestures of the speaker. This oral messenger, this diegetic relayer of others' words, solicits play-belief according to the supplementary principle that *hearing is believing.* But, as we know, talk being cheap,

---

7. This produced a kind of closed circuit of semiotic reference. See my introduction to *Daphnis and Chloe,* pp. 7–8.

hearing is *not* believing. Speech is ordinarily even less reliable than visual demonstration as a source of truth. Yet this very factor of unreliability qualifies it for other uses. The truth that speech is the very medium of the lie makes it also a suitable medium for human play. The very fact that hearsay is less credible than perception gives to the oral image the privilege of an incredibility of which spectacle is incapable: the portrayal of superhuman feats, the revocation of the laws of nature, and vast leaps in space and time. Its capacity for (dis)simulation, which makes the spoken word less reliable than ocular evidence, liberates it in poietic play to carry other, ulterior and tropological, significances. Hence the superior semiotic plasticity of verbal over visual representation in myth and other as-if speculation.

Of all modes of communication, writing is, and ought to be regarded as, the least credible. Spectacle and speech are at least present to the spectator and can be examined, even talked back to, by the addressee, but, as Plato's Socrates pointed out to Phaedrus, no written text can be interrogated. If its author is a liar, this liar is absent, and no twitch or evasive gaze is there to betray his dissimulation. Writing, being least credible, then, is the readiest vehicle of the incredible and the supreme medium of imitative play. As a simulation of perception and as an object of made belief, the written image is the ultimate play equipment of human intelligence.

Individual writers may strive for truthfulness and succeed in conveying reliable information. I would not want to deny the usefulness of the very medium I have chosen to use in this thoroughly unplayful study of poietic play. Writing, a perilously slippery mode of information exchange at best, becomes an instrument of social control when it is docilely received as truth by a literate population; such obvious points sometimes need to be mentioned and accounted for. Why should writing, so suited to the earnestly tendered lie, be so earnestly received? The answer is also obvious. For the fact that written documents, particularly printed publications, are afforded the presumption of truth—until, that is, they are proven guilty of untruth—we can thank the institutions that have depended on literacy to extend their influence. These institutions—religious, cultural, academic, economic, and in every instance *political*—have needed to maintain their own credibility by asseverating the truthfulness of their written messages, wrapping themselves in the word and disingenuously going forth to preach the virtues of literacy. To the extent that such institutions are anti-poetic, they are so because verbal poiesis demonstrates all too well the manipulability of the word and especially the *written* word. Such institutions are iconophobic in regard to the written image, because this verbal construct is the quintessential poiesis, the supreme fiction that belies the verity of writing. The written image is, to use Bakhtin's term, the ultimate *carnivalization* of literate systems of control, a play that, when it is tolerated at all, must be sequestered and strictly regulated.

The Image of Made Belief

The image-regulation in which literary theorists over the past half-century have been complicitous has used as its principal methods analysis and classification. Without wishing to seem hostile to these two generally useful approaches to the knowing of complex objects, I will restate my opposition to their inappropriate, essentially iconophobic, application and then investigate the possibilities of a unitary model of the written image.

Textual analysis, when it was based on formalist principles, could complete its work once all syntagmatic elements within a text were separated, labeled, and evaluated. When structuralism expanded critical attention to include paradigmatic networks of meaning, analysis seemed to have more work to do, for it was now expected to refer to linguistic and broader cultural codes within which the analyzable elements of the text stood in determinable relationships. When this critical recourse was questioned and poststructuralist principles were applied, the relation of any given set of signifiers and applicable paradigms became, to say the least, unstable. To be more specific, the meaning of written images, once these mental constructs were equated with their constituent words, dissolved when these words were shown to have no stable paradigms in language or culture to connect with. For example, suppose one encounters — or, shall I say, suppose one supposes one encounters — the image of a hawk in a poem of Jeffers or Hopkins. What does such an image *mean*?

> The term *hawk* does not merely signify a species of bird. Obviously, it brings into play the paradigms of relative coloration, predatoriness, and migration, to name only a few taxonomic relations. Beyond these of course, no term exists independently of conventional associations and connotations — good/evil, aggressive/non-aggressive, free/confined, and so on in the case of the hawk. But the complexity accelerates when we take into account the essential fact that no term ever occurs in isolation; it is always textualized as part of the discur-

sive system of the speaking subject, a speaker whose language is foreign to himself as subject, who speaks in a voice inherited from culture. (Alwin Baum, in Spanos, 90)

Yes, but. . . . As Horatio murmured, "'Twere to consider too curiously, to consider so." Poststructuralist signification becomes something like a highway system that no sooner gets travelers to one town than it leads them to another on-ramp to another route to another town. Any good road map will show that all the towns in a country are connected by a relational network. It is useful that they should be and necessary for the traveler to know this in order to plan an itinerary, but trips need not be perpetual. This sort of traveling, this sort of reading — it is undoubtedly possible, but is it obligatory? According to some theorists, if one aspires to the status of a "rigorous reader," one must undertake such a procedure: without that rigor one becomes that sort of traveler/reader who, when he or she gets to a place, immediately flops down on the first available signified and drops off to sleep in the warm glow of a covert cultural code.

The method of rhetorical classification seems to offer some relief, both to the weary paradigm-wanderer and to the quester after methodological rigor. Instead of focusing on the atomic and sub-atomic levels of the text, this method focuses on the molecular and observes how different kinds of images serve different functions. It tries to identify some images as "literal," others as "figurative," and yet others, which seem both literal and figurative, as "symbolic"; groups of similarly derived images it notes as "clusters" or "iterative" images; and of course it divides figurative images into six or seven tropological image-types.

This taxonomic approach ceases to reassure us, however, as soon as we examine particular images. Then it is often the case that we cannot decide whether to place an image in the literal, the figurative, or the symbolic bin. Then, if we grit our teeth and drop it in the figurative bin, we are faced with the dilemma of its tropological function. (How many tropes are there anyway — scores of them, six or seven major ones, four "master tropes," or do they all collapse into two?) Finally, having completed this desperate taxonomic exercise, we are left with the queasy feeling that these rhetorical categories are not exclusive and that they seem useful only after we have convinced ourselves (and are prepared to convince others) by the deployment of other rhetorical devices disguised as explanatory arguments.

A descriptive approach, one that describes the manner in which a written image describes its signified, might be a satisfactory solution to our problem.

As I have argued earlier, the conceptual distinctions between space and time make clear sense to us as abstractions, but, when applied to our experiences and our mental images, these distinctions become blurred. It is evident that perceptual and imaginal representations, though they usually first strike us as spatial entities, are never without their temporal aspects. Written images, moreover, are borne upon the temporal trajectory of language and therefore come into being word after word.

Mikhail Bakhtin, concerned with the problem of novelistic representation, attempted to study the "process of assimilating real historical time and space in literature" by merging them in the concept of the "chronotope" ("Forms of Time and the Chronotope in the Novel"). This word, which combines the Greek words for time and space, he says he borrowed in 1925 from A. A. Ukhtomski, a physiologist who, like Bertalannfy, had become intrigued by the advantages of applying a relativity model to biology. All living things, he reasoned, have built into their central nervous system the capability to perceive and respond to spatial and temporal input simultaneously, a faculty that Michael Holquist has characterized as "a clock combined with a range finder" (69). "The special meaning it has in relativity theory," wrote Bakhtin, "is not important for our purposes; we are borrowing it for literary criticism almost as a metaphor (almost but not entirely)." Not entirely, because the same animals who write and read literature make their way daily through this chronotopic *Umwelt*. "In the literary artistic chronotope," he goes on to explain,

> spatial and temporal indicators are fused into one carefully thought-out, concrete whole. Time, as it were, thickens, takes on flesh, becomes artistically visible; likewise, space becomes charged and responsive to the movements of time, plot and history. This intersection of axes and fusion of indicators characterizes the artistic chronotope. (Bakhtin, 84)

Michael Holquist further defines this concept in his glossary to *The Dialogic Imagination*:

> [The chronotope is a] unit of analysis for studying texts according to the ratio and nature of the temporal and spatial categories represented. The distinctiveness of this concept as opposed to most other uses of time and space in literary analysis lies in the fact that neither category is privileged; they are utterly interdependent. The chronotope

is an optic for reading texts as x-rays of the forces at work in the culture system from which they spring. (Bakhtin, 426)

In the chronotope we have perhaps a conceptual means of coming to terms with imagery. But, when one does attempt to apply this "optic" to verbal images, one quickly recognizes that the spatial and temporal coefficients that appear to account for differences on the scale of the narrative do not suffice to do so on the scale of the word or phrase, that is, the scale of the written image. Pursuing the Einsteinian metaphor, "almost as metaphor (almost but not entirely)," we may conclude that the quanta of literature do not conduct themselves in the same manner as do the massive bodies of literature. They exhibit, in other words, a behavior that cannot be sufficiently accounted for in spatiotemporal terms. The generic conflict between prose fiction and poetry, which Bakhtin analyzes in terms of voice, may also be a conflict in the aesthetic value that Aristotle called *megathos,* or proportionate size (*Poetics,* 450b24–451a15). The incompatibility of these two broad genres, especially in their modern representatives, the novel and the lyric poem, may be a function of scale: the longer text seems to situate its every image upon a space-time grid, while the shorter text invites the reader to examine up close the tropological shiftiness of images in addition to their spatiotemporality. Any future search for a unified-field theory of literature may well depend on establishing the parameters of the written image, as well as of the dialogic voice.

The model I will here propose (diagram 4) incorporates not only Bakhtin's chronotope, but also a third force, the verbal medium itself. The analogy upon which this model is based is not relativity theory but the rather more comprehensible solid geometry of Euclid. To "save the phenomena" while accounting for them, I would suggest that every written image may be located upon a coordinate determined by the intersection of three axes:

1. The axis of *temporal change,* ranging from the pole of static image to that of kinetic image; change on this axis includes growth, relative size and motion, decay, and modification due to agency of other objects; the importance of this axis is considerably enhanced by the left-to-right reading process that lends even to static images, arranged serially, a kinetic character;

2. The axis of *spatial complexity,* ranging from the pole of nominal image to that of relational image, the former merely a generic noun, the latter a noun situated within a space relative to other nouns; while the nominal image seems to float in space, the relational image is firmly

Diagram 4

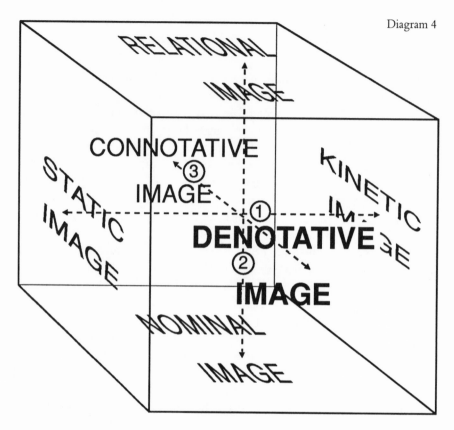

1. axis of temporal change   **2.** axis of spatial complexity   **3.** axis of semantic extension

moored to a network of other images and forms part of a relatively detailed spatial context (see Talmy); and

3. The axis of *semantic extension,* ranging from the pole of denotative image (literal, concrete, referential) to that of connotative image (tropical); at the denotative pole an image is the representation of a particular object; at the connotative pole it is a collection of abstracted properties that are shared with other objects or with universals;

(In the diagram the arrows that are shown arbitrarily meeting at the center are so drawn simply for the sake of convenience and to illustrate their relative orientations.)

The axes of temporal change and spatial complexity together define the appearance, position, behavior, and duration of every mental image, that is, its chronotope. Composing an internal replica of the visual field, these chronotopic elements constitute the stage upon which verbally cued images manifest themselves and act out their scripted roles. Evoked, though they are, by language, these imaginal signifieds, once they are conjured into being, pretend to be purely visual, that is, quasi-perceptual objects of attention. As such, they are virtual iconic signs. But insofar as they function in narrative action as consequent effects of prior causes and prior causes of subsequent effects, such images point indexically both to the past and to the future, both to the left and to the right of the passage that evokes them. As iconic representations, written images may be said to exist in a state of plus or minus spatial complexity; as indexical representations, they become, metamorphose, and pass away in a process of plus or minus temporal change. It is therefore as *indexical icons* that such images are the objects of poetic focus during enactive interpretation.

The words, the symbolic signs that create the visual illusion of indexical icons, are instrumental to these spatiotemporal representations and, as instruments, are held in peripheral awareness during the enactive performance of the text. Yet, as the distinctive medium of literature, these instrumental devices draw attention to themselves and often "bare themselves," as the Russian Formalists used to say. Though our concern in this study has been the written image, we must acknowledge that language seldom restricts itself to the representation of perceptual objects. Besides formulating propositions with little or no image-value, as in "To be or not to be, that is the question," language takes imaged objects and converts them into concepts, as in, "Whether 'tis nobler in the mind to suffer / The slings and arrows of outrageous fortune. . . . " In this latter example these implements of war have lost much of their image-value and have become emblematic attributes of an abstraction, or at most an allegorical figure, "fortune." Upon the axis of semantic extension every image is assigned its function: at the one extreme as a particular object that merely happens to belong to a nameable genus of objects and at the other extreme as a generic type that surrenders up to another term its cargo of conventional and natural associations. To the degree that it maintains its integrity as an unextended item, the narrowly bounded semantic content of the image resists immediate dissolution. But to the extent that it serves a tropological function, its connotative contents burst the bounds of the concrete image and, as abstracted properties, spill out and reassemble themselves about another term, stated or implied. An image thus extended, for example, as the vehicle of a metaphor, is like a nova that blazes out for an instant, distributes its contents, and then, its energy expended, vanishes from sight.

Like this nova-simile of mine, a simple tropical image is designed to be a non-reusable container of meaning, no sooner used than discarded. If compared with the images that reading projects upon the spatiotemporal play frame, these tropical images are fleeting, insubstantial wraiths, not only because they convert themselves quickly into connotative abstractions, but also because on the axis of spatial complexity they usually occur as simple nouns, that is, as nominal images upon the axis of temporal change these simple tropical images, like Hamlet's "slings and arrows," are briefly glimpsed pictorial entities at the static extreme: no stone is fitted to the sling-pouch, no arm extends the leathern thong, the arrows have no determinable speed or measurable trajectory.

Yet despite the virtuality of the tropical image, poetic faith can substantiate it if on the axis of spatial complexity this image is situated near the relational extreme. That is, for such a wraithlike analog to seem more real and present on the imaginary inner stage of the reader's mind than those things that the text asserts *are* real and constitute the tenor of the discourse, all it needs is detail and relational development as in the conceit and the *paysage moralisé.* Additionally or alternatively the tropical image can substantiate itself if on the axis of temporal change it situates itself near the kinetic extreme—if, that is, by moving and changing it simulates narrative action, as in the Homeric simile and in the allegory. Shakespeare's sonnets provide countless examples of tropical images that do not spill their meaning and forthwith vanish. A summer's day, a court session of sweet silent thought, a morning sun early beclouded, bare ruined choirs—none of these vehicles enjoys the same ontological status as their tenors yet have by a kind of poetic *trompe l'oeil* achieved an imaginal status that far exceeds their tenors and the personae to whom these tenors are attributed. To be construed *as an image* of any sort is therefore to be projected within a spatiotemporal field, an interior visionary place. Even the tropical image, even the most conventionalized of metonyms, situated toward the connotative pole of the axis of semantic extension, must also find its position intersected by the planes of time and space. It is within this space-time field that enactive interpretation focuses on its percept-like objects and does so with the playful credulity with which the mind visualizes any fictive entity.

Yet despite the fact that the enactive interpreter focuses upon the indexical icons projected simultaneously in space and time, this reader still maintains a tacit awareness of the semantic function of the text. Similarly a reader automatically decodes graphemes in order to process sememes. At issue in the reading of written images is, if I may repeat myself with all the emphasis of a conclusion, *the distribution of attention*. No performance is skillful unless most of the performer's efforts are executed by the peripheral consciousness—not the *un-,* or *sub-,* or even *pre-*conscious, but that wide-angled awareness, that capacity for parallel processing that is the "second nature" of the trained practitioner. For the reader of literature, this skill is one of linguistic and literary competence, and, since it is exercised in the processing of symbolic signs, it uses the verbal medium as an instrument that it engages in peripheral consciousness. At the risk of redundancy, I will stress one final time that peripheral awareness should never be confused with absent-mindedness: it is an alert responsiveness that is the highest achievement of any performer's training.

Enactive interpretation preserves the integrity of imagery *as illusion* by focusing on images only insofar as they are locatable on the spatiotemporal axes. Its instruments are the words, the symbolic signs, that constitute the performance script and these serially cued entities alone are its focalized objects. The axis of semantic extension upon which this script of symbolic signs does its propositional work must, during enactive interpretation, be processed peripherally. There are occasions, of course, when for purposes of technical instruction, or comprehension, a reader must focalize this semantic axis. In the reading of non-play texts, texts that declare themselves to be critical or theoretical, critical interpretation is a requisite maneuver, but its earnest and habitual application to texts that solicit poetic faith has seemed to me a misdirected effort, an essentially anti-poetic activity. Critical analysis in its endeavor to explicate what it has called "the text" has had only one access to the *poema,* entering it by one axis only, along which it has attempted to draw off only the semantic content of words using for conveyance its own words, as though these were equivalent symbolic signs.

This procedure, I have argued, not only fails to achieve its hermeneutical objectives, but diverts attention from the performance that is indeed the made thing, the *poema,* the play of words in the game of pretending to transcend language. Symbolic signs *in play,* in the process of generating iconic and indexical signs, become metalinguistic. Their evoked images are indexical icons that have a finite sign function. As such, these image-cues do not promote what Peirce referred to as an "infinite series" of signification and what Eco called "unlimited semiosis," but vanish into the images that they signify, images that are signifieds having an object-like finality.

The written image, no matter how it may be constructed in the mind of the enactive interpreter, has this finality because this interpreter chooses not to accompany the words being read with a running commentary or a series of interrogations. When reading a set of image-cues such as those in Keats's "Ode to a Nightingale" that assert that the bird's song

> ofttimes hath
> Charmed magic casements, opening on the foam
> Of perilous seas, in faery lands forlorn,

this reader constructs a mental image one detail after another—a piece of architecture linked to elements of a seascape and a landscape, views that begin in rectilinear clarity, enlarge in scope, and, as they do so, evanesce into a generic geography of "faery." The reader would be sensitive to the connotations of these words and to the iconographic allusions in this desolately romantic setting but would not stop to try to specify them. I am not suggesting that such interrogation should not, but that it *cannot,* be done in enactive interpretation: the two interpretive modes are mutually interferent. During the interior enactment of a text, by definition a trusting surrender of the will to the verbal cues of the text, the reader simply does not engage the text in colloquy—*cannot* do so, because the only language the reader "for the moment" possesses is that by which he or she "for the moment" is possessed. The words the enactive interpreter reads speak through him or her and cancel out the normal flow of inner speech, which, as propositional thought, would otherwise be an available means of interrogating the text.

This total, albeit temporary, commitment of poetic faith has always been easier for the performer to achieve in an oral reading, that is, a recitation, especially if the text has been memorized. Anyone who recites a poem or speech from memory becomes so absorbed in the recollection and proper production of the words that all other verbally mediated thought is excluded. While it offers many advantages for verbal poiesis, writing poses its own problems. Since words are securely captured on the page and the long-term memory is not normally exercised in the performance of texts, readers may stop at any point to question a word or reread a phrase and may proceed at a pace determined not by the text, but by the fluctuations of their interest. Writing thus promotes desultory approaches to the text-reception that range from the close reading of formalist critics to the pleasurable "browsings" of Roland Barthes. Writing fairly invites its own inquest and dissection.

But can written texts be re-oralized—"brought to life" and performed within an inner *theatron?* If we intuitively agree that they can, we have yet to elaborate a method by which to examine how this is done, especially how words prompt mental representations. Except for a handful of inquirers, most notable among them I. A. Richards in his *Principles of Literary Criticism* and Jean-Paul Sartre in his *Psychology of Imagination,* the relation of mental processes to imaginative play has been a taboo field of inquiry. Those literary theorists who had the hardihood to venture into this interdisciplinary no-man's-land ran the risk of being labeled "psychologistic." It is apparent now that one of the tactics of latter-day iconophobes has been to deny the relevance, sometimes even the reality, of what they like to call "subjective states." Their logic seems to be that, if the workings of the conscious mind are not directly observable, then how it forms images from verbal cues is merely idle speculation. Some have gone even further and have argued that since, as they have concluded, there really is no mental entity, there can be no mental imagery— only signs that pass between signers in ceaseless commutation. Any further study of the written image must squarely face the issue of mental imaging and must do so, it seems to me, within the disciplinary context of cognitive psychology.

BIBLIOGRAPHY

Abrams, Meyer. *The Mirror and the Lamp.* New York: Norton, 1958.

Addison, Joseph. *Essays in Criticism and Literary Theory.* Ed. John Loftis. Northbrook, Ill.: AHM, 1975.

Albright, William F. *From the Stone Age to Christianity.* Baltimore: Johns Hopkins University Press, 1957.

Bachelard, Gaston. *La Formation de l'esprit scientifique.* Paris: J. Vrin, 1947.

Bailey, R. W., L. Matejka, and P. Steiner. *The Sign: Semiotics Around the World.* Ann Arbor: Michigan Slavic Publications, 1980.

Bakhtin, Mikhail. *The Dialogic Imagination.* Ed. Michael Holquist; trans. Caryl Emerson and Michael Holquist. Austin: University of Texas Press, 1981.

Barthes, Roland. *Elements of Semiology.* Trans. Annette Lavers and Colin Smith. London: Jonathan Cape, 1967.

———. *The Pleasure of the Text.* Trans. Richard Miller. New York: Hill and Wang, 1975.

———. *Image, Music, Text.* Trans. Stephen Heath. New York: Hill and Wang, 1978.

Bateson, Gregory. "A Theory of Play and Fantasy." *American Psychiatric Association Reports* 2 (1955): (Reprinted in his *Steps to an Ecology of Mind.* New York: Chandler, 1972.)

Berlyne, Daniel E. "Curiosity and Exploration." *Science* 153 (1966): 25–33.

———. "Laughter, Humor, and Play." In *Handbook of Social Psychology,* ed. G. Lindzey and E. Aronson. New York: Addison-Wesley, 1968.

Bertalannfy, Ludwig von. *Problems of Life: An Evaluation of Modern Biological Thought.* New York: John Wiley and Sons, 1959.

———. *General Systems Theory: Foundations, Development, Applications.* New York: Braziller, 1968.

Birdwhistell, Ray L. *Kinesics and Context: Essays on Body Motion Communication.* Philadelphia: University of Pennsylvania Press, 1970.

Bleich, David. *Subjective Criticism.* Baltimore: Johns Hopkins University Press, 1978.

Block, Ned, ed. *Imagery.* Cambridge, Mass.: MIT Press, 1981.

Brown, Roger. *Words and Things.* Glencoe, Ill.: Free Press, 1958.

Bundy, Murray Wright. *The Theory of Imagination in Classical and Medieval Thought.* Urbana: University of Illinois Press, 1927.

Butcher, S. H. *Aristotle's Theory of Poetry and Fine Art.* 1894. Reprint. New York: Dover, 1951.

Caillois, Roger. *Man, Play, and Games,* trans. Meyer Barash. New York: Free Press, 1961.

Chapman, Gerald Wester, ed. *Literary Criticism in England 1660–1800.* New York: Alfred A. Knopf, 1966.

Chatman, Seymour, Umberto Eco, and Jean-Marie Klinkenberg, eds. A *Semiotic Landscape: Proceedings of the First Congress of the International Association for Semiotic Studies, Milan, June 1974.* The Hague: Mouton, 1979.

Chomsky, Noam. *Current Issues in Linguistic Theory.* The Hague: Mouton, 1966.

Collins, Christopher. *The Uses of Observation: Correspondential Vision in the Writings of Emerson, Thoreau, and Whitman.* The Hague: Mouton, 1971.

——, trans. *The Daphnis and Chloe of Longus.* Barre, Mass.: Imprint Society, 1972.

——. "Figure, Ground, and Open Field." *New York Quarterly* 10 (Winter 1972): 118–26.

——. "The Moving Eye in Williams' Earlier Poetry." In *William Carlos Williams: The Man and the Poet,* ed. Carroll F. Terrell. Orono, Maine: National Poetry Foundation, 1983.

——. "Groundless Figures: Reader Response to Verbal Imagery." *The Critic* 51 (Fall 1988): 11–29.

Crane, Hart. "General Aims and Theories." In *The Poetics of the New American Poetry,* ed. Donald Wilson Allen and Warren Tallman. New York: Grove Press, 1973.

Croce, Benedetto. *Guide to Aesthetics,* trans. Patrick Romanell. Indianapolis: Bobbs-Merrill, 1965.

Crystal, David. *Prosodic Systems and Intonation in English.* London: Cambridge University Press, 1969.

Davis, Robert Con, ed. *Contemporary Literary Criticism: Modernism Through Poststructuralism.* New York: Longman, 1986.

Downey, June E. *Creative Imagination: Studies in the Psychology of Literature.* New York: Harcourt, Brace, 1929.

Eagleton, Terry. *Literary Theory: An Introduction.* Minneapolis: University of Minnesota Press, 1983.

Eco, Umberto. *A Theory of Semiotics.* Bloomington: Indiana University Press, 1976.

——. *The Role of the Reader: Explorations in the Semiotics of Texts.* Bloomington: Indiana University Press, 1979.

Ehrmann, Jacques. *Game, Play, Literature.* Boston: Beacon Press, 1968.

Eliot, T. S. *Collected Poems 1909–1962.* New York: Harcourt, Brace, 1964.

Empson, William. *The Structure of Complex Words.* New York: New Directions, 1951.

Engell, James. *The Creative Imagination: Enlightenment to Romanticism.* Cambridge, Mass.: Harvard University Press, 1981.

Erlich, Victor. *Russian Formalism: History—Doctrine.* The Hague: Mouton, 1965.

Finnegan, Ruth. *Oral Poetry: Its Nature, Significance and Social Context.* Cambridge: Cambridge University Press, 1977.

Fish, Stanley E. *Self-Consuming Artifacts: The Experience of Seventeenth-Century Literature.* Berkeley and Los Angeles: University of California Press, 1972.

——. *Is There a Text in This Class? The Authority of Interpretive Communities.* Cambridge, Mass.: Harvard University Press, 1980.

Frank, Joseph. "Spatial Form in Modern Literature." *Sewanee Review* 53 (Spring, Summer, Autumn 1945); revised and reprinted in his *The Widening Gyre.* Bloomington: Indiana University Press, 1968.

——. "Spatial Form: An Answer to Critics." In *Critical Inquiry* 4, no. 2 (Winter 1977): 231–52.

Friedrich, Paul. *Language, Context, and the Imagination,* comp. Anwar S. Dil. Stanford: Stanford University Press, 1979.

Frye, Northrop. *Anatomy of Criticism: Four Essays.* New York: Atheneum, 1970.

Fustel de Coulanges, Numa Denis. *The Ancient City: A Study on the Religion, Laws, and Institutions of Greece and Rome.* Garden City, N.Y.: Doubleday Anchor, 1956.

Garvin, P., trans. and ed. *A Prague School Reader on Esthetics, Literary Structure and Style.* Washington, D.C.: Georgetown University Press, 1964.

Ghiselin, Brewster, ed. *The Creative Process: A Symposium.* New York: Mentor, 1955.

Girard, René. *Violence and the Sacred,* trans. Patricia Gregory. Baltimore: Johns Hopkins University Press, 1977.

——. *Des Choses cachées depuis la fondation du monde: recherches avec J. M. Oughourlian et Guy Lefort.* Paris: Grasset, 1978.

——. *To Double Business Bound.* Baltimore: Johns Hopkins University Press, 1978.

Goffman, Erving. *The Presentation of Self in Everyday Life.* Garden City, N.Y.: Doubleday Anchor, 1959.

——. *Encounters: Two Studies in the Sociology of Interaction.* Indianapolis: Bobbs-Merrill, 1961.

Gordon, Rosemary. "A Very Private World." In *The Function and Nature of Imagery,* ed. Peter W. Sheehan. New York: Academic Press, 1972.

Hall, E. T. *The Hidden Dimension.* New York: Doubleday, 1966.

——. *Beyond Culture.* Garden City, N.Y.: Doubleday, 1977.

Hans, James S. *The Play of the World.* Amherst: University of Massachusetts, 1981.

Hartman, R. R. K., and F. C. Stork. *Dictionary of Language and Linguistics.* New York: John Wiley and Sons, 1972.

Havelock, Eric A. *Preface to Plato.* Cambridge, Mass.: Harvard University Press, 1963.

Hebb, D. O. *The Organization of Behavior.* New York: John Wiley and Sons, 1958.

Heidegger, Martin. *Being and Time,* trans. John Macquarrie and Edward Robinson. Oxford: Basil Blackwell, 1967.

Hirsch, E. D., Jr. *Validity in Interpretation.* New Haven: Yale University Press, 1967.

Holland, Norman N. *The Dynamics of Literary Response.* New York: Oxford University Press, 1968.

——. *Poems in Persons: An Introduction to the Psychoanalysis of Literature.* New York: W. W. Norton, 1975.

Holquist, Michael. "Answering as Authoring: Mikhail Bakhtin's Trans-Linguistics." In *Bakhtin: Essays and Dialogues on His Work,* ed. Gary Saul Morson. Chicago: University of Chicago Press, 1986.

Holt, Robert. "Imagery: The Return of the Ostracized." *American Psychologist* 19 (1964): 154–64.

Huizinga, Johan. *Homo Ludens: A Study of the Play Element in Culture.* Boston: Beacon Press, 1955.

Husserl, Edmund. *Cartesian Meditations: An Introduction to Phenomenology,* trans. Dorion Cairns. The Hague: Nijhoff, 1960.

Ingarden, Roman. *The Cognition of the Literary Work of Art,* trans. R. A. Crowley and K. R. Olson. Evanston, Ill.: Northwestern University Press, 1973.

Iser, Wolfgang. *The Act of Reading: A Theory of Aesthetic Response.* Baltimore: Johns Hopkins University Press, 1978.

——. *Prospecting: From Reader Response to Literary Anthropology.* Baltimore: Johns Hopkins University Press, 1989.

Jakobson, Roman, and Morris Halle. *Fundamentals of Language.* The Hague: Mouton, 1956.

Jameson, Fredric. *The Political Unconscious: Narrative as a Socially Symbolic Act.* Ithaca, N.Y.: Cornell University Press, 1981.

Jaynes, Julian. *The Origin of Consciousness in the Breakdown of The Bicameral Mind.* Boston: Houghton Mifflin, 1976.

Klinger, Eric, ed. *Imagery: Concepts, Results, and Applications.* New York: Plenum, 1981.
Korzybski, A. *Science and Sanity.* New York: Science Press, 1941.
Krieger, Murray. *Theory of Criticism: A Tradition and Its System.* Baltimore: Johns Hopkins University Press, 1976.
Kuhn, Thomas. *The Copernican Revolution: Planetary Astronomy in the Development of Western Thought.* Cambridge, Mass.: Harvard University Press, 1957.
Lawall, Sarah. *Critics of Consciousness: Existential Structures of Literature.* Cambridge, Mass.: Harvard University Press, 1968.
Lentricchia, Frank. *After the New Criticism.* Chicago: University of Chicago Press, 1980.
Lessing, G. E. *Laokoon oder Ueber die Grenzen der Malerei und Poesie.* In *Gotthold Ephraim Lessing Werke,* ed. Uwe Lassen. Hamburg: Hoffmann und Campe, 1963.
Levich, Martin, ed. *Aesthetics and the Philosophy of Criticism.* New York: Random House, 1963.
Levy, Joseph. *Play Behavior.* New York: John Wiley and Sons, 1958.
Lewin, Bertram. *The Image and the Past.* New York: International Universities Press, 1968.
MacDermot, Violet. *The Cult of the Seer in the Ancient Middle East: A Contribution to Current Research on Hallucinations Drawn from Coptic and Other Texts.* Berkeley and Los Angeles: University of California Press, 1971.
Macrobius. *Commentary on the Dream of Scipio,* trans. William Harris Stahl. New York: Columbia University Press, 1952.
Matejka, Ladislav, and Irwin R. Titunik. *Semiotics of Art: Prague School Contributions.* Cambridge, Mass.: MIT Press, 1976.
McGuigan, F. J. "Imagery and Thinking: Covert Functioning of the Motor System." In *Consciousness and Self-Regulation: Advances in Research and Theory.* Vol. 2. New York: Plenum, 1978.
Merton, Thomas. *The Ascent to Truth.* New York: Harcourt, Brace, 1951.
Miller, J. Hillis. "Stevens' Rock and Criticism as Cure, II." In *Contemporary Literary Criticism: Modernism Through Poststructuralism,* ed. Robert Con Davis. New York: Longman, 1986.
Mitchell, W. J. T., ed. *The Language of Images.* Chicago: University of Chicago Press, 1980.
——. *Iconology: Image, Text, and Ideology.* Chicago: University of Chicago Press, 1986.
Ong, Walter J. *The Presence of the Word.* New Haven: Yale University Press, 1967.
——. *Orality and Literacy: The Technologizing of the Word.* New York: Methuen, 1985.
Ortega y Gasset, José. *La Deshumanización del Arte.* Madrid: Revista de Occidente, 1962.
Paivio, Allan. *Imagery and Verbal Processes.* New York: Holt, Rinehart, and Winston, 1971.
Pearce, Roy Harvey. See Whitman.
Peirce, Charles S. *Collected Papers.* 8 vols. Eds. Charles Hartshorne and Paul Weiss. Cambridge, Mass.: Harvard University Press, 1931.
Piaget, J. *The Origins of Intelligence in Children.* New York: International Universities Press, 1952.
——. *Play, Dreams and Imitation in Childhood.* New York: W. W. Norton, 1962.
Pick, Herbert L., Jr., and Linda P. Acredolo. *Spatial Orientation: Theory, Research, and Application.* New York: Plenum, 1983.
Polanyi, Michael. *Personal Knowledge: Towards a Post-Critical Philosophy.* Chicago: University of Chicago Press, 1962.
Polletta, Gregory T., ed. *Issues in Contemporary Literary Criticism.* Boston: Little, Brown, 1973.
Posner, Roland. "Poetic Communication versus Literary Language or: The Linguistic Fallacy in Poetics." In *A Semiotic Landscape,* ed. Seymour Chatman, Umberto Eco, and Jean-Marie Klinkenberg. The Hague: Mouton, 1979.

Pound, Ezra. *ABC of Reading.* New York: New Directions, 1960.

Richards, I. A. *Principles of Literary Criticism.* Reprint. New York: Harcourt, Brace, 1930.

Riffaterre, Michael. *The Semiotics of Poetry.* Bloomington: Indiana University Press, 1978.

———. *Fictional Truth.* Baltimore: Johns Hopkins University Press, 1990.

Rosenau, Helen. *Vision of the Temple: The Image of the Temple of Jerusalem in Judaism and Christianity.* London: Oresko Books, 1979.

Rosenblatt, Louise M. *Literature as Exploration.* New York: Appleton-Century-Crofts, 1937.

———. *The Reader, the Text, the Poem: The Transactional Theory of Literary Work.* Carbondale: Southern Illinois University Press, 1978.

Rugg, Harold. *Imagination.* New York: Harper and Row, 1963.

Sapir, Edward. *Language: An Introduction to the Study of Speech.* 1921. Reprint. New York: Harcourt, Brace and World, 1949.

Sarbin, Theodore R. "Imagining as Muted Role-Taking: A Historical-Linguistic Analysis." In *The Function and Nature of Imagery,* ed. Peter W. Sheehan. New York: Academic Press, 1972.

Sartre, Jean-Paul. *The Psychology of Imagination.* New York: Philosophical Library, 1948.

———. *Being and Nothingness,* trans. Hazel E. Barnes. New York: Philosophical Library, 1956.

———. *What Is Literature?,* trans. Bernard Frechtman. New York: Washington Square Press, 1966.

Saussure, F. de. *Course in General Linguistics,* trans. W. Baskin. Glasgow: Fontana, 1974.

Scholes, Robert. *Structuralism in Literature: An Introduction.* New Haven: Yale University Press, 1974.

Segal, Sydney Joelson, ed. *Imagery: Current Cognitive Approaches.* New York: Academic Press, 1971.

Singer, Jerome L. "Imaginative Play as the Precursor of Adult Imagery and Fantasy." In *Imagery: Concepts, Results, and Applications,* ed. Eric Klinger. New York: Plenum, 1981.

Slatoff, Walter J. *With Respect to Readers: Dimensions of Literary Response.* Ithaca, N.Y.: Cornell University Press, 1970.

Snyder, Gary. *Myths and Texts.* New York, Totem-Corinth Books, 1960.

Sokolov, Aleksandr Nikolaevich. *Inner Speech and Thought,* trans. Donald B. Lindsley. New York: Plenum, 1972.

Sontag, Susan. *Against Interpretation.* New York: Farrar Straus and Giroux, 1967.

Spanos, William V., Paul A. Bove, and Daniel O'Hara. *The Question of Textuality: Strategies of Reading in Contemporary American Criticism.* Bloomington: Indiana University Press, 1982.

Stekel, Wilhelm. *Sadism and Masochism: The Psychology of Hatred and Cruelty,* trans. Louise Brink. Vol. 1. New York: Grove Press, 1964.

Stewart, Dugald. *Elements of the Philosophy of the Human Mind.* Vol. 1. London, 1792.

Suleiman, Susan R., and Inge Crosman, eds. *The Reader in the Text: Essays on Audience and Interpretation.* Princeton: Princeton University Press, 1980.

Talmy, Leonard. "How Language Structures Space." In *Spatial Orientation: Theory, Research, and Application,* ed. Herbert L. Pick, Jr., and Linda P. Acredolo. New York: Plenum, 1983.

Tedlock, Dennis. *The Spoken Word and the Work of Interpretation.* Philadelphia: University of Pennsylvania Press, 1983.

Tompkins, Jane P., ed. *Reader-Response Criticism: From Formalism to Post-Structuralism.* Baltimore: Johns Hopkins University Press, 1980.

Tyler, Stephen A. *The Said and the Unsaid: Mind, Meaning, and Culture.* New York: Academic Press, 1978.

Van Peer, Willie. *Stylistics and Psychology: Investigations of Foregrounding.* London: Croom Helm, 1986.

Vernant, Jean Pierre. *Myth and Thought among the Greeks.* London: Routledge and Kegan Paul, 1983.

Vygotsky, L. S. *The Psychology of Art,* trans. Scripta Technica. Cambridge, Mass.: MIT Press, 1971.

———. *Thought and Language,* ed. and trans. Eugenia Hanfmann and Gertrude Vakar. Cambridge, Mass.: MIT Press, 1978.

Wallas, Graham. *The Art of Thought.* London: Jonathan Cape, 1926.

Wasson, Gordon R., Carl A. P. Ruck, and Albert Hofman. *The Road to Eleusis.* New York: Harcourt Brace Jovanovich, 1978.

Weber, Samuel. *Institution and Interpretation.* Minneapolis: University of Minnesota Press, 1987.

Wellek, René, and Austin Warren. *A Theory of Literature,* 3d ed. New York: Harcourt, Brace, and World, 1956.

Wilner, Eleanor. *Gathering the Winds: Visionary Imagination and Radical Transformation of Self and Society.* Baltimore: Johns Hopkins University Press, 1975.

Whitman, Walt. *American Primer.* Quoted by Roy Harvey Pearce in his introduction to *Leaves of Grass:* The Facsimile Edition of the 1960 Text. Ithaca, N.Y.: Cornell University Press, 1961.

Whorf, Benjamin Lee. *Language, Thought, and Reality.* Cambridge, Mass.: Technology Press, 1956.

Wilson, Richard Albert. *The Miraculous Birth of Language.* New York: Philosophical Library, 1948.

Wimsatt, W. K. *The Verbal Icon: Studies in the Meaning of Poetry.* New York: Noonday Press, 1960.

Winnicott, D. W. *Playing and Reality.* London: Tavistock, 1971.

Yates, Frances. *The Art of Memory.* Chicago: University of Chicago Press, 1974.

INDEX